HELPFUL HINTS FOR HARD TIMES

HELPFUL HINTS FOR HARD TIMES

HOW TO LIVE IT UP WHILE CUTTING DOWN

HAP HATTON
LAURA TORBET

Facts On File Publications
460 Park Avenue South
New York, N.Y. 10016

HELPFUL HINTS FOR HARD TIMES

Library of Congress Cataloging in Publication Data
Hatton, Hap
  Helpful hints for hard times.

  Includes bibliographies.
  1. Consumer education.   I. Torbet, Laura.   II. Title.
TX335.T62   640.73   81-12498
ISBN 0-87196-617-4   AACR2
ISBN 0-87196-672-7 (pbk.)

Printed in the United States of America
10 9 8 7 6 5 4 3 2 1

*Dedicated to Alix Elias,
a loyal and dear friend*

CONTENTS

ACKNOWLEDGMENTS

Our special thanks go to the following individuals, some more instrumental than others, in putting this book together:

Diane Cleaver
Alix Elias
Pat Ethridge

Rod Hardesty
Christine and Earl Hatton
Bob Hutchins

Mike Kennedy
Milly Klingman
Heide Lange

Michael McNeil

Wallace Orr

Allison Pearl
Delmar Ronning
Craig Steadman

Kath Twohill
Jamie Warren
Craig Widmar

Our indebtedness to the hundreds of sources we called upon also warrants mention. It's reassuring to see so many dedicated to the pursuit of better living with less.

Hap Hatton
Laura Torbet

New York City
June 1982

INTRODUCTION LIVING WITH LIMITATIONS: AND LIKING IT

These days it's not only counterculture dropouts who cultivate their own plots of land, and not only members of the Sierra Club who are careful about turning out lights every time they leave a room. You don't have to be a fanatic about conservation to buy a small car. And it's not only the poor who have to settle for meat loaf, who are skipping their vacations this year, or who haven't put a penny into savings lately.

Out of awareness or necessity, almost everyone today is involved somehow in economizing or conserving. Everyone, at some level, feels the economic pinch, whether it's a matter of not trading in the car this year, or eating meat less often, or moving to a smaller house and keeping the thermostat turned down.

This is quite a change from the affluent—and recent—past. The American who lives in the lap of luxury is fast becoming an exception to the rule. We'd come to expect abundance, a reliable sequence of cause and effect from our work to our earnings to the goods and services they purchased—an infinite flow of milk and honey. But, almost without realizing it, we've moved into an age of scarcity and diminished expectations. We own cars and homes designed when hardly a thought was given to efficiency or economy—energy-eaters that are increasingly costly and wasteful to keep up. We're working just as hard, earning as much or more money, spending more than ever, and using up as much energy as ever—yet we have less to show for it.

Moreover, it doesn't look like this is a temporary situation, an aberrant blip in the economic curve or a brief summer drought. Belt-tightening is here to stay. Certainly the diminishing of energy resources is irrevocable, although we had closed our eyes to it until recently. Just as we were thinking about abandoning materialism, it has abandoned us. We're fast coming to the point where there's little alternative to "alternate lifestyles" for everyone.

So what do we do? Living in the new less-is-more world is going to require considerable adjustment. Most of us have not always been penny pinchers. It wasn't so long ago that we went to the movies on a whim and thought nothing of running the air conditioner day and night during the summer. We never gave a thought to how long we ran the bath water or how far we drove the car. Now we're being forced by economic necessity to change our ways, and to rethink many old habits as we become aware that the world's resources are limited—as are our own.

Making changes isn't easy, but it's necessary. Many of us are poorly equipped for living in this new age. Suddenly we need information and skills we don't have and aren't sure how to acquire. We may feel left behind, at a loss to cope with new requirements, changed rules. And because we're ill-prepared, we're also irritated at being forced to live with what we regard as undeserved deprivation. We feel inefficient and bumbling in our attempts to try new ways, and don't know where to begin.

Helpful Hints for Hard Times is designed to facilitate that beginning. It's a primer on economy, conservation, and cooperation.

Helpful Hints for Hard Times distills the best information from countless books and pamphlets written on everything from home-buying and insulation to car repair and money management. It is a collection of the most pertinent background information and hints for efficiency in each area. It extracts the juiciest tidbits buried in these publications and lists the most useful sources of further information. It presents realistic new strategies that don't require highly specialized skills or a tremendous expenditure of time. It concentrates on non-technical, easily implemented suggestions with high-yield results.

The good news is that all this recycling and penny-pinching, bartering, and saving needn't be thought of as hardship or deprivation. There seems no question that we'll have to cut down, be more careful, learn new habits, do without. But acquiring the skills to cope with scarcity and adopting a lifestyle compatible with new economic and social demands can be rewarding and beneficial. We can learn to take pleasure in new, and simple, things. We can have the satisfaction of stretching our current income and resources by eliminating a good deal of waste. We can become closer to our friends and community and learn the benefits of sharing and cooperation. We can regain a sense of control over our lives and a sense of personal accomplishment and of contribution. *Helpful Hints for Hard Times* espouses a philosophy not of miserly, bare-bones existence, but of fulfillment through planning and through personal and group energy.

To start, take a look at your needs and skills and way of life to see what kind of changes will benefit you most. Try to form an honest view of how you spend your time and money and how you feel about it. Ask yourself the following questions:

- *Are your concerns economical?*
- Are you habitually short of money? Do you want things you can't afford? Do you have trouble meeting your regular bills? Is this a new situation?

- Will your economic situation change in the near future? Will you be earning more money? Less? Will you incur more obligations? Do you earn a regular salary? Or do you freelance?

- Have you ever lived on a budget? Are you used to spending money freely? Do you save any money? Invest? Buy on credit? Do you hate having to pinch pennies? Or do you enjoy being thrifty?

- Where would you cut down if you had to? Travel? Taxis? Dry cleaning? Babysitters? Hairdressers? Eating out? The second car? Club memberships? Magazine subscriptions? Movies? Theater? Clothes? What would you find it hard to do without?

- *Are you concerned about conservation?*

- What things do you do now to conserve? Are you careful to turn off lights? To save water? Do you keep the thermostat turned down in the winter? Use the air conditioner conservatively in the summer? Do you use public transportation? Do you check the energy efficiency rates on appliances? Recycle bottles or paper? Use leftovers?

- What kinds of things might you do? Any of the above? Are you likely to give up your daily bath for a shower or to use cloth napkins? Or are you more likely to insulate your home or cut down further on the use of your car?

- *What are your skills and interests?*

- Can you change a tire on your car? Change the oil? Balance your checkbook? Negotiate a mortgage? Fix a leaky faucet? Install carpeting or hang wallpaper? What things do you like to do most? Least?

- *What kinds of community and cooperative facilities and groups are available?*

- What's available in your community? A food coop? A recycling center? Day care? A community college? Legal aid? A tool rental service?

- Are you involved in a car pool or any cooperative ventures? Do you share ownership of anything—a car, a boat, an electric lawn mower? Do you share clothes with a friend? Do you have any barterable skills? Typing? Bookkeeping? Sewing? Carpentry? Car repair? Babysitting?

- Do any of these things interest you? Or are you a loner? Can you think of a way to trade your skills for others? Any possessions you wouldn't mind owning on a shared basis?

Answering these questions should help you pick and choose among this book's many suggestions and tips according to your needs, skills, and the amount of time and effort you're willing to spend. For example, you may not want to bother lighting the stove by hand each time to save the energy consumed by the pilot light, but may very well follow HHHT's suggestion to turn off the pilot light on the heating system just once at the beginning of the summer, and turn it on again in the fall, something surprisingly few people do. You may find it convenient to recycle your paper waste, but not aluminum cans, or may be willing to skimp on heat in the winter, but not on air conditioning in the summer. The idea is not to make you a lawyer, a mechanic, a do-it-yourselfer, a coupon clipper, or a miser, but to build self-reliance—and to develop a comfortable, long-term approach to living—by capitalizing on the skills and concerns that you do have.

Sometimes just knowing the facts, or hearing an interesting statistic, is startling enough in itself to change your habits. For example:

- Every person discards four pounds of waste *per day*. An aluminum can takes 1,000 years to decompose. A three-foot-high stack of newspapers—perhaps two week's worth—uses up a whole tree.

- In the first ten years (or 100,000 miles) of a car's life, it is never cheaper to trade it in than it is to repair it.

- One-half of all the energy in this country is expended by automobiles (*not* including the energy consumed in their manufacture). The cost of operating a car varies drastically according to its size and efficiency—from $.10 a mile to $.35.

- A pinhole drip can waste up to 170 gallons of water a day. If it's in the hot water faucet, it adds $10 to $20 per month to the fuel bill.

- A ceiling fan is very useful in the winter. It keeps the heat low in a room, saving 20 to 40 percent of that heat, and costs no more to run than a 15-watt light bulb.

Some of the helpful hints require almost no effort to follow up on:

- If you buy gasoline in the early morning you'll get more for your money, because the heat of the sun hasn't yet had a chance to expand the gas in the fuel tank.

- You may be able to negotiate a better deal on a new car at the end of the month, when the salesperson is getting anxious about meeting his or her quota.

- 40 percent of the water used in the home is consumed in flushing the toilet. A plastic jug filled with water or sand and placed in the tank can displace a good deal of that water and save many gallons per day.

- There are probably half a dozen "personal" possessions that you could purchase cooperatively with friends or neighbors—an electric typewriter, a calculator, a lawn mower, a magazine subscription, a bulk food order, etc.

- There are probably half a dozen "services" that you could barter with others: driving, typing, shopping, haircutting, babysitting, bookkeeping. Electrical work in exchange for legal advice, carpentry in exchange for mechanical work.

- The best months to buy a refrigerator are January and July; the best time to buy books is January; you can get a better price on fuel oil in July.

- It is often more economical and energy-efficient to have an air-conditioned car! Most cars are aerodynamically designed so that at certain speeds the drag created by open windows wastes more fuel than the air conditioner.

The yield from just small changes can be great, both to you and to your community:

- If everyone washed his or her clothing in warm or cold water, we'd save the equivalent of 100,000 barrels of oil a day, enough to heat 1,000,000 homes through the winter.

- If everyone ran one less load *per week* in the dishwasher, it would save enough oil to heat 140,000 homes through the winter.

With an understanding of your own needs, skills, and goals, and with some basic information, you're ready to proceed, in your own way, at your own speed. Every small step is helpful; it's not necessary to revolutionize the way you live. But every little step that saves you money or that saves resources for the larger community is worthwhile.

MONEY

MONEY

Probably nowhere are our individual and idiosyncratic ways as apparent as where money is concerned. Everyone's ideas of what constitutes extravagance, economy, or deprivation differ. People with similar incomes and needs spend their money quite differently. One person's idea of poverty might be not having all his or her clothes and linens professionally laundered or dry-cleaned. Another person with an income twice as high might not dream of such extravagance.

HHHT is concerned primarily that you manage your money in a way that works for you and enables you to have as many of the goods and services you want as possible with as little worry and waste as possible.

This chapter contains very little advice on how much you should spend or how much of your income you should save. Those matters are covered elsewhere. Rather, this chapter offers information and advice concerning such matters as banking (choosing a bank and the correct type of bank account), budgeting and money management, insurance, wills, investments, credit, debt, even bankruptcy.

Learning about money, and getting a better look at the way *you* use and misuse it, is the best way to implement the habits and economies that will serve *you* best.

STARTING POINTS

"Annual income twenty pounds, annual expenditure nineteen, nineteen and six, result happiness. Annual income twenty pounds, annual expenditure twenty pounds ought six, result misery." This advice hasn't been improved upon since Charles Dickens put these words in Mr. Micawber's mouth over 100 years ago, in *David Copperfield*.

- *You earn your own money with your own time.* Your money is as intertwined with your being as your breath. It should bring you pleasure, not anxiety and grief.

- *You will never have enough money to satisfy all your desires.* You will constantly have to choose among the things you want. So for everything you choose to buy, you will have to forgo something of similar value. But for everything you let pass, you will have in its place something you value more.

- *You decide how every dollar of income leaves your hands.* Unless you bury them where no one can find them, you're going to be disbursing your earnings somehow. The money may dribble away on taxis and lunches, or you may leave it in one big lump in the bank when you die. But the decisions are yours. Problems with money can be solved if you recognize how you make your spending decisions and alter your decision-making process accordingly.

- *You may be married or living with someone whose pecuniary values are exactly the opposite of yours, yet whose values and needs are just as real as yours are.* The conflicts such a situation creates must be faced and understood before they can be solved. If you can't understand your partner's desire to buy a fishing pole, then don't be surprised that he or she doesn't share your interest in a new stereo system. You *can* learn to acknowledge and accommodate your partner's different financial habits, and the two of you can work to get each of your habits in line with the realities of your incomes and bank accounts. Resolving this problem isn't easy, but the alternative is constant conflict and a deteriorating relationship, as well as an eroding credit rating.

- *If you've got to make changes in your ways of handling money, do it in a way that you find comfortable.* If it is easiest for you to change your habits by thinking of your new course of action as a budget, then do so. For some people, however, budgets are like a nagging, disapproving parent. If it's psychologically less burdensome to think of your new habits as a fiscal plan, a spending strategy, a saving plan, or a set of monetary goals, then use one of those images.

- *No one can avoid this society's constant exhortations to spend.* The media would have us think that everyone except us wears designer originals, lives in a perfect house in a perfect neighborhood, and can travel anywhere at the drop of a hat. These images so saturate the media that, whether we like it or not, they are ingrained in us. No wonder many Americans feel that budgets are old-fashioned, lower-class, and plainly for someone else. To have to live on a budget and be constrained by its limits represents failure to many of us, especially if we've embraced the goal of unfettered consumption. If you're resistant to budgets (and most of us are), think of your budget as a spending plan that accents what you *can* buy, and how you *can* stay in the mainstream as a consumer—a *wiser* consumer.

- *There are two ways to be rich: acquire great wealth—or acquire few needs.*

SPENDING

REVISING YOUR SPENDING HABITS: AN APPROACH TO NEW SPENDING POLICIES

1) *Set specific, sensible goals.* You have to know where you want to go before you set off. Write down what you want to do with your money, how much money you'll need to do it, how much money you have coming in, and how much money you're spending. Set a firm, unbreakable date by which you will have completed this task, and then let yourself daydream about it from time to time until then. You'll recognize goals and dreams you may have buried, resistances and fears you will have to struggle against, and, probably, some creative ways to make the adjustments you need.

2) *Commit yourself to spending an hour a week dealing with your money.* That doesn't just mean writing checks and balancing your checkbook. It means reviewing your expenses, your savings, and your spending objectives for the week—every week. This kind of constant analysis is what you need so you can . . .

- *Identify and reduce the largest expenses in your budget.* If your food bills amount to $50 a week and you can save $15 of that amount one week a month by shopping only for sale items, you'll have reduced your food budget by nearly 7 percent with minimal effort. And at the end of one year you'll have an extra $180 to put towards a new house, or towards an investment fund. This kind of paring can also be done with other "constant" expenses such as transportation, clothing, and utilities.

- *Take note of how often you pay for nonessential small items.* Doing without things like milk shakes, pinball games, and movies you don't really care whether you see can put money in your pocket. This is often a helpful way to start training yourself in new spending habits; once you see your fiscal health improving through the reduction or elimination of these small but recurring expenses, you'll be encouraged to make bigger savings.

- *Think twice before making purchases that turn into sources of constant expense.* For instance, if you feel you need a second car, analyze the additional costs for repairs, gas, insurance, parking, and depreciation that a second car will involve in terms of the number of times a week you need a second car. Decide whether using an occasional taxi or rented car is cheaper than subjecting yourself to additional fixed expenses.

3) *Expect some difficulty with this new way of approaching your spending.* No one adapts easily to a basic change in living style. If you haven't imposed much direction on your spending in the past, you can expect to feel cramped from time to time once you begin. The key to maintaining your new spending style will be the excitement and pleasure of seeing your spending goals being met, your credit problems being rectified, and your long-term spending projects becoming more than pipe dreams as special accounts devoted to them grow.

4) *Indulge yourself now and then.* Treat yourself to a new record, shirt, magazine—whatever—every week or so. If you're too strict you'll build up anger and resentment, jeopardizing your whole plan.

HINTS FOR EFFICIENT SPENDING

1) *Never go to the store without a list.* You may know that this works well for grocery shopping, but you should try it when you go shopping for clothes, sundries, and other purchases. Your wardrobe, for instance, can be managed more effectively—and more cheaply—if you go shopping for a pink blouse or a green polo shirt, not just "something to wear after work."

2) *Avoid going shopping with a friend or with the kids.* Shopping with a friend can lead you to purchase something you'll never use. And grocery-shopping with the kids is both distracting and expensive—they always want you to buy things they've seen advertised on television.

3) *Don't go to sales unless they are for something you intended to buy* before you heard about the sale.

4) *While you are shopping, check for upcoming sales.* Ask the clerk when the next price reduction is scheduled. You may find out that the very thing you came to buy will be on sale in a few days.

5) *Remember that what looks like a sale price may well be the standard price.* "Going Out For Business—Everything Reduced 50%" signs can also be misleading. Passersby often misread the "for" as "of" and rush in to take advantage of prices that haven't been reduced at all.

6) *Get friendly with a sales clerk at each of your favorite stores.* Find out what their hours are. They may be able to steer you to good buys, or tell you about new bargains. Leave them some self-addressed postcards so they can notify you of sales.

7) *Check the phone book for wholesalers who deal in items you want to buy.* You may locate a wholesaler who is willing to sell directly to you at a substantial discount.

8) *Don't overlook auctions.* Some of the best are run by local, state, and federal agencies. You'll find them advertised in local newspapers, so keep an eye out.

- The local police or sheriff's department may auction off unclaimed articles that have been stolen or found.
- The General Services Administration auctions off surplus government items such as used vehicles and used office furniture and business machines. For information call the Federal Information Center (listed in the phone book under U.S. Government) for the GSA location nearest you, and contact its personal property division.
- The U.S. Postal Service auctions off unclaimed parcels in 20 states across the country.
- The Internal Revenue Service auctions off property seized from delinquent taxpayers, and the Small Business Administration auctions off property taken from failed businesses.

9) *Make discount purchases through buying clubs.* Membership fees range around $25, and you save about 10% off prices at participating stores. A further benefit is the guide to local discount sources that most buyer's clubs provide.

10) *Suggest that your block association sponsor a* supervised *tool closet.* You may be able to avoid buying a chain saw, a lawn mower, or some other expensive equipment. The only pitfall here is that the use and upkeep of these tools must be supervised; otherwise, people may handle them carelessly.

11) *Try the same approach for infrequently used appliances.* If you don't have a block association, try your athletic, sewing, or bridge group. It may be the way to get a floor waxer or some other appliance that's useful to have—occasionally.

12) *Or, rent seldom-used tools and appliances.* If you can't rouse any enthusiasm for group purchasing, find a rental service for items like rug shampooers and electric sanders. Or check with a local repair shop. You may be able to rent anything from a crowbar to a padlock there for a nominal fee and a deposit. It doesn't hurt to ask.

13) *Exchange services instead of paying for them.* It may be possible to trade babysitting time for a round trip to the shopping center or for tutoring, gardening services, woodworking, auto repairs, or whatever.

14) *Be careful with credit.* Use credit only if you've calculated a payment plan, taking into account the projected life of the item as compared to the length of time it will take you to finish paying for it.

15) *Whenever you can, pay cash for your purchases and ask for a discount.* You may save 2% to 10% of the purchase price, particularly in small stores.

16) *Don't* ever *buy from door-to-door or telephone salespeople.* If you were going to try to put something over on people, wouldn't you choose the place where they feel most secure . . . their own homes? Wouldn't you avoid a store or office or other location where you could be found and confronted by dissatisfied customers?

17) *Give children financial responsibility.* Set them up at an early age with an allowance—even a checking or savings account—and never bail them out. Specify what the allowance is to cover and renegotiate at regular intervals. For costly items, such as bikes or stereos, pay a percentage of the cost. Take into account what your child's friends are getting—don't make his or her allowance too large or too small in comparison. The responsibility of having to pay for some of their possessions encourages children to take better care of them. This saves you money!

BARGAINING

Bargaining is a skill that most Americans associate with Middle Eastern bazaars or wheeler-dealer businessmen. But in these hard times, bargaining is a survival tactic that can win you big savings on your personal purchases. Statistics show that many retailers and most contractors feel women are pushovers and therefore charge them more than they would men. So in many cases it's essential that you bargain. In any case, it's always worth a try, and you can bargain anywhere. Here's a set of strategies that work:

1) *Know who you're dealing with and what his or her powers to reduce prices are before you try to bargain.* You're likely to succeed in a small store when you're dealing with the owner or in a larger store when you're dealing with someone in authority. A floor manager, a commissioned salesperson, or a department head can help you. Sales clerks usually can't.

2) *Shop when the seller can give you full attention, and bargain in private.* Don't expect to strike a bargain around Christmas, or in the middle of the Saturday rush. You want to be able to talk with the seller at some length. The more time and attention the seller has lavished on you, the more eager he or she will be to compensate for it with a sale.

3) *Be charming.* It helps to regard the bargaining process as a peaceful game, not warfare. It doesn't pay to be nasty, harshly critical, or overbearing. In fact, if you treat the seller as an equal, you are more likely to make the kind of bargain you want.

4) *Be sympathetic.* Listen to the seller. Commiserate about the long hours, the busy or slack sales, the competition, even the weather or the economy. You'll learn things that you can use when you really begin bargaining.

5) *Express surprise at the listed price.* You may have been looking at bags for 20 minutes, but the last thing you should intimate is that you've actually seen the price tag. When you do finally let the seller watch you look at it, register surprise and ask why the price is so high. The seller will probably tell you all the reasons why it's the best bag for the money. Remember those advantages and use them as ammunition if you're encouraged to take a lower-ticketed item later on.

6) *Admire quality and demand it.* It doesn't hurt to show that you're a practical shopper who appreciates quality. Agree when the seller praises the material and features.

7) *Find the flaws.* After you've expressed your dismay at the price but agreed to the high quality of the item, begin pointing out its flaws. As one veteran bargainer says, "If you can buy it, you can find a flaw." All it takes is a poorly–stitched seam, a smudge, a scratch, a loose door, a quirk of design that you can criticize. One woman we know managed to get $3 off on each of three pairs of shoes for her kids because the holes for the buckles were too small. She told the salesman that a shoemaker would charge that much to enlarge them, and that enlarging them was necessary so the kids could put their shoes on and take them off without help. (She fixed the holes herself with a roasting fork when she got home.)

8) *Be candid and specific.* Ask for help with the price. Offer a specific amount that's less than you're actually prepared to pay. If you're vague, the seller may not acknowledge that you want to bargain seriously.

9) *Blame a bad guy for your low bid.* Any third party will do, maybe even a fictitious villain. Blame the budget, or your spouse. Explain that you'll get killed if you spend one dollar more than what you've offered.

10) *Exploit the competition.* Compare the price to that in another store, either the closest one that offers the same merchandise, or the store's most aggressive competitor. Mention the difference to the person in charge. This works well. Or simply carry in a shopping bag from the other store and display it prominently. It will probably put the owner in a mood to bargain.

11) *Get tough.* If you're buying a big-ticket item, it's unlikely that you'll come back often, as you might for smaller things. Most people don't get more than one refrigerator at a store. (But you can mention that you need other appliances as you look at the appliance or product you're shopping for.) You should feel free to take a hard-line approach to your bargaining in this situation. This is also the approach to take if you're dealing with a professional commission seller. Ask right away how much the salesman really wants for the item. If the first offer is substantially less than the ticket price, be bold and bargain for an even lower price. An easy re-

duction is a good indicator of a big markup. Another indicator is an across-the-board markdown for a whole group of people—conventioneers, employees of a company, union members, students, or other special groups. Use all the techniques you can here, because you're dealing with experienced people who know to the penny how much leeway they have to maintain a profit.

12) *Search for successful combinations.* If you're having a hard time negotiating a lower price, look for ways to encourage the seller's cooperation. Get a friend to come back in with you and buy the same item, as long as you get a discount on the double sale. Try for a cash discount, as described above. If you can, point out that you are responsible for buying decisions at your place of business and may be able to send business along to the store. (This works well at restaurants.) The combination of a new advantage to the seller with a cash payment often swings the bargain in your favor. For instance, you may get your deal if you offer to pay cash *and* pick the item up, or to pay cash *and* take the floor sample.

13) *Be ready to compromise.* You won't negotiate a discount every time you try . . . but you may get a credit towards your next purchase, or free delivery, or a bonus like a tie, a matching belt, or a super scratch-proof enamel finish.

14) *Be persistent.* If you can't negotiate a discount on your first visit, or if the merchant has a reputation as a hard case, make a few visits to the store. One woman saw a chair she wanted in December. She visited the shop three more times, each time making a point of admiring the chair and complaining about her budget. She closed her deal in mid-March, getting a hefty discount.

15) *Be a good customer.* The woman who bought the chair also brought the dealer more business. She always came with a friend, and they made a point of buying something each time they visited the shop. Their small purchases marked them as buyers, so when she put in her bid for a discount, it was well-received. If you're a regular customer at a small grocery store, for instance, you should aim at negotiating bulk discounts on things like cat food, paper towels, or deli items.

SAVING

SIX SAVINGS TECHNIQUES

1) *Save your change.* Take all the coins and $1 bills out of your pockets or change purse every day and put them in your piggy bank. Deposit the money in your savings account once a week. Don't let it sit where you can dip into it.

2) *Make one week a month a "no frills" week.* Stay home in the evening, keep your meals simple, take your lunch to work, substitute a walk around the block for a cup of coffee at break time, skip the post-work cocktail at the local bar. Or do it one day each week. You'll save and you'll appreciate the little luxuries during the rest of the month all the more.

3) *Bill yourself for savings just as though you were paying off a loan.* Buy a cash receipt book and make up a page for each of your paychecks for the next year. In advance, enter deposit requirements that add up to the savings goal you set for the year. Keep the book where you keep your bills and tear off a page every time you make the required deposit. By the time you've gone through the payment book, you will have added substantially to your savings account.

4) *Set up a fully automated savings plan.* Find out whether your employer's bank will make payroll deductions—then you'll never see the money outside of your savings account. Next best is a plan that automatically takes money from your checking account each month and puts it into your savings account.

5) *Never spend gift money or tax refunds.* Put them directly into your savings account. Try to get a raise and do the same with the additional income, or at least half of it.

6) *Cut out the habit you want to break most.* Each time you want to buy cigarettes or cookies or booze, take the money *out* of your pocket and put it into your piggy bank. You'll be paying yourself to fight a troublesome habit, adding to your savings by keeping your pockets empty enough to resist temptation.

The thing that makes these savings ideas work is getting the money *out* of your pockets and *into* the bank. None of these savings devices will work unless you get the money you would ordinarily spend into a bank account.

BANKING

Now that you have something to put into the bank, it's time to look at some of the ways you can make your bank work harder for you.

CHOOSING A BANK

- *Look for accessibility to your home and/or workplace.* Better to pay charges than to have to depend on mail deposits or to be caught short of cash and have to spend time and money to get to the bank.

- *Look for convenient hours.* The usual 9:00 a.m. to 3:00 p.m., even at a bank near your workplace, forces you to bank during your lunch hour, along with all the other people who have to bank during *their* lunch hours. It may be better to walk an extra block to a bank that's open after work, before work, or on Saturday, or even to pay an extra fee, than to put up with long lines and aggravation in the middle of the workday.

- *Look for good bookkeeping.* A bank may score well on charges, but when you ask around, you may find that it scores badly on misposted deposits and checks.

- *Look for a good interest rate on loans—personal and mortgage.* If you expect to be in the market for a home sometime in the future, it may be wise to establish a relationship with a bank that offers good terms on mortgages or personal loans. It may simplify getting a loan when you need it if you're already known as a dependable bank customer.

- *Make sure deposits are registered as individual checks clear.* Some banks will not make your deposit final until *all* the checks listed on your deposit slip clear . . . so you may be unable to draw against the local checks you deposited until the out-of-state checks you deposited along with them have cleared.

- *Make sure that your deposits are insured.* Most banks are covered by some sort of federal or state deposit insurance, but you wouldn't want to be stuck with an exception.

- *Consider banks that offer a 24-hour automatic teller and a banking card that lets you write checks at any branch.* There's nothing like being able to do your banking at 7:00 in the morning when you're out walking your dog. But this feature can also make it more difficult to break bad spending habits. It also usually means added charges. If you have a bank with convenient hours and locations, you should try to do without this service.

THE THIRD ACCOUNT

Most of us make do with a checking account, or with checking and savings accounts. You should consider maintaining three accounts: 1) a checking account, joint or personal, for day-to-day bills; 2) a savings account for accumulating money for investments (see the section on investments, pages 31–38; and 3) a savings account for bills you pay once a year. Savings accounts for accumulating funds and checking accounts are discussed in separate sections.

Why a Third Account?

That third account, devoted to savings for annual bills, is useful for a number of reasons. First, you have to figure certain kinds of annual expenditures into any spending plan or budget, including life, health, and auto insurance; magazine and newspaper subscriptions; club memberships; Christmas and other holiday expenses; donations to charity; and a vacation fund. The third account allows you to put away some money each month for these expenses. It also serves as an interest-paying substitute for the Christmas, Chanukah, or vacation clubs advertised by your bank. These clubs are good *only* for the bank, since they give the bank the use of your money without providing even the usual bank interest rates. The third account will bring you a better return on your money.

SAVINGS ACCOUNTS

The level of interest banks can pay you for the use of your deposits is fixed by law. Right now, that means that you may earn much less money with a standard savings account than you can by putting the money into a savings certificate or money market fund.

How Interest Rates and Inflation Affect Your Savings

Interest rates are now so low that your deposits will not keep pace with inflation. A television that sells for $100 may well cost $120 in a year. But $100 placed in a savings account that compounds interest daily at 5.25 percent will be worth only $105.47 after the same period of time. So why bother with a savings account? Because your television set can't earn you any money at all.

If you save $50 a month for two years, even at disadvantageous bank interest rates, you'll accumulate well over $1200 to put into higher-interest investments. So if you dream of putting together a nest egg, a savings account is still the place to start. In it you can amass the capital necessary to meet the minimum requirements of higher-interest-earning investments. (There is an exception: Alliance Capital Reserves [see page 32] will accept investments from small depositors.)

Questions to Ask Before Opening a Savings Account

1) *How is the interest figured?* There are more than 140 different ways for banks to tabulate interest payments, so it's hard to say definitively which way is best. But some ways of figuring interest are definitely better than others. For instance, interest that is compounded quarterly gives you a smaller return than interest that is compounded daily.

2) *When does your deposit begin to earn interest?* If your money earns from the day of deposit to the day of withdrawal, it is doing its best work.

3) *How much of your money earns interest?* Some banks give you interest only on the lowest balance you have during an interest period. So if you have $20 in your account on January 1 and deposit $1,000 on January 15, when you check your interest on April 1, you may be shocked to see that you've earned interest only on the $20 that was in the bank at the beginning of the quarter.

4) *How many "grace" days does the bank provide?* Some banks credit your account with full interest even if you deposited your money one or two days after the period began, or withdrew it a day or two before it ended.

5) *Does the bank penalize you for frequent withdrawals?* Does it give you a bonus if you leave your money alone for a year?

6) *What is the APY?* This is the Annual Percentage Yield; it tells you how much each $100 earns. It takes into account all the bank's idiosyncracies and is the best figure to use in comparing interest rates offered by different banks.

Our Advice

In general, look for the highest APY, day-of-deposit to day-of-withdrawal interest, grace days that are calculated in business days instead of calendar days, and the fewest service charges or penalties. Banks work for themselves, not for you. And even when two banks offer the same interest and the same compounding frequency, one's policies can put more interest in your pocket than the other's. Don't be satisfied that your money is doing the best it can where it is. Keep asking around . . . you may even find an out-of-state bank that affords an attractive bank-by-mail home for your long-term savings.

How Bank Credit Cards Can Jeopardize Your Savings

Your savings can be endangered by disputed or overdue bills. Here's how it happens: When you have a bank credit card at the same bank that holds your savings, the bank can take your savings in payment for disputed or overdue bills charged to your credit card. To protect yourself, don't keep a savings account at the same institution where you have a bank card. Or, if that is impractical, remember to close your account and move it to another bank if you find yourself unemployed or over your head with "easy monthly payments."

The Cash-Rebate Savings Account

The rebate has even found its way into savings accounts. Banks in about 250 cities now offer special "Save System" or "Savings Plus" accounts that entitle depositors to rebates averaging 7 percent when they pay cash at local supermarkets, restaurants, department stores, pharmacies, etc. The rebates are credited monthly to the savings account. To find the bank nearest you, call Savings Plan Systems' toll-free number: (800) 328-5107.

CHECKING ACCOUNTS

Electronic banking is convenient, but the old-fashioned checking account has some distinct advantages:

1) Cancelled checks are receipts that prove payments have been made.

2) You can stop payment on a check for an unsatisfactory service or product.

3) You can "float" or "kite" a check, writing it on Friday, for instance, and depositing the cash to cover it on Monday.

4) Electronic payment arrangements often involve automatic deductions from your paycheck, and that takes away your freedom to choose when to pay which bills.

Our Advice

Stick with a checking account rather than opting for electronic funds transfer; let the bugs be worked out on other people's accounts.

If you opt for a computerized checking account, go for one that offers you the most convenience and service for the least amount of money.

Free Checking Accounts

- *There are banks that offer free checking.* Remember—banks use your cash balance and are making plenty of profit from it. About one-third of American banks offer free checking accounts requiring no minimum balance. Usually these banks are smaller ones with perhaps only one office. If there is such a bank near where you live or work, consider using it. Another one-third of the country's banks offer free checking to students, senior citizens, or other segments of the population; so as you shop around, be sure to ask about free accounts and who is eligible.

- *Keep convenience in mind when you shop for a bank.* Unless you can easily make deposits by mail and can wait not only for checks to clear but also for them first to reach your bank, then opening an account at a more conveniently-located bank may be worth the additional cost.

NOW Accounts

- *The next best thing to free checking is an interest-bearing checking account.* If you can't find a convenient bank that offers free checking, then go for this alternative. Federal law prevents banks from paying interest on checking accounts, so banks have come up with some creative ways to get around the regulations. The best-known, most flexible of these are NOW accounts, so-called because you use a "negotiable order of withdrawal" to get funds from the account. There's no difference between a check and a NOW draft. And you'll earn interest on the money in your account until the order clears.

- *Because a balance requirement is customary, choose a bank that offers a NOW account requiring a minimum average balance.* This is more advantageous to you than one requiring a minimum *lowest* balance. Your account can dip lower with an average balance requirement than it can against the unyielding floor of a lowest balance.

If you can find neither a convenient NOW account nor a free checking account, the next step is to shop for a regular or special checking account.

Regular Checking Accounts

A regular checking account requires you to keep a minimum balance but doesn't charge you for the checks you write. When you're comparing banks for a regular checking account, keep two things in mind:

1) *As in shopping for a NOW account, ask whether there is a minimum average balance for the month or a flat minimum dollar balance.* With the minimum average you can deposit a few hundred dollars at the beginning of the month and write checks against it until you reach a zero balance at the end of the month; you may still have maintained the minimum average balance you need. That's why the minimum average balance offers you better use of your money than the minimum dollar balance.

2) *Find out whether there are fees and charges and, if so, how much they are.* You may find that there is a service charge or a stiff penalty for letting your account fall below the minimum; or there may be a ceiling on the number of free checks and deposits you can make.

Special or "Economy" Checking Accounts

Unlike a regular checking account, no minimum balance is required for a special account—*but* you can be charged:

1) a flat monthly service charge plus . . .
2) a fee of $.10 or more for any or all of the following:

- each check,
- checks *and* deposits, or
- checks, deposits, *and* each check you deposit, even though several may be listed on one deposit slip.

The obvious lesson here? Shop around. Some "economy" accounts are anything but that. Keep in mind how may checks you write and how many deposits you make in a year. This can determine whether or not special checking makes sense for you.

A Helpful Hint for the Checkbook That Won't Balance

If you're tearing your hair out because you can't balance your checkbook, divide the discrepancy by 9. If it divides evenly, there's a good possibility that your problem is a transposed figure. This is an old accountants' test that may help you balance your account.

JOINT ACCOUNTS

Joint accounts are a useful part of any family's money management system because household bills can be paid by either partner. But they can pose problems, especially if they're the family's only account or if there are serious marital difficulties.

Joint Checking

Disadvantages
The chief disadvantages of joint checking accounts are:

1) *Death and taxes.* Taxes are levied on the accounts of the first person to die. If you're to avoid taxes on the portion of the savings that you contributed, you must be able to prove which funds belong to you. And immediately after your partner's death, the account will probably be frozen, so you won't be able to use the account when you'll probably need it most. At best, you'll have access to only part of the money in the account.

2) *Your partner has the right to empty the account and vanish, and you haven't any recourse.*

3) *The main problem with a joint account, however, is the continuing struggle to keep the accounting straight.*

Two Suggestions for Dealing with Your Joint Checking Account

1) *The one-checkbook method.* Whenever you take a check, put your initials on the stub so that it's clear who is supposed to record the amount.

2) *The two-checkbook method.* Leave one at home for regular expenses. At regular intervals reduce the balance it shows by a specified amount, which is allocated to the second checkbook. You can draw against that amount as though it were a separate account for your unbudgeted expenses . . . and your funds won't get out of control.

In either case, the key to keeping your accounting straight is to keep your deposit slips in one place and to record your expenditures as they occur.

Joint Savings: Why You Shouldn't Bother

1) *Just as with a joint checking account, if your partner dies, you must be able to prove which funds in the joint account belong to you. Otherwise, the entire account will be taxed as though it belonged to the deceased.*

2) *Upon your partner's death the account is frozen.*

3) *The account can be cleaned out by the courts if either one of you encounters a lawsuit.* So if your partner has a car accident and must pay damages, your savings will be swept up with your partner's to pay the court settlement.

4) *If your marriage dissolves, a joint account is not a secure source of support for a non-working partner, as a separate account in that partner's name would be.* Studies have shown that it would cost tens of thousands a year to replace the services of a spouse who is a full-time homemaker. An independent savings account for him or her is one way to acknowledge and reward the years of service that constitute an enormous financial contribution to a marriage.

CREDIT

As the prime lending rate (the interest rate banks charge their *biggest* business customers) soars, the cost of credit rises with it. Missouri, for one, now allows credit-card issuers to charge their card-holders a record 22 percent interest rate. Other companies tack annual fees onto their regular charges as well. This is in effect an attempt to discourage credit spending, which many economists believe is one of the causes of today's double-digit inflation.

And the economy isn't the only victim of credit cards—millions of people seriously over-extend themselves, spending money they don't have. Here are some tips on credit and credit card usage.

ABOUT CREDIT

Three Ways to Make Credit Cards Work for You

1) *Always be aware of timing.* By making credit-card purchases within approximately five to seven days before your billing date, you can take 50 to 60 days to pay for your purchase *without* interest because the amount charged will not appear on your statement until the following month. The time that elapses from when a transaction takes place to when it's posted to your account to when your monthly bill is sent out to when you pay 21 to 30 days later can involve a substantial grace period. Make the most of it.

2) *If possible, cross companies.* With credit cards, especially gasoline company cards, this can work to your advantage. Buy Exxon gas; pay with a Texaco card. The bill is sent to Exxon, which sends it to Texaco, which sends it to you. The result? Several months' reprieve.
Note: If you disapprove of this kind of transaction, remember that banks use *your* money in a similar way to earn enormous sums of money each year. Adopting "float" tactics yourself is both fair and sensible.

3) *Bank credit cards charge lower interest rates for loans than they do for purchases.* At times it's worth the trouble to borrow money to make a large purchase.

Are you planning on taking a trip? Since you'll be charged, say, 22 percent interest on your $500 plane ticket, but only 18 percent for the $600 loan you take out for spending money, make your loan larger and use the extra cash to pay for the ticket.

Our Advice

- *Limit the number of credit cards you hold.* The interest rate drops on many cards after a certain level of debt is reached. So you may find yourself paying 18 percent on 10 accounts when you might instead be paying 12 percent, for awhile, on one. Additionally, and importantly, it will be easier to keep track of your debt level if you are using only one or two cards. A small number of credit accounts also provides a psychological obstacle to wild spending. Owing $50 on each of 10 accounts doesn't seem nearly so burdensome as owing $500 on one.

- *Shop around for low interest rates.* Comparative shopping can pay off. A credit union, for instance, may offer lower interest rates than a credit-card company. And borrowing against your life insurance can be a cheaper source of money than taking out a personal loan.

- *Finally, keep a running tab of your charges.* Failure to do so can result in disastrous spending.

Reminders

- *You pay for credit.* Creditors are lenders. They make money from your use of credit. Unless inflation and your credit purchases are carefully considered factors in your spending program, your use of credit is probably an unrecognized drain on your income.

- *Credit problems have only one genesis: you've bought something that is too expensive for you* (or you've bought lots of things that, added together, are too expensive for you). They also have one cure . . . you must stop spending until you get out from under your existing credit burden.

PROS AND CONS OF CREDIT

What's Good About Credit

Let's start on the positive side and look at the good things that credit cards and small personal loans offer:

- *You can buy expensive items economically,* because the interest you'll pay may be less than the price increases inflation will cause if you wait and save to buy them.

- *You can set up a moderately comfortable household,* and make the credit payments as though they were savings account deposits while enjoying your appliances and furniture.
- *You can avoid carrying cash.*
- *You can cushion yourself financially in a pinch.*
- *Your monthly statements can help you keep track of your spending and thus help you plan for the future.*

When to Use Credit

1) *If you really need an item that is on sale, it pays to borrow to take advantage of the sale price.* This goes for everything from paper towels to a new winter coat, but use credit only if the purchase would otherwise stretch your budget.

2) *If you need extra cash, instead of cashing in securities and incurring heavy penalty fees, take out a loan to see you through.* The interest on the loan will likely be less than the interest you would lose on early withdrawal of the invested funds.

3) *Take out a home improvement loan in order to improve your present home rather than moving.*

4) *Use credit to save you money.* A new washer and dryer can, for example, make expenditures for disposable diapers, diaper services, and laundromats unnecessary. And the gas guzzler on which you spend $150 a month for fuel can be traded in for a car that costs a third as much to operate.

5) *Use credit to get a better job and increase your earning power.* For example, a loan to pay for a college course that can advance your career is money well borrowed.

When Not to Use Credit

1) *Don't charge routine purchases.* Pay cash for your groceries, booze, etc.

2) *Charging for entertainment can be like quicksand.* Pay in cash—you'll spend less.

3) *On a vacation, when the tendency is to splurge, pay as you go instead of accumulating charges large enough to cramp your style for months to come.*

4) *If your income drops for any reason—because of cutbacks at work or because you've switched jobs—don't rely on credit cards to sustain your old lifestyle.*

CREDIT PROBLEMS

Signs That Your Use of Credit is Out of Control

1) You're putting out 20 percent or more of your take-home pay in credit installments.

2) You're buying the groceries with your credit cards.

3) You're charging goods that will be used up or worn out by the time you're finished paying for them.

4) You're being dunned. You've gotten a second notice about your department store charge, or a turn-off notice from the electric company.

5) You're paying monthly interest charges for credit, yet you have no cash cushion—nothing in your checking or savings accounts or even in the cookie jar.

6) You're paying credit card installments each and every month as though they were utility bills, without reducing the balances in your accounts.

7) You're sending out partial payments.

8) You're paying close attention (or avoiding paying attention) to the ads for loan consolidation (the ones that suggest you can exchange your monthly payments to 20 creditors for one simple, larger payment).

Credit Cures

If you are in the early throes of a credit collapse, you're eligible for the first level of cure:

The Scissors Solution

1) Take out all of your credit cards.

2) List them, including account numbers, and the telephone numbers you should call if they're lost or stolen.

3) Take a pair of scissors.

4) Cut *all* your credit cards in half. Spare none. Throw the pieces away.

5) Pay your bills. (See pages 24–29 if you need to make special arrangements to do this.)

6) When you've made your next-to-last payment on the last account to be paid off, take out your list of credit cards.

7) Choose two oil company cards, an international credit card (preferably American Express, Carte Blanche or Diner's Club—most of the charges on these cards must be paid in full every month, and the only fees ordinarily applicable are the annual card fees) and two store credit cards (a card from a major department store and a card from a store that features first-rate clothing).

8) Call and report them lost so you can get replacements for the ones you cut up.

9) Call the numbers for all the others and cancel them.

10) Now use your cards only when you need to, as tools that contribute to your spending plan, not as accomplices on impulsive spending sprees.

The Alternative

You might be reluctant to try the scissors solution. But unless you curb your credit spending entirely you will wind up in greater trouble.

- You will have to deal with collection agencies.
- You will have to deal with lawyers.
- You may put a permanent blot on your credit record.
- You may be forced into bankruptcy, or into a court-supervised plan to avoid bankruptcy.

Disaster Signs

It's too late for the scissors cure when:

- The bank wants its overdue installment on your personal loan.
- You're right up to your $500 credit line at the department store, and you're already a month behind in your payments to them.
- You could only pay half of the last oil company bill, and the new one has arrived already.
- You just got a letter from a collection agency about your bill at the clothing store.
- You went into your neighborhood grocery store and there, taped to the cash register where you and everyone else can see, are two of your checks with your name, address, and the words "Insufficient Funds" stamped across them.

It's time for stronger medicine.

The Bite-the-Bullet Cure

When you're in trouble with your creditors and there's just no way to placate them, given your income, your first impulse may be to avoid the calls, neglect the letters, and just try to evade the whole issue.

Don't.

Your best strategy is to be aggressive about getting your debts settled. It is time for you to intervene on your own behalf. The only way to improve your reputation with yourself and your creditors is to face up to the problems you've created and to create some solutions.

1) *Start with what you can do.* If you're working, figure out how much you can afford to pay to your creditors each week or month. Be realistic and be fair to yourself and to them. The key at this point is to find the level of payment that you can maintain without fail. You will probably have to face curtailed spending for a year or more to get rid of your debts, so

when you try to figure how much of your take-home pay you can devote to credit payments, be sure you have set aside sufficient amounts for rent, food, household expenses, essential clothing (nylons, shoes, and one or two replacement garments), transportation, and a curtailed leisure budget. It is only fair to aim at putting 15 percent of your take-home to the task of getting yourself out of debt. Twenty percent is even better, but it will probably strain you—you must commit yourself to a very Spartan lifestyle to keep up such a heavy repayment rate.

2) *Get out your scissors!* Especially if you couldn't or didn't restrict your credit card buying earlier, you must now. In fact, your credit card buying may already have been restricted by the card companies. At any rate, now is the time to put the brakes on . . . with one possible exception.

3) *Put aside one international credit card* (if your credit on the account is unimpaired). Since you are going to be devoting most of your disposable income to getting out of debt, it may be wise to put aside one major card in case you have an emergency, like a pair of eyeglasses that need replacement.

4) *Make the card as unavailable as possible.* Some suggestions:

- If you have a trustworthy friend or relative, give him or her the card to keep until you have an emergency.
- Best of all is if you have a tax accountant or money manager who can hold the card for you until you've gotten your debts straightened out.
- If you have a safety deposit box, lock it up there.
- And if none of these alternatives are open to you, drop the credit card behind your refrigerator or stove, whichever is more inaccessible. (Note: if it's the refrigerator, when you remove the card, take the opportunity to vacuum the coils—this makes your refrigerator more energy-efficient.)

5) *Set up a debt repayment plan.* Once you've got an accurate idea of what you *can* pay back, it's time to look at how much you've *got* to pay back and to whom.

- Make a list of *all* your creditors, how much you owe each of them, and how much you'd be paying them each month if you were financially healthy.
- Arrange them in order of the size of your obligation to each and divide the amount you are able to pay proportionally among them.
- Figure out how long it will take you to pay off the debts at the rate you can manage. (And don't forget that the interest will be greater

than it would otherwise have been because of the additional time you're taking for repayment, increasing your debt.) Be accurate here because if you must go into bankruptcy at some later point, the court can make you honor your debts to creditors if *all* of them haven't been paid fairly.

6) *Call each of your creditors in order of your obligation.* Talk to someone in authority—the head of the credit department, for example, not just the clerk or worker who happens to answer your call. Your creditor may have a credit consultant who assists people with credit problems. Whatever the case, be absolutely straight with them: if overspending got you into your jam, then don't give a lame excuse about illness. If you're out of a job, just say so.

Explain your plan. Tell them that you have worked out a way of paying back the money you owe. If necessary, give the larger picture by mentioning your total monthly debt burden and your total income. At best, your plan will be accepted as it stands.

The key elements at this point are to be 1) in command of the facts, 2) clear in the reasoning you've put into the plan, and 3) forthcoming about the reasons you're in this fix and how determined you are to discharge your obligations.

7) *If you can't bring yourself to make these calls, disguise yourself.* Make yourself a concerned relative. There is no denying that being in this predicament is very distressing, and it's better to fabricate a concerned relative to help you than to let things ride until you're sued. Call the creditor or the creditor's lawyer, explain that you are your own married sister or brother-in-law. Decline to give your name; just explain that you are interceding for your relative. Explain the facts. Explain the repayment plans. This approach lets you emphathize with the creditor about your own feck-lessness without losing face. It's a way of getting around your own im-mobility and embarrassment. The key here is to be truthful about the facts, even if lying about your identity is necessary.

8) *Or, look for a formal intercessor.* If you can't stand to make these calls in your own name or under an assumed name, or if you've received negative responses on your first couple of calls, a debt counselor may be your best bet. Using a debt counselor is especially prudent if you're asking your creditors to be patient for an extended period. The counselors are familiar with your creditors, and this may be an aid in getting your creditors to cooperate with your plans.

The credit explosion has made casualties of many of us, so merchants and bankers across the nation have set up non-profit agencies to work with debtors and creditors to solve payment problems.

On the other hand, if you're going through a debt counselor that is sponsored by businesses and bankers, remember that you are dealing with people whose first allegiance is to your creditors. There are instances when bankruptcy is the path you should take, but credit counselors who work for your creditors might not be candid with you about this option.

Chances are good that your community has a credit counseling service of some sort. The National Foundation of Consumer Credit, 1819 H Street, NW, Washington, DC 20006 will refer you to the nearest credit counseling service. The Family Service Agencies also offer financial counseling. You can find out if there's an agency in your community by writing to the Family Service Association of America, 44 E. 23rd St., New York, NY 10010.

Your church may have some sort of debt counseling. Catholic Charities, for example, offers guidance in setting up a budget and in some cases can help with creditors—it depends very much on local diocesan policy. If you're in the military, there are debt counselors available to you. You should also check with your bank, your employer's personnel department, and the local legal aid society for their recommendations. Finally, your creditors themselves may recommend a debt counseling service.

The fee for debt counseling should be nominal.

The Legal Cure

Some bad financial situations have to be solved under the law. Your problems may be too big to be settled voluntarily between you and your creditors. Your reputation may have been weakened by past credit problems. A consolidation loan may be out of the question. You may be facing an enormous medical bill or some other debt that would drain your income for a big part of your working life.

In cases like these, you need the protection of the law; otherwise, you'll suffer from repossession, collection agencies, lawsuits, and garnishments.

See a Lawyer

When you seek a legal remedy to your credit problems, you'll probably be able to choose between two options: the Wage Earner Plan and the total "clean slate" bankruptcy petition. A lawyer can advise you as to which course you should follow.

If you file for bankruptcy, use a do-it-yourself bankruptcy kit and do the preliminary paperwork yourself. This will lower your legal fees. But once you've done what you can, bring your papers to a lawyer. It's worth the fee of $150–$250 or so for a lawyer's professional review and guidance through the initial steps of your petition.

If you have a house, professional advice may save it from the auction block. And if you have a lot of creditors, such advice may relieve you of debts that you might not have included in your own petition.

Bankruptcy: What It Does and Doesn't Do

- It discharges all your listed, non-exempt debts by requiring that all your non-exempt assets and belongings be sold and the proceeds given to your creditors.

- It doesn't discharge exempt debts—like overdue rent payments—and it does deprive you of non-exempt belongings—like a vacation home or a pleasure boat.

- It bars you from filing for bankruptcy again for six years. If you're unfortunate enough to have a major hospital bill right after you're declared bankrupt, you're stuck with it.

- It exposes any friends or family members who co-signed loans for you. The creditors can proceed against those people for full payment of the loans on which you defaulted.

- It appears on your financial records and credit rating reports for fourteen years. It may take years for you to reestablish a decent credit rating, and even then it may be impossible to get more than one or two loans at a time, to get a large personal loan, or to get a loan to start a business. (You'll have less trouble, however, getting an auto loan or loans for other purchases that can easily be repossessed.)

- It leaves you with the tools of your trade, the clothes you own (with some possible exceptions, like furs), a small amount of savings and life insurance, some furniture and appliances, your house (perhaps), a car, and personal belongings whose value doesn't exceed a specified limit.

- It leaves intact your obligation to pay for alimony, child support, loans you got by lying about your finances, most taxes, student loans, debts you owe because you stole or embezzled money, and any debts that you forgot to list in your bankruptcy proceedings.

The Wage Earner Plan: An Alternative to Bankruptcy

Bankruptcy may be easy to contemplate and easy to get done, but it is hell to live with. It marks you for a long time as a financial pariah and wipes out your assets.

But there is an alternative that gives you the protection of the law without the stigma of a bankruptcy decision. It is the Wage Earner Plan. This is a provision of the Federal Bankruptcy Act that gives you a chance to pay off your debts. It amounts to a last-ditch effort to fend off bankruptcy.

WHAT THE WAGE EARNER PLAN DOES

- *It entails the development of a plan for paying off debts which is submitted to the court.*

- *It relieves loan co-signers of their obligation to "pony up" for you.*
- *It generally allows 36 months for 100 percent repayment (with no interest accruing during that time).*
- *It provides for a reduction in debt, if necessary;* you might pay only 60 to 80 cents on the dollar. Creditors will sometimes accept this; after all, it's 60 to 80 percent more than they'd get if you declared bankruptcy.
- *It prevents bankruptcy and keeps its long-term consequences off your financial record.*
- *It relieves you from debts that a bankruptcy petition doesn't dissolve.* Under the Wage Earner Plan, you can get out from under a student loan, a debt you incurred by lying about your finances, certain fines, taxes, court judgments, even a long residential lease.
- *It protects you from being sued by your creditors, from having your goods repossessed, or from being thrown out of your house or apartment.* When the plan is fulfilled, these dangers are over because your debts are regarded as discharged.
- *It can protect you if you lose your job or become unemployed later on.* The court can extend the plan or reduce the debt in that situation.
- *It leaves you with a viable credit rating because you've proven that you're committed to paying off debts,* even when it's an uphill battle for you.
- *It removes control of your finances to the court and your trustee.* You may be forced to sell some of your assets, turn all of any raises over to your creditors, and live a very frugal lifestyle under the supervision of the court and your trustee. You will be on a strict budget, with little room to improve your lifestyle.

WHAT YOU HAVE TO DO TO USE IT

1) *Get a lawyer to help you apply.* The lawyer should set up your financial plan, help you negotiate with your creditors, and administer the repayment.

2) *Get court approval of a detailed plan to pay your debts.* You'll have to show your income and expenses and how much you can repay each month. If 36 payments (covering the three years of the Wage Earner Plan) can't cover your debts, the court may agree to a reduction of your debt.

3) *Get a court-appointed trustee to administer this plan.* The trustee accepts your monthly payment and disburses shares to your creditors.

Our Advice

If you want to do your homework before seeing a lawyer, Wage Earner Plan forms can be obtained for $4.95 from Enterprise Publishing Company, Suite

501, Beneficial Building, Wilmington, DE 19801. Don't pay $10 or $20 for the useless pamphlets advertised in newspaper ads.

If you are in serious trouble, the Wage Earner Plan is certainly a better option than bankruptcy, especially if you have obligations that would be exempt from a bankruptcy petition. But if your creditors won't cooperate, or if you're in enormous debt, bankruptcy is almost inevitable.

What to Avoid If You're In Too Deep

- *Avoid letting things slide.* That's how you got into trouble, and further procrastination will only get you in deeper. Make yourself face up to your financial problems—then get on the phone with your creditors and see what you and they can work out.

- *Avoid debt-poolers, even if things have gone beyond the stage where you can work things out alone.* These people may sound like debt counselors, but instead of being privately sponsored agents who charge nominal fees, they may soak you for as much as 20 percent of your income. They have even been known to take money without ever disbursing it to the proper creditors. If you need money counseling, be sure you know what you're getting into.

- *Don't waste money on mail order plans for getting out of debt;* if they're worth anything at all, they're simply descriptions of the Wage Earner Plan above.

- *Generally, try to avoid a consolidation loan.* The interest rates are too high, and you'll struggle with the large, long-term monthly debt as much as you did with 10 smaller debts.

BILLING MISTAKES AND THE FEDERAL TRUTH IN LENDING ACT

Always protect yourself against billing errors. Here's what you must do to preserve your rights under the Federal Truth in Lending Act.

1) *Write, don't phone,* when responding to an error or making a query. You need to have a record of your correspondence.
2) *Don't send original credit slips, etc.,* unless you have a photocopy.
3) *In your letter, include the following:*

- your name and account number
- a description of the error, the exact dollar amount, and an explanation
- a request for copies of sales slips, etc., if you need only information
- any other information that is pertinent.

4) *Send your letter to the address that is listed on your bill after the words, "Send inquiries to."*

Companies are required to answer your inquiry within 30 days. If you don't get satisfaction, then you and the company may have to have it out in small claims court. This initial correspondence establishes your claim.

TAXES

OUR ADVICE

The best way to save money on your taxes is to have a *reputable* tax accountant do them for you. It will cost you about $200 or so, but it may save you thousands in payments to the government. If your economic situation is straightforward and simple, you can probably do your income tax yourself. But there are very few people who can't benefit from having their taxes done for them. Even an uncomplicated economic situation might provide an opportunity for income averaging once in awhile. (That's when you average your income in a year when your earnings were high against your lower income during the preceding years to bring down your taxes.) So if you handle your own taxes regularly, consider having them done periodically, every third year or so, just to make sure you're taking all the deductions and tax advantages you're entitled to.

ADVANTAGES OF HAVING AN EXPERIENCED FULL-TIME TAX ACCOUNTANT

- *Advice from the Internal Revenue Service, while free of charge, is not necessarily the final word.* The IRS may give you bad advice and then penalize you for taking it. It may not recommend all the deductions you deserve. In fact, when some enterprising people took a sample tax case to several IRS offices, they were given advice that varied so dramatically that the resulting tax bills differed by thousands of dollars. You'll probably do better if you hire your own expert who is familiar with your profession and lifestyle.
- *You don't want to be found guilty of tax evasion for bogus deductions* a fly-by-night tax person dreamed up to impress you.
- *You want a tax accountant who will go to the IRS with you if you're audited.*
- *You want the tax accountant to be accessible during the year* when you have questions about the best way to make an expenditure deductible.

CHOOSING A TAX ACCOUNTANT

- *Ask people in your line of work for recommendations.* Tax law is complex and wide-ranging, so you'll do best to use someone who knows about the deductions to which your profession entitles you. A small business tax specialist may not be up to date on tax decisions affecting free-lance artists, for example.

- *Ask your lawyer and banker if they have recommendations.* If your business affairs are complex, these sources may be your best bet.

- *Avoid the ephemeral tax outfits that spring up in December and disappear in May.* You need to know your tax advisor will be available if the IRS calls you in for a chat in August.

AUDITS AND DEALING WITH THE IRS

Only a very small percentage of returns are audited each year. If you file your taxes late without permission, however, you're asking for an audit, or at least for attention from the IRS. If you make use of a full range of deductions, you're also more likely to be called in—and that's where your tax consultant will come in handy.

For more information about dealing with the IRS, see the concise discussion in *Guide to Consumer Services,* Revised Edition, by Consumer Reports Books (see p. 00). It is a compendium of advice from the Consumers Union and will give you some orientation in case of an audit.

INVESTMENTS

If you're looking for some way to make your savings work harder but don't have enough money to go into the stock market, there are several alternatives. Consider these if you can invest:

UNDER $1,000

All Savers

These one-year certificates are sold in most banks. The minimum you can invest is $500, and your money is federally insured. But the real advantage here is the fact that up to $1,000 in annual interest is tax-free, and it's $2,000 if you're filing a joint tax return.

The interest rate fluctuates with the market and changes monthly throughout the year, though you are locked into the interest rate that is effective at the time of your purchase.

Money Funds

Once upon a time, while most people of average income lent their money to banks in the form of savings for a mere 5 percent interest, those with $100,000 on hand were able to make a loan to, say, General Electric for a return of 15 percent.

Thanks to money funds, this better rate of return is now available to almost everyone. Money funds pool the relatively small investments that we once marked for savings accounts and then make short-term, high-interest loans to big business or government. During 1981, money market funds paid between 12 percent and 17 percent on investments.

These funds are *not* federally insured, which may be a disadvantage for some. On the other hand, loans are usually made only to the biggest banks, major corporations, or the U.S. Government.

The advantages of these funds include:

1) *High interest.* On "no-load" funds there are no commission charges for putting money into the fund or taking it out.
2) *No minimum length of deposit.* You can take your money back at any time and keep all the interest it earned up to withdrawal.
3) *You can withdraw your money easily* by phone, wire, letter, or special check.
4) *You don't have to put a lot of money into the account.* Most money funds do have a minimum initial investment of $1,000 to $5,000, and minimums on successive deposits. But some don't. For instance, Alliance Capital Reserve at 140 Broadway, New York, NY 10005, has no minimum requirements at all as we go to press. For information about Alliance, call (800) 221-5672 toll-free; in New York State, call (212) 635-3400 collect.

You can find out more about money market funds in general from the Investment Company Institute, 1775 K Street, NW, Washington, DC 20006. Ask for a list of money funds (there are about 130 different companies) and their toll-free numbers. Mention that you're especially interested in "no-load" funds to avoid sales charges and increase your earnings.

30-Month Savings Certificates

Some savings institutions offer "small-saver" accounts for those with a balance of $500 or less. You put your money into the bank for 2½ years and the bank pays you a fixed rate of interest that may be as high as 15 percent or more. This is the best rate of interest available on a federally insured account of this small size, but you must be able to commit your funds for 30 months, or else forfeit much of the interest you would have earned.

$1,000 OR MORE

Repos

These are short-term bank accounts that mature in 10 to 89 days. Some banks require a $3,000 deposit, but there are repos available for $1,000. These are a new offering on the money market, so you can expect to find widely varying interest rates, minimum deposits, and fees. But generally you can expect interest rates of up to 16 percent. Repos are also called Investors' Group Fund, Flexifund, or Investment Certificates. They are not federally insured, but the banks are required to use the money only for U.S. Government securities, making the account a secure, conservative investment with a short life and a good return.

Treasury Notes and Bonds

The U.S. Government sells Treasury notes in $1,000 minimum denominations. These notes mature in one to 10 years and pay a high interest. For instance, a four-year note might earn 14 percent, bringing you $560 above your $1,000 investment over the course of its life. But redeeming Treasury notes early does result in severe penalty.

You can also purchase Treasury bonds for $1,000 apiece. Bonds take 10 years or more to mature, and also pay interest that is better than what is available on regular savings accounts. But 10 years is a long time to tie up your money.

The big advantage of these securities, aside from their safety, is that the interest can't be taxed by state or local governments. You pay only the federal income tax on these earnings.

You can buy notes and bonds at your bank or brokerage office, but you will be hit with substantial fees for this service. It's easy to buy your notes and bonds directly from your local Federal Reserve Bank.

The Federal Reserve Bank in Richmond, Va., has published a free booklet, "Buying Treasury Securities at Federal Reserve Banks." Write to the Federal Reserve Bank, P.O. Box 27622, Richmond, VA 23261, for your copy, or contact your local Federal Reserve Bank.

Corporate Bonds

These bonds mature in five to 40 years. A 10-year $1,000 bond at 13 percent pays $130 each year and then returns its original investment. You earn $1,300 for putting your $1,000 aside for the term of the bond. You can get Bell Telephone Company bonds in $1,000 denominations. Most other bonds call for investments of $5,000 or more.

Bonds are available through your banker or broker. If you buy when the bond offer is issued, you won't pay a fee. If you buy a bond from another investor after the issue is made, you'll pay a commission.

Standard & Poor and Moody's are independent services that rate bond issues. A triple-A rating is most secure. Bonds rated less than triple-B offer more interest on your investment because your loan is less secure. The additional return recognizes the greater risk you take that the issuer will default and you'll lose your money. You should ask your banker or broker about a bond issue before you give the order to buy.

To find out more about corporate bonds, write to The Guide Series,

Thomson McKinnon, 1 New York Plaza, New York, NY 10004 and ask for its free booklet on corporate funds.

$3,000 OR MORE

Certificates of Deposit

You can get a six-month Certificate of Deposit for $10,000 at your local bank if you have as little as $3,000 on hand. The bank accepts your deposit and lends you the balance of the $10,000 for the certificate. The bank charges you interest on your loan of 1 percent more than the interest on the CD. Your portion of the investment earns less than the going rate of the CD because of this charge.

For instance, if you open a six-month CD account with $3,000, with the bank providing the remaining $7,000, if the CD earns 15 percent, your $3,000 will earn about 12.25 percent. Your interest has been reduced, but when you compare it with the 5.25 percent or 5.5 percent ordinarily available on savings, the advantage is obvious. Your investment is federally insured, and you have to tie up relatively little of your money to get a CD under this arrangement.

Treasury Bills

If you have $10,000 to invest, you can get a Treasury bill which matures in less than a year. The same general rules apply to these as to Treasury notes and bonds. See page 33.

The Stock Market

The adventurer in you may be strongly drawn to the stock market. Unless you have about $10,000 in spare capital—that's *after* buying adequate life insurance and *after* accumulating a comfortable amount of additional money in savings—you should avoid the impulse.

Most brokers simply do not offer good enough service to their smaller accounts. You may be fortunate enough to know a broker, or to be related to one, so your situation may be different. But unless you're in this tiny group you should avoid direct investment in the stock market. Decide instead in favor of alternatives like All Savers and money funds (see pages 31–32) or mutual funds.

Mutual Funds

If you're able to put small amounts of money aside for investment, you should consider mutual funds. These are investment companies that invest in many different types of stocks and bonds. In the long run, these funds do about as well as the stock market averages, but they are not totally without risk. That's because mutual fund companies have distinct investment personalities that reflect the investment philosophies of their managers.

Some funds are much more speculative than others. Some funds invest in a very specialized group of stocks, bonds, or securities. These funds are quite susceptible to declines in the general economy or in the specific areas where their investments are concentrated. On the other hand, even funds that invest in a broad range of stocks, or in the specific stocks used by analysts to determine market trends, rise or fall with the general tides of the market.

So while mutual funds give you the power to invest small sums of money along with other people so that you become part of a significant investment group, they are not foolproof. Minimum investments vary from fund to fund, but it's easy to find funds that accept as little as $25 to $50 a month under periodic purchase (or accumulation) plans.

Different Types of Mutual Funds

This list will give you some idea of the wide range of funds for you to consider. It isn't exhaustive, but it's indicative of the flexibility of mutual funds and of the importance of knowing exactly what you want for your money.

- *Balanced funds.* The accent here is on secure investment. The disadvantage is that your money experiences only moderate growth.
- *Bond funds.* These portfolios consist of securities from major companies.
- *Commodities funds.* These invest in commodities like cattle, cotton, and wheat, rather than in stocks and bonds. These are much more risky than stocks in general.
- *Common stock funds.* These concentrate on stocks, but the funds range from conservative, blue-chip portfolios to highly speculative risk portfolios.
- *Funds of funds.* These companies invest in other mutual funds. Their portfolios naturally offer broadly diversified investments, and diversification is generally a sign of secure and conservative investment.
- *Growth funds.* These offer more risk than balanced funds (see above), but also more return. A fast-moving growth fund should earn 12 percent a year over a period of at least five years. Growth funds are good investments for younger people.
- *Income funds.* These are generally the most conservative of the mutual funds. The goal here is to provide a regular dividend that is paid to the investor. Speculation is out—secure, steady-earning investments are the focus. Income funds are a good choice for people who are

about to retire. Many investors move their money into income funds once they stop working.

- *Index funds.* These funds invest in the same stocks that Standard & Poor uses to compile its 500 Stock Index. The performance of these funds thus duplicates the general performance of the market.

- *Junk bond funds.* These funds invest in poorly-rated, high-interest bonds. The prospect of these bonds is default or high yield, so this kind of fund is obviously not a conservative investment.

- *Municipal bond funds.* These tax-free funds offer good advantages for middle-income people who need a tax shelter. The tax exemption can turn even a 5.5 percent yield into an 8 percent effective gain on your investment.

- *Special purpose funds.* These funds invest in a single industry or area. A fund may concentrate on mining stocks or energy stocks, in companies in the mountain states, or in U.S. Government securities. These funds' narrow portfolios make them very responsive to specific situations affecting the industry or area in which they concentrate. Obviously, a special purpose fund that invests in U.S. Government securities is extremely conservative, while one that invests in energy issues may be adversely affected by unpredictable developments.

- *Venture capital funds.* These funds invest in young companies that are not yet registered with the Securities and Exchange Commission. Their stock is not yet traded on the market. While some of these companies prove to be big gainers once they are eligible for over-the-counter trading, these funds are still very speculative.

The Advantages of Mutual Funds

1) *You can invest small sums.* If you're a small investor in corporate stocks and bonds, your investment will probably not get adequate attention from a regular broker, and you'll have to allow for stiff brokerage fees, unless you have enough money and confidence to do your own investing through a discount broker, whose services are even more restricted.

2) *Mutual funds are required by law to diversify,* even within a portfolio that concentrates on a specific type of stock. For instance, even if you've invested in a mutual fund that concentrates on energy stocks, you're protected because the fund is allowed to invest only a relatively small percentage of its capital in any single company's stock.

3) *The funds are tightly regulated* by state and federal law to prevent irregularities, such as fund supervisors investing your money in corporate stock in which they have an interest.

4) *The funds provide all sorts of services,* from IRA and Keogh retirement accounts (see pages 39–41) to automatic reinvestment of your earnings.

5) *Mutual funds come in a broad array of investment types,* and you can find one to fit your specific needs, even as your needs change.

Selecting a Mutual Fund

You can see by the list above that mutual funds offer lots of choices for your investment money. In order to make a good choice, you must first consider the following:

- The size of your income.
- The size of your family.
- How long it will be until you retire.
- The size and variety of your other financial arrangements.
- If you are very well off, with money to gamble, then you can try one of the more speculative portfolios.
- If you have a family to think about, and years of hard work ahead of you, a growth fund is the best choice.
- If your working days are over, your family is grown, and your need to accumulate capital is just about gone, then look for a fund that maximizes your income.
- Begin narrowing your choices of funds once you have a good understanding of why you're putting your money into a certain kind of fund.
- The best way to do this is to send for a prospectus from each of the funds you're considering.
- The more conservative your goals, the larger the fund you should consider.
- Funds that are run by one person, rather than a group of investment specialists, reflect the limits of that person. If your investment strategies happen to coincide with his or hers, it may be a good bargain for you; but if his or her judgment is faulty, there are no other people to balance the direction of the fund.
- You should be sure that the company's investment record and present holdings reflect general objectives that are compatible with your own.

A Vital Way to Save on Mutual Funds

When you do decide to put money into a mutual fund, there is one very effective way to save. Shop for a "no-load" fund. These funds don't have salespeople or sales charges, so there's no load of service charges on your investment. When you put your money into a no-load fund, all of your money goes to work. When you invest in a load fund, you may lose as much as 9 percent of your money off the top as a sales charge.

There is no difference in performance between these two types of funds: there's only a difference in the amount of money you can earn. Over 10 years or so, no-loads offer a much better return.

You must seek out no-load funds, however, since they don't have sales forces. To begin your search, look in your newspaper's mutual fund section. Funds that have the same price in "bid" and "asked" columns are no-load. Sometimes they are marked "N.L." to distinguish them from load funds. Once you've identified a group of no-load funds, you can write directly to the No-Load Mutual Fund Association, Valley Forge, PA 19481 and ask them for information.

Sources of Information

For additional information about mutual funds, see *Investment Companies*, a yearly publication of Weisenberger Financial Services; *Moody's Bank and Financial Manual*, which includes evaluations of the top 100 mutual funds; and *Mutual Funds Scoreboard*, a quarterly publication, and *Mutual Funds Almanac*, a yearly publication, both by the Hirsch Organization.

PREPARING FOR THE INEVITABLE

PLANNING FOR RETIREMENT

The chances are one in three that you'll live your retirement in poverty. The chances are much better than one in three that you'll be closer to poverty during retirement than you've ever been. To trust the government or your employer to provide for your retirement is an enormous miscalculation. Accept the task of planning for retirement right now, rather than evading this frightening task until it's too late.

Standard Sources of Retirement Income

Social Security

Social Security remains in question as an adequate source of retirement income; fears that the system is bound to collapse are not entirely unfounded.

Social Security pays its beneficiaries out of the taxes it receives from those who are still working. It takes the taxes of about three workers to keep a single Social Security beneficiary going. That's fine right now. For every 18 people of retirement age there are about 100 people in their working years. Only 54 have to have jobs for the system to work. By the year 2010, however, for every 100 people of working age, there will be 30 Americans of retirement age. The future of the Social Security system depends on the willingness of Americans to pay astronomical Social Security taxes during their working years and to face less than astronomical returns during their retirement.

Private Pensions

Only about half of the work force is covered by private pension plans. Many of these people will pay into the plan for years and never collect: They may die before they retire or the plan may shut down, stranding them without benefits. Even if your pension plan does last, you're likely to find that it isn't keyed to inflation, so you'll be stuck on a fixed income—and it will probably be quite small.

You may also have to be a certain age before you can start investing in a company pension plan. You may have to work for a firm for 14 years, for example, before its pension plan will admit you. If you follow a career strategy that calls for lots of mobility—job-hopping—you may never qualify for a pension plan at all. And when you finally do settle down to one employer you may find that you're too old to be admitted to the pension coverage.

Finally, if you interrupt your employment with a leave of absence, you may lose your pension rights and have to start all over again. This is, often the case with women who take maternity leaves.

Women may also find that pension plans discriminate by requiring that they pay in larger amounts and accept smaller pension checks because of their statistically longer life spans.

These factors add up to the depressing truth that depending heavily on your private pension plan may be as unwise as counting solely on Social Security for your retirement.

Other Options

If the two most common plans are undependable, what can you do to take care of yourself as you age? Some of the best deals for your retirement are the IRA (Individual Retirement Account) and the Keogh plans. Both of these retirement plans are approved by the U.S. Government; they are tax-sheltered—the money that goes into them and that which they earn is for the most part tax-free—and they're easy to use.

The IRA Plan

As of January 1, 1982, almost anyone can open an IRA. You can put away $2,000 every year, tax-free. But you must leave the money alone until you are $59\frac{1}{2}$ (under threat of a 10 percent tax bite). Then you can begin to draw on the account and pay tax on your income from it, although at a rate that is probably going to be lower than your present taxes. You must begin to draw on the account by the time you are $72\frac{1}{2}$, even though your contributions can continue afterwards. Before January 1, 1982, IRAs had been limited to those whose employers had no pension plan, but the Government has widened eligibility to include about 40 million more Americans.

The Keogh Plan

Keogh accounts are for those who are fully self-employed or who work part-time for themselves. The new regulations let you put away up to $15,000 a year tax-free for retirement and, like the IRA, you can start to collect at age $59\frac{1}{2}$ and must begin to collect by age $72\frac{1}{2}$.

Over 20 or so years, yearly sums as great as $15,000 (it used to be $7,500) invested will grow into a fund that you can draw on generously for the rest of your life.

A Final Word about the IRA and Keogh Plans

- Most economic experts agree that IRA and Keogh accounts are two of the best deals available for those planning for their old age.

- You can put the money to work in a savings account, in annuities, money market funds, stocks, mutual funds, bonds, or other approved investments. You can change your investments as you wish, although you cannot withdraw the money for your own use.

- The funds are immune from bankruptcy attachment, but they are not insured per se. So if you want to play it safe, invest your funds at the highest available interest in a federally insured savings account at a bank. This is a conservative way to have your investment safe and growing, although you will not have the growth potential that you would by moving your IRA or Keogh assets from investment to investment as economic conditions dictated.

- You must set up an IRA or Keogh account through a trustee or administrator. The plans are available from banks, mutual funds, and insurance companies. *Don't* use an insurance company. Their carrying and service fees are exorbitant.

- For more information, write Lord, Abbott & Co., *Retirement*, P.O. Box 666, New York, NY 10005 and request their free "Guide to Retirement Planning." Also, for $2.25, "A Shopper's Guide to IRAs and Keogh Plans: Choosing a New Plan and Evaluating the One You Have" is available from N.R.O.C.A. Press, P.O. Box 12066, Dallas, TX 75225.

Annuities

Another very secure place for your retirement fund is in annuities. Basically, annuities are arrangements by which you pay an insurance company premiums up to a certain date, after which the insurance company pays you, either for a stated length of time or for the rest of your life. Annuities are helpful in that they force you to save and won't let you dip into your savings.

The hitch is that the return you get on the money you gave to the insurance company is *much* less than the return you are likely to have gotten by investing the same amounts of money in stocks, bonds, or other investments. And if you're a woman, you will once again have to face smaller monthly payments because the insurance company figures you'll be getting checks longer than the average man would.

Despite the fact that annuities pay back less for your investment, you may want to consider this option, not because it provides a great income, but because it is very secure. If inflation continues, your annuity isn't going to be worth much; but if inflation comes to a stop, an annuity with a big, secure insurance company is relatively secure from the economic readjustments that reduced inflation would involve.

As with Social Security and the private pension, the annuity is not in itself the answer to your retirement needs. It has a place as a conservative hedge, but continued inflation could make the payback insubstantial.

Real Estate

The other "best-bet" investment for retirement is income-producing real estate. The optimum arrangement for many retirees is to own a small apartment house with two or three rental units or a two-family suburban dwelling that gives the retirees a comfortable place to live, plus a reliable source of income that is tied to inflation. The main disadvantage of this kind of arrangement is the worry and responsibility it involves—maintenance, taxes, depreciation, and tenants.

But, all in all, real estate investment offers a secure, conservative return combined with a permanent roof over your head.

LIFE INSURANCE

Life insurance is like poker. Essentially, you and the life insurance company are gambling. They are betting that you won't die during the time they insure you. You are betting that you will.

Should You Ante Up for the Life Insurance Game?

Life insurance is probably superfluous for you if:

- *You have no family depending on you for its support.* (Even if you're single, however, you may need to consider life insurance to care for elderly, or soon-to-be elderly, parents in the event of your death.)
- *Your family is mature and your spouse is working or has a marketable skill or profession* that would produce adequate income in the event of your death.

- *You have savings or some other kind of investment sufficient to support your survivors.*
- *You're collecting Social Security benefits, and your spouse is 62 or older.* (If you die before your spouse turns 62, he or she must wait until then before collecting benefits from your Social Security.)

If you don't fit into these categories, *life insurance does protect your family because:*

- *Most life insurance death benefits are not taxed by the federal government.*
- *Life insurance benefits are paid independent of your estate.* Even if your estate gets tied up in probate court, your survivors will have enough to live on.
- *Your premium payments create a cash value for your policy* that is more secure from your creditors than most other assets in the event of bankruptcy. That value is much more secure from economic fluctuations (except inflation) than are investments in the stock market or in bonds.

Note: You can get more interest by putting money into a savings account than by using the same amount to pay insurance premiums, so a policy isn't the best way to save. But because insurance companies are so stable, there are few more secure ways of investing your dollars. One company's logo isn't the Rock of Gibraltar for nothing—but it isn't a gold mine either.

How Much Life Insurance Should You Consider?

Until you marry, your life insurance needs are likely to be minimal. Your parents are still likely to be working so your death will not create too many hardships for your survivors. Once you marry, the picture shifts radically.
You'll need to have enough insurance to:

1) *Cover your family's living expenses.* Figure that your death will reduce family expenditures between 10 percent and 20 percent. If there are no children, your spouse might be able to get by on as little as 40 percent of your current income.

2) *Cover mortgages and other outstanding debts.* This includes your credit cards, your car loan, and any personal loans you may have outstanding.

3) *Educate the children.* Make a generous allowance here. Costs will continue to rise as higher education reacts to the contraction of population, inflation continues to swell costs, and federal funds for education dry up.

You can subtract from these basic expenses:

1) *Whatever income your spouse can definitely earn.*
2) *Whatever Social Security benefits will be due because of your death.* (Don't forget that your wife will be without Social Security benefits from the time your youngest child turns 18 until she turns 62.)
3) *Whatever pension or group insurance coverage you carry.*

The result will be the amount of coverage you should provide for your family. A simpler formula involves multiplying your yearly income by six and buying life insurance in that amount.

Life Insurance Options

Term Insurance

For this form of insurance, you don't need a big bankroll. You pay the insurance company very little, and they hedge their bet very tightly. They cover you only for a certain number of years: the shorter the length of the term, the less expensive the policy. This is a good kind of insurance for young marrieds as long as it's *convertible* term insurance, which allows for a switch to one of the broader policies without requiring another physical examination. If you have children, you'll especially need the conversion feature.

Straight Life

This kind of insurance, also known as whole life or ordinary life, is the kind you can borrow against. Not only does it cover you in case you die; it also accrues a cash value that you can get back in a lump sum or in monthly payments. It is a good way to build up savings if you absolutely can't save any money on your own. Over a normal life span, you can build a policy with a cash value worth half or more of the face amount. Whether you get the value back in a lump or in installments is determined by the particular policy you buy. You usually redeem it at your retirement or at some specified age.

Endowment

This kind of insurance is designed to pay off at some future date. The face value of the policy provides protection in case of your death, while the endowment provisions of the policy build up a specific amount that can cover your kids' education or your own retirement. It pays off in a lump or in periodic installments. It is the most expensive kind of insurance, and inflation is its worst enemy. The sums paid to you are fixed, so you're in danger of paying in today's relatively hard dollars and getting out dollars that have been damaged by years of inflation. On the other hand, if inflation is brought under control, this can be the most secure way to provide for a future income.

Riders

These are just the basic policies. You can make the game much more interesting with riders. For instance, you can get a straight life policy that carries a rider providing your survivors with a monthly income of a given amount for 20 years after your death. Riders can tailor-make a policy to your specific needs.

Rules of Thumb for Securing Your Loved Ones

- *Cover your family's breadwinner thoroughly.* If you really depend on two incomes for your family, make sure that both earners are covered.

- *Know who you're dealing with.* You want an insurance company that is financially strong, long-lived, and very, very secure. It's probably a good idea to be as conservative as you can in selecting your insurer. *Best's Insurance Reports* rates the companies; it is probably available in your local library.

- *Inform your beneficiaries.* Once you've gone to the trouble of covering your loved ones, you must take the next step to make them feel really secure. Tell them who your insurer is, for how much they are covered, and where you policy is kept. Thousands of people lose their insurance benefits because their benefactors put off telling them the details of the policy, neglected to put the papers in a safe place, or didn't even tell them that the policy existed.

- *Put all your policies together in a fireproof box.* Put a letter in the box listing your policies, the companies that carry them, and the benefits they pay. Give a copy to your lawyer. Tell your beneficiaries about the policies and how to get them in the event of your death. Revise the letter if you cash in a policy or let one lapse. Let your insurance company know when you change your address. Your insurance policy is an investment in the future for your loved ones. Don't provide by half measures; keep the benefits accessible by keeping your beneficiaries informed.

Rules of Thumb for Saving on Your Life Insurance

- *If you buy term insurance, make sure it is a convertible policy* so that you can move on to straight life coverage without having to take a medical exam.

- *Make your life insurance payments in as few installments as you can.* Life insurance premiums are a key ingredient of that third bank account we've recommended that you keep (see pages 13–14), and you can not only earn money on the monthly share of your yearly or quarterly premium, but you also save money in additional interest and processing charges levied by the insurer.

- *Never buy entirely new policies once you've got an insurance policy.* You can probably arrange any additional coverage you may need by having riders added to your policy. You'll save large amounts on the heavy "front end" charges that are often attached to new insurance policies.

- *Review your policy from time to time.* A change in your occupation can result in a lower premium for you. A change in your lifestyle, like retirement, may mean that you don't need life insurance at all any more.

WILLS

Strictly speaking, making a will won't save you any money. But it is a way to make sure your goods and money go where they should. Since you earned your belongings and money, the state allows you to dispose of them as you want . . . provided you follow all the protocols that have evolved.

If you know who you want to leave your assets, even if those assets don't amount to a great deal, you should have a will. Some states will accept a handwritten (holographic) will even if there are no witnesses, but why take a chance? A will removes some of the elements of chance, and at very little expense.

Your will can result in great savings for your beneficiaries, even if you personally don't have much to leave. If you stand to inherit your spouse's estate, for example, and if both of you should die at the same time, and it can be *proved* that you died last, there are all sorts of consequences advantageous to your heirs in the form of taxes and rules of inheritance and probate—if you have a will.

If you are unmarried, widowed, or divorced, you'll need a will more than ever to leave your estate to the people or causes that you want to provide for. Your lovers, friends, favorite charities, and even some of your closest relatives could be out in the cold unless you specify what you want them to inherit.

So spend the few hundred dollars that a simple will costs and protect your assets for the people you want to have them.

Tips on Making a Will

1) *Get a lawyer.* If you have a substantial estate, or if you have complicated family ties, get someone who has experience in handling wills. You may

be satisfied that you can express your desires clearly in the will you write for yourself, but the probate court may find confusion because of laws you didn't know about, or wording that some lawyer found questionable. Unfortunately, just as the range of goods you can leave behind has expanded, so have the provisions of the law. Between estate taxes, legal fees, and the consequences of vague wording, a lawyer can be invaluable. Confusion means that your loved ones suffer in loss of time and money.

2) *There are money- and time-saving automated will forms* that use modern word processing technology to create wills. These forms have the capacity for adding special clauses as you need them in constructing an individualized will. Ask your lawyer if such automated will drafting is available, and be sure to have your lawyer check the final draft.

3) *Get special advice if you have a retarded child or relative for whom you wish to provide.* The Association for Retarded Citizens has local and state offices that can refer you to a legal expert. Send $.50 to the National Association of Retarded People at 2709 Avenue E, East, P.O. Box 16109, Arlington, TX 76011 for a booklet called "How to Provide for Their Future."

4) *Discuss your tax arrangements with a specialist in wills and estate planning if you've put money into tax shelters.* Otherwise, death may cause great financial loss to your survivors.

5) *Pay special attention to real estate holdings other than your home*, if you have such holdings.

6) *If you have property in another state, your will may have to go into probate there.* One way to avoid this is to arrange joint ownership with the person you wish to have the property. When you die—or when your joint owner dies—the property passes in its entirety to the co-owner without passing through probate.

7) *Make sure you have enough cash assets in your estate to cover the estate taxes.* If not, your real estate assets may have to go on sale to pay the government. Here again, you need the advice of an expert.

What Not to Do with Your Will

1) *Don't hide it.* You may do too good a job. Be sure that several other people know that you have a will and where you keep it.

2) *Don't leave your will in your safe deposit box.* Keeping a copy there is fine, but your safe deposit box will be sealed on your death. So have your lawyer keep your will. That way it's accessible.

3) *Don't revise your will without consulting your lawyer.* Changing anything in your will may invalidate the whole thing. If you let your lawyer keep your will, you'll have to consult him or her about changes.

4) *Don't depend on your will to detail your wishes for your funeral.* The will may not be read until after you're buried. Make a separate statement for funeral wishes, and let your spouse or close friend or lawyer keep a copy of that as well.

DOING YOUR OWN INVESTIGATING

The advice in this chapter has been gleaned from the best sources available, but which financial strategy is best is a matter of opinion. Let this material make you aware of financial options you may not have considered; then go out and do the research you need to determine what sort of investments, insurance, or borrowing is best for you.

There are good sources of information at several levels beyond that of this chapter. Two are Sylvia Porter's *New Money Book for the 80's* (New York: Avon Books) and Jane Bryan Quinn's *Everyone's Money Book* (New York: Dell Publishing).

In addition, you should look for the most recent publications available at your local library, including financial periodicals like the *Wall Street Journal, Fortune, Barron's,* and the financial pages of major newspapers, especially the *New York Times.* It is not unreasonable to study your money and investment options for several months before deciding how to distribute your money.

Don't overlook any free courses that might be available in the areas that interest you. They might be offered by brokerage houses. Colleges and universities also offer courses on economics and money management that are good starting points for your money studies.

A SAMPLING OF AVAILABLE SOURCES

The Consumer Credit Handbook (587-k), free. A general guide to obtaining credit, available through the Consumer Information Center, Pueblo, CO 81009.

Everybody's Guide to Small Claims Court by Ralph Warner, $6.95. A flawless guide to fighting your case in small claims court. Addison-Wesley Publishing Co., Jacob Way, Reading, MA 01867.

A Guide to Budgeting for the Family (#108), $.35 and *Credit Shopping Guide* (m-01-1), $1.00. Two of the many practical booklets about family economics available through the Superintendent of Documents, U.S. Government Printing Office, Washington, DC 20402.

"Net Worth Statement" (CEH-6), $.25 and "Do You Know Your Valuable Papers?" (E 963), $.85. Two pamphlets about handling money and documents from the Distribution Center, 7 Research Park, Cornell University, Ithaca, NY 14850.

The Seven Laws of Money by Michael Phillips, $4.00. Provides some wise, smart, almost cheeky advice that can revolutionize your ways of dealing with money. Random House, 455 Hahn Road, Westminster, MD 21157.

Successful Investing—A Complete Guide to Your Financial Future, edited by Ronald K. Mills, $8.95. A basic, conservative approach to keeping your savings safe, including definitions of the terms of the marketplace and an overview of the problems of economics. Simon & Schuster, 1230 Ave. of the Americas, New York, NY 10020.

There's More to Credit Cards Than Meets the Eye by 275-52-3902 and 302-52-9965, $3.50. This book is "Dedicated to the hundreds of retailers who overcharge thousands of their customers millions of dollars due to the unfair subsidizing of credit card percentages." Interstate International Publishing of Cincinnati, P.O. Box 29047, Cincinnati, OH 45229.

You Can Negotiate Anything by Herb Cohen, $12.00. A somewhat aggresive but practical approach to dealing with negotiating at all levels. Practical reading, especially for the timid. Lyle Stuart, Inc., 120 Enterprise Ave., Secaucus, NJ 07094.

Your Inflation Guide: Dollars and Sense. Free advice from the federal government . . . who should know better? Available also from the Consumer Information Center, Pueblo, CO 81009.

BUYING A HOME
AND MOVING IN

BUYING A HOME
AND MOVING IN

Generally speaking, you have two very basic choices when it comes to shelter. You can rent or you can buy. There are some very good reasons to rent, not the least of which is that buying has never been tougher. The United States is experiencing the biggest housing crunch in its history. People born during the "baby boom" just after World War II are now ready to buy homes, but the supply is short, so prices are high, and money is so tight that mortgage interest rates are at unprecedented levels. But despite these difficulties, and despite rising taxes and the responsibility that comes with ownership, almost two out of every three Americans still want to buy.

Most people know that there are good financial reasons to buy a home, but the real motivation to buy is the psychological payoff. A private home is a tangible reward for one's efforts, and a family seems more secure in a home of its own than in the hands of a landlord. If you feel this way, but don't own a home, then it's time to start making your dream real. This chapter presents a number of ways in which you may be able to get your first home, even if the financial odds seem stacked against you. It also includes tips for the more experienced buyer and ways to save on moving into a new home.

THE BUYING PROCESS

Many people stumble into buying property without really understanding the steps involved. These are distinguished neatly below, although once you get involved in the process, you'll find they overlap.

1) *Decide exactly what you want in a home.*
2) *Analyze your finances and decide how much you can afford to pay.*
3) *Accumulate or acquire your down payment.*
4) *Begin house hunting*—zero in on the community and neighborhood you want and narrow down the range of homes.
5) *Begin to shop for financing.*

6) *Find the house you want and have it inspected and appraised while negotiating with the seller.*

7) *Draw up the contract to purchase.*

8) *Secure the mortgage.*

9) *Complete the purchase and celebrate the closing.*

People most often have complaints about their home-buying experiences for these reasons, according to the Better Business Bureau:

- They bought bigger or more expensive homes than their budgets allowed.

- They now pay more to maintain their homes than they can easily handle.

- They found serious flaws in the construction of their homes.

- They bought property that fell in value.

- They suffered a loss of income and had to carry mortgages on their reduced incomes.

- They bought too hastily.

- They bought in a neighborhood they came to dislike.

These problems can be avoided only by careful consideration of each step in the buying process.

DECIDING WHAT YOU WANT

Recognize your needs. For instance . . .

- Are you interested in a coop or a condominium? (See "Condominiums, Cooperatives, and Other Housing Options," pages 71–76.)

- Do you want a house in the city, close to your job but short on trees, grass and acreage?

- Do you need a house surrounded by land, where you can garden, raise some kids, and yodel without complaints?

- Can you take on the chores involved in maintaining an older home—keeping those picturesque wooden shakes (shingles) in order, for instance?

- Are you working from your home, so that additional office space or electrical lines are necessary?

- Do you entertain a lot for pleasure or for business and therefore need extra kitchen and living space?

- Do you need extra bedroom space for growing children?
- Do you want a neighborhood with lots of children, or is a quiet, decorous neighborhood more to your liking?

Don't kid yourself about your needs. Your image of the country estate will pale soon if you need to get home quickly and easily after late sessions at the office. And that sophisticated townhouse will prove cramped, noisy, and inconvenient if you're really geared to the split-level and patio style of the suburbs.

DECIDING WHAT YOU CAN AFFORD

Traditional Formulas

Plan conservatively. Look at the problems inflation has created for those who thought fixed incomes could provide an adequate standard of living. Here are three conservative formulas:

- *You can afford a house that costs two to two and one-half times your gross annual income.* If you're earning $20,000 a year, you can safely consider a home costing $45,000 to $50,000.
- *The average combined monthly costs of all your housing expenses should equal about one and one-half week's take-home pay.* Your mortgage payment should equal no more than one week's take-home pay. The remaining half-week's take-home pay must cover your monthly expenses for utilities (oil, gas, electricity, water, and garbage collection); insurance payments; local, state, and school taxes; and repairs and maintenance inside and outside your home.
- *The difference between your total expenses and your take-home pay can determine your mortgage payment.* Add up your expenses for each month— food, clothing, savings, utilities, and entertainment. Don't forget to figure in about one-twelfth of what you pay yearly for vacations, holiday presents, and credit card purchases. If you are careful to include all your monthly expenses, the difference between those expenses and a month's take-home pay will be a suitable mortgage payment.

You should stick to a less expensive house or a mortgage requiring monthly payments that are less than one week's take-home pay if:

- you live in a cold climate
- your house is all or mostly electric

- your taxes are high or soon will be (if you move into a booming community, you can bet they will)
- you have college-age children or will have in five years or less
- your house is older and will therefore require a substantial budget for upkeep
- your family is already large, or a new home will mean family expansion
- your credit burden is large (be especially attentive to educational loans, car loans, and credit card debts to department stores or major credit companies)
- the cost of living in your neighborhood is high
- your line of work requires frequent moves
- your work brings in an irregular or fluctuating income.

You may consider a slightly more expensive home or a larger mortgage payment if:

- you have no other debts
- you are an accomplished—or at least a committed—do-it-yourselfer
- your line of work entails likely advancement and pay raises
- your family is small and will remain so
- your community has low taxes and is likely to maintain present rates
- you are interested in a house requiring low maintenance, with all major appliances in good condition.

The Latest Trends

Some lending institutions still use the time-tested formulas described above to compare your housing selection with your income, but others now consider these approaches, even if adjusted, irrelevant in the current market. You may find that the lender to whom you apply for your mortgage will be more interested in your total assets: savings, investment holdings, the value of your current house, your life insurance, art or collectibles, even your car. From your total assets, the prospective lender will subtract the money you owe for your current mortgage, the balance you have yet to pay on your car, your credit obligations, bills, and other items. At that point you should have an amount sufficient to cover your down payment, closing costs, and moving costs, plus at least two or three months' salary as a cushion against illness, an accident, or an unforeseen cash crunch.

How to Miscalculate the Costs of a New Home

- *Forget to adjust your commuting expenses.*
- *Forget to adjust the cost of utilities.* These may be substantially different from where you now live; you may have to pay a water bill that accounts for a new lawn, or an electric bill for double or triple the number of rooms you're used to lighting.
- *Forget that the insurance costs for the new home are likely to be considerably higher* than for your current home or apartment.

Strategies for Making Home Ownership Economically Feasible

- *If you're a one-income couple, become a two-income couple.* Half of all home buyers are families with more than one wage-earner. The second earner contributes between one-third and one-half of the family income in about 30 percent of these families.
- *Relocate to a smaller city in the heartland.* The cheapest homes are most abundant in north-central cities with fewer than 250,000 residents. The worst place to shop is on the West Coast or in cities like New York, Washington, and Boston and their suburbs.
- *Postpone having children.* You can afford a home much more easily if you don't face the expense of raising kids.
- *Share a home.* Urban areas that don't restrict the number of unrelated people who can live together are perfect for various combinations of singles and couples. There are pitfalls—zoning restrictions, psychological barriers, legal and living hassles. But sharing works well for lots of people, even when children are involved.

THE DOWN PAYMENT

Once you have an idea of the total package you can afford, it's time to take a look at your down payment. Under ordinary conditions, lenders require down payments of up to 35 percent of the cost of the home. With inflation at a higher rate than the interest on an ordinary savings account, how in the world can you save enough money to make the down payment? This can certainly be discouraging, but there are solutions. Home buying is the best way to fight inflation because home values appreciate even faster than your dollars shrink, so the time and effort required to put together the down payment are worth it.

How to Get the Money

- *Start saving immediately.* Some people spend years lamenting about their inability to make a down payment, but they never take the first step towards making their fantasies real. A savings account is not the best way to put your money to work, but it is a way to accumulate the capital for some earnest investment. Save hard until you have enough to buy into the money market; it may take less than six months to save enough to buy high-interest certificates of deposit. If you need more than willpower, sign up for an automatic savings plan at your commercial bank or at your workplace. Talk with an officer at your bank, explain your home-buying goals, and listen to his or her advice. Together you can work out a plan to get your down payment. Arrange to be notified about 60 days before you have saved the required amount, so you can begin your house hunting in earnest. (Also refer to the savings and investment suggestions in Chapter One, "Money".)

- *Borrow the money from your parents.* Many, many home buyers get a large part of their down payments from their parents. It may be a no-interest loan or a very low-interest one, but make it formal, to protect your parents in case you can't pay them back. If the money is an outright gift, think about taxes. Each of your parents can give you and your spouse $10,000 each ($40,000 total) in a year that's not subject to gift taxes. If you arrange to borrow a larger sum from your parents, do so in more than one year. You can get $12,000 at the end of December and another $12,000 at the beginning of January without your parents' having to pay the gift tax.

- *Borrow against your assets.* If you own a car that's been paid for, a fur coat, a diamond ring, or a stock portfolio, offer it as collateral. Not only will you get your loan, but the collateral will probably give you an advantage of a point or part of a point in the interest rate.

- *Find a seller who is willing to defer the down payment.* You may be able to do so if the market has been tight because of high interest rates and the unavailability of mortgage loans. You give the seller a second mortgage at a fairly steep interest rate, but it allows you to make payments in installments, and sometimes postpone payment for two or three years. This is a particularly good deal if the house has been held by one owner for a long time, and if you can buy it on the low end of its value range. Because you will see the house's value rise more steeply in this situation, the overall cost of the second mortgage will be reduced.

- *Rent with an option to buy.* If a home has been on the market for awhile, or if the owner is under pressure to sell and move away, you may be able to arrange a deal by which you rent the property and a percentage of your monthly payment is put aside to accumulate the down payment. Once you've completed the down payment, you can go on to buy the house and secure the mortgage as in a standard deal.

- *A low-interest second mortgage can cover a good part of your down payment.* If you're buying a new home, the builder may agree to this. It is most likely when money is tight or when there's a local building glut.

- *Private mortgage insurance may enable you to borrow 90 to 95 percent of the cost of your home.* You pay an annual insurance premium (that also includes the mortgage payment) to a private mortgage insurance company until it holds a loan in the normal amount of 70 to 80 percent of the selling price. Then you can cancel the insurance. If you forget to cancel it, the insurance will continue and you'll be paying unnecessary premiums. You may have to hunt around for a lender who offers this kind of private mortgage, and availability may depend on local conditions. This is sometimes easier to secure through the bank where you've been accumulating your down payment in savings, so if a bank officer doesn't mention it, be sure to bring it up.

Unless you're fortunate enough to accumulate your down payment through savings or investment or through gifts or no-interest loans, that process will be a real financial burden, particularly because of the interest you'll be charged. Your justification is that the property you are going to buy will appreciate, quickly reducing your debt to a reasonable proportion of your assets. And those assets, consisting largely in the value of your home, will continue to grow long after your debt is paid.

How Much Should You Put Down?

There are several reasons to try to make only a small down payment, but because of inflation and the tight money market, you may not find a lender who will agree to it. The choice of percentage may be pretty well out of your hands, depending on your financial record, local conditions, the age of the home you're buying, and other disparate factors. You may, however, be rewarded for putting down as much as you can possibly afford. The major arguments for both alternatives are presented below.

Advantages of Large Down Payments
- *You may be able to cut the interest rate on your loan by a half-point or so by making a larger down payment.* If you manage to lower an interest rate from, say, 11.5 percent on a $40,000 loan to 11 percent by putting down a big down payment, you'll save almost $5,500 over the term of the loan.

- *The more you pay up front, the lower your interest costs will be over the course of the loan, even if you don't get the half-point.* Assume that you have an option on a home worth $60,000, and the best rate you can get for your mortgage is 14 percent. If you put down 20 percent of the total, or $12,000, you'll repay $74,556 over the course of the loan. If you put down 10 percent, or $6,000, you'll have to repay $95,015. The $6,000 difference in the down payment compounds to a $20,459 difference over the life of the loan. (This is less important if you expect to move well before your mortgage is paid in full. Also, mortgage interest is tax-deductible, so smaller interest payments may be less advantageous than they seem.)

Advantages of Smaller Down Payments

- *You can keep your finances more flexible, more "liquid," if you make a smaller down payment and put other savings into different kinds of investments that leave the money accessible.* That way you won't need additional loans in case of emergencies or for upcoming expenses like tuition or travel.

- *The less money you put down, the bigger your profit if you have to sell your house quickly.* A smaller down payment means that if you decide to sell the house, you will be more likely to find a buyer who will be able to reimburse you your collateral. More buyers assume a small down payment and a large mortgage than vice versa.

HOUSE HUNTING

As soon as you've got some idea of what you can actually afford and have the better part of your down payment together, you can settle down to the serious business of house hunting.

Comparing Communities

Once you have a general sort of environment in mind, you can begin comparing communities. *It is generally advisable to look for a well-established neighborhood with stabilized land values and a solid sense of community.* In the long run, this will have a greater effect on the value of your home than any improvements you make or any other special features your home may have.

- *Research the tax rates in the areas you're considering.* Property taxes are the second largest item, after mortgage payments, in the home buyer's budget, and you'll be paying them as long as you live in the home. So ask neighbors, town officials, and your real estate agent about these things, especially:
  - *Reassessment customs*—some localities hit new owners with hikes in the valuations of their homes
  - *Scheduled reassessments* facing the whole community
  - *Special assessments* in the wings for sewers, roads, or schools

— *The services your taxes pay for*—it may save you a few hundred dollars per year (or more) if your community provides garbage removal, outstanding schools, special recreational facilities, or an excellent hospital.

Remember that local word of mouth is pretty reliable. In most communities the people know what financial surprises the local government may have in store for you, so add the gossips' forecasts into your project outlays, no matter what reassurances the seller gives you to the contrary.

- *Remember to compare communities on the basis of the cost of commuting, in dollars and in time.* You may spend as much as one-fifth of your working day commuting, so be sure the roads and public transportation are good. A two-dollar-a-day difference in commuting costs swells to about $500 annually.

- *Make sure that all of the stores, services, and educational and recreational facilities that you need are within easy reach and that their prices are in keeping with your budget.* You may find that choosing one community over another makes a difference of several dollars a day in various costs.

- *Make sure that you don't get stuck with bad zoning.* Your dream house may be on the market because the lovely wooded land behind it has just been zoned for an apartment house. Zoning ordinances may regulate whether house guests can park their cars in the street overnight, or whether you can put up a garage or add a patio or swimming pool. The lack of a plan is just as undesirable as bad planning, so find out what kind of zoning commission the community has and what kind of impact it has on the neighborhood you are considering. Visit the local building department or the planning agency and ask for the zoning maps. Be wary if there aren't any. Even if there are, ask what zoning variances have been granted, and what policies govern them.

- *If you have kids or plan on them, check out the schools carefully.* Is there a busing program? How much does the school district spend per year per child? What are the teachers' salaries and budget levels for ancillary programs like sports and art education? Is there a nearby community with a more attractive package? Is there a high school? You'll need it sooner than you can imagine. What about bond issues for the schools? Will they be at the mercy of "Proposition 13"-type movements? Talk to the local administration or principal about the school. If you meet with evasion or stonewalling, there may be a problem in the district. The best thing you can do for your child is to visit the school when it is in session and see for yourself how it's run. Lunch time especially will give you an idea of the nature of discipline at the school and the kinds of students that attend. In any case, be sure to investigate the curriculum. You may be surprised at what is taught or not taught.

Rules for Shopping

- *Give yourself enough time to investigate a good selection of homes and communities and to make the appropriate decisions.* You're probably making the biggest investment of your life. You may be buying the place where you'll spend the next 20 years, and even if you sell your home in a few years, the profit you make then depends on your decision now. You should budget about three months for serious house shopping, beginning when your down payment is ready. If you have a restricted budget or specific needs, then figure that it may take a good deal longer to find the place you want. Of course, you may happen onto the perfect place the very first weekend you look—and if you do, don't hesitate to buy it. But generally you can expect that it will take some time to find your house, so be easy on yourself and allow enough time to shop sensibly.

- *Keep your information organized.* Get a notebook (a loose-leaf one is probably best) and take lots of notes. You'll be meeting dozens of people and seeing scores of houses, and you'll need to weigh a lot of considerations before making the crucial decisions. Keep specific information on each house—total house area, condition of the basement, type of landscaping, size of school classes, tax rates, commuting costs, mortgage rates, heating plants, and so on. Keeping the details straight and the figures accessible will not be possible unless you have an organized way of keeping track. Notes become even more important if you're planning to share the property in some way and you must pass the facts along to a spouse or partner.

- *Have the house inspected and appraised by professionals and get the findings in writing.* This will prevent unforeseen and crippling maintenance expenses. In addition, those findings can be bargaining points in the negotiations with the seller. Look for inspectors and appraisers who are members of their professions' national organizations. If you are getting a government-backed mortgage, you'll need an inspection and/ or assessment in any case. Also, lenders will have the home assessed to determine how much they will loan you, and inspected to insure that it will stand for the length of the mortgage. You'll be charged for these evaluations at closing, so try to have them done by the bank's usual people before you actually apply for the loan. That way you'll have the information early enough to use it while bargaining and won't have to pay for it twice. If you cannot have evaluations done in advance, be sure to make the purchase agreement contingent on the finds of the lender's assessor and the inspector.

Shopping for Maximum Savings

If saving money is a very high priority, and if you have the time to look for the deal that can save you the most, then consider these tips:

- *Only visit houses that are for sale by the owners.* You'll save some money because there will be no broker's fee.

- *Buy an older home.* The owner has probably made a large profit on his or her equity—the appreciation of the home since it was built—and may therefore come down a bit on the price. Newer homes are priced high to recover the inflated costs of recent construction, finishing, and landscaping. *The advantages of an older home include:*

  — established landscape features
  — better materials and workmanship
  — lower taxes
  — "character"
  — structural faults that have already been discovered and corrected through years of use
  — an established neighborhood.

- *The disadvantages may include:*

  — the need for repairs (major sore spots might include the electrical system, plumbing, and the heating plant)
  — older major appliances
  — an inefficient energy profile
  — a declining neighborhood (watch our for a flock of "for sale" signs or lots of ads or listings for houses in the neighborhood.

- *Shop for your home during slow months.* Most people try to move as soon as school's out, so they shop in the early spring. The market gets very busy again in the early fall, when companies that are fully staffed after the summer vacation are ready to make new assignments. Few people are eager to move in the dead of winter, so if you can stand it, look for your new home in December, January, and February.

- *Shop for a house that's been on the market for some time; its price will have dropped.* In many cases it will still be on the market because it needs work and is a little "different." If you're willing to take the chance that you may have a hard time finding a buyer when it comes time to sell, you may find a very good deal on a home that has a strong and eccentric character of its own. And if you can do the work yourself, you can make a substantial profit when the time comes to sell.

- *Look in a neighborhood that's marginal.* This can be very chancy, but there are run-down neighborhoods shoulder-to-shoulder with better neighborhoods in every city. So buying a house on a borderline street and gambling that urban renewal will make you a pioneer in a reviving neighborhood may turn out as well for you as it did for people who invested in areas like Park Slope in Brooklyn or Greenwich Village in Manhattan.

- *Look for a home in a condominium that has failed, a development that has gone bankrupt, or a house that has been foreclosed.* The bank or receiver, eager to turn it over before the housing begins to fall apart from vandalism, lack of maintenance, or neglect, will sometimes offer such housing at a bargain price.

Real Estate Agents

One of the biggest assets you can have in house hunting is a good real estate agent. There are good agents in firms of all sizes, but make sure that the agent you choose belongs to the National Association of Realtors and to the local real estate board. That way you will have some recourse if you can prove that you were pressured into a purchase or that the broker misrepresented some fact about the house. Keep the following tips in mind when dealing with real estate agents:

- *Use several agents in the area you're considering.* After all, you don't pay agency fees, the seller does. Even when listings are shared, they sometimes don't become common knowledge for a few days or more. Your dream house could be someone else's bargain if you confine yourself to one broker. There's one precaution to recall when you are dealing with more than one agent, though. IF YOU'VE SEEN A HOUSE WITH ONE AGENT, OR THROUGH THE OWNER DIRECTLY, DON'T GO INSIDE IT WITH A SECOND AGENT. When you pull up outside a house you've already been shown, simply say that you've seen it. Otherwise you could be slapped with a lawsuit.

- *Cultivate your agent a bit.* A luncheon date to talk over your needs and to get acquainted may move you to the front of your agent's mind when new listings come in. It's a small expense compared to the time and money you're investing in your home.

- *Be frank about your finances and your needs.* You'll save time and make the house hunting experience easier for everyone.

- *Avoid brokers who begin to sell you houses without even finding out what you have in mind.*

- *Don't expect the broker to work to bring the price down.* The broker is paid a percentage of the selling price, so it is to his or her advantage to keep the house price at the high end of the price range.

- *Be clear about the contract terms relating to the broker.* Get the details of the escrow arrangements for your deposit. If the deal collapses just before closing, does the broker keep the deposit? If you decide to change your mind about buying, do you get your money back? (You should, no matter how hard the broker has worked and how whimsical your change of mind may be.)

SHOPPING FOR FINANCING

Once you've picked a neighborhood, you'll need to shop among lending institutions for financing. You're most likely to find a lender in the community where you're buying your house because the lenders prefer to return the funds they're loaning to the community that produced them. The exception may be if you've established a healthy savings account for your down payment in your original community, but the new neighborhood must be nearby for your savings bank to provide the mortgage.

The most important consideration in your financial shopping is to get the best possible mortgage interest rate. A difference of half a percentage point can amount to more than $6,000 over the course of the loan. You should also compare different lending institutions to find what policies each follows regarding down payments, what each requires in closing costs, which ones offer VHA-backed loans and rollover mortgages, and which ones demand "points" *before* you find the home you want. These topics will be discussed later in the chapter; the advice here is that you should be selective when shopping for a lender, just as you are when shopping for a home.

NEGOTIATING A PRICE

Once you've found the place you want, shoot for the best price possible. Keep these basic tips in mind as you negotiate with the seller.

- *Make your first bid substantially lower than the asking price.* If the initial price is $60,000 or less, your first offer should probably be 80 to 90 percent of that figure ($48,000 to $54,000 for a house priced at exactly $60,000). For homes priced at over $60,000 you can offer an even smaller percentage of the asking price. Be bold; people are sometimes successful with bids of 50 percent below the quoted price.

- *If you're interested enough in the house to have it inspected by a professional, do so before you begin bidding.* The inspector will tell you what ought to be done to the house and how much it will probably cost. Subtract this figure from your first offer, which should already be lower than the asking price, as discussed above. If about $4,000 worth of work needs to be done on a $60,000 house, for example, the opening bid should drop to between $44,000 and $50,000.

- *Don't be afraid to walk away.* If the seller turns your bid down firmly, but you don't want to pay anything more for the house than you bid, you should be equally firm. You won't be happy if you pay more than you think is just, but you may find that over time (in one to two months) your bid becomes more attractive to the seller.

- *Don't be rushed into a deal on the seller's terms.*

- *As your original bid sits on the table, keep researching real estate in the area.* The research may convince you to increase your bid a bit; by that time the seller may be willing to come down a little. If you keep investigating other options, you'll be less likely to make a bad deal out of desperation.

MAKING THE CONTRACT TO PURCHASE

Once you've agreed to terms in principle, and the time comes to sign a contract, you definitely need a lawyer. You're about to bind yourself with a contract to buy the property, and when you think of the time and money involved, you can see why the protection of an attorney is absolutely essential. If you don't have a lawyer already, get one in your new community. You can get advice on picking a lawyer from your local lending institution, the bar association, or a friend in the community.

The contract you sign will be a conditional agreement to purchase. The condition is usually that you find a lender willing to make the mortgage loan. The contract also fixes the amount of the earnest money you will be asked to put down on the purchase. The usual binder is about 1 percent of the price of the house.

Your contract can cover such matters as the date you expect to move in; special arrangements for the seller to stay on, including the amount of rent he or she will pay you, if necessary; and the penalties, if any, should the deal fall through. *But be sure that the following more fundamental terms are covered in the contract:*

- *description of the property*—both the house and the land
- *selling price and terms of payment*
- *provision for an inspection* (if one has not yet been conducted) before the deal becomes final

- *details about peculiar legal aspects of the property,* such as mineral rights held by a third party or an easement for the property
- *date of the closing, date you can move in, and date when title to the property passes to you*
- *the legal names of all the people involved in the sale*
- *details about the type of mortgage*
- *arrangements to apportion the seller's and buyer's shares of taxes, insurance, utility bills, and other costs.*

Once again, it is absolutely necessary to have a lawyer working with you at this point and hereafter. The legal costs now will protect you from heavier losses later on.

SECURING THE MORTGAGE

Once you've got the contract to purchase, you're ready to make the final arrangements for your mortgage. You'll have found out about the local availability of financing, and you'll have discovered that mortgages come in all shapes and sizes. Make your final decision carefully.

Following is an outline of the various kinds of mortgages and their chief drawbacks and advantages.

General Tips About Mortgages

- *Shop hard to get a mortgage with a prepayment clause that allows you to pay off your mortgage early.* This way you can, if you wish, work to reduce the principal of the loan before mortgage terms begin to put a dent into it. If interest rates fall after you've taken out the mortgage, a prepayment clause will allow you to take a new mortgage at the lower interest rate and use it to prepay the balance of the old high-rate mortgage.
- *Watch out for "points" and origination fees.* These administrative charges have mushroomed as a means by which lenders can make more money on the loans they give you. "Points" are charges that the lender makes at the time the loan is made; origination fees are charged at the time of the closing. Both have the same effect. If you borrow $70,000 and the lender charges two points, you'll actually get $68,600 to pay for your home, while you'll have to pay back the full $70,000. Over the course of a 15-year mortgage, a point is equal to about one-eighth of 1 percent additional interest. So when you shop for financing, keep these charges in mind. You may find a lender who charges 17 percent interest but tacks on a four-point origination fee; you'd be better off with another lender at 17.25 percent, without any points or origination fees.

- *The factor determining whether your loan will be granted may be the length of time it takes to secure it.* If you need to close quickly, government-sponsored loans may be out of the question unless you can make special arrangements in advance.

- *Find out whether you can extend your mortgage.* As long as the terms don't work against you, it can be to your advantage to lengthen the term of your loan.

- *Do you have to carry insurance to satisfy the lender?* If so, make sure *you* can do the shopping. If the lender wants to restrict your right to look for a better price on the insurance, then try another lender. As long as the coverage you arrange has the same provisions for coverage, you should be able to have any company you want write the policy.

- *Find out about late charges.* If you can't make the payments on time, is there a grace period? How long is it? Once the grace period is over, what are the charges? (Six percent is about average.)

- *Find out about the closing costs.* You can save money by getting the seller to agree to pay some of them.

Traditional Approaches

Conventional Mortgages

In this type of loan, the lending institution itself is the only agency you deal with. If you qualify, the loan can come through in a few days or, at most, a few weeks. There's no limit to what you can qualify to borrow, but you may have to make a down payment of 35 percent of the purchase price of your home to get the mortgage. You can reduce this burden in some cases by taking out a mortgage insurance policy (see page 57); the down payment on a loan of up to $60,000 can drop as low as 5 percent, and you still get the loan fast. The major problem with conventional loans is that they now carry heavy interest rates. Also, it may be hard for you to qualify for one of these mortgages, or to find a reasonable down payment.

Veterans Administration Loans

It is hard to find a lending institution that will write a VA mortgage, but if you're an eligible veteran, it's worth your while to try. The mortgage is underwritten by the federal government, but the money is made available by a bank or other lender. And since VA loans carry a lower-than-average interest rate, lenders have been reluctant to make them. If you do find a lender, you'll have to pay to have the home you're considering appraised. (This is a reasonable precaution in any case, since it may give you ammunition to lower the asking price if you find defects in the house.) But once the assessment is complete, you can ask for a loan of 100 percent of the appraised value of the house. Usually the lender will insist on a down payment, but it may be less than an ordinary loan would require. Once you've got your home, you will have the right to prepay part of your mortgage without penalty, further reducing your interest costs. And if you should run into financial problems and have trouble making mortgage payments, the VA will do its best to keep the lender patient as you get back to making regular payments. For details about VA loans, write to the Veterans Administration, Washington, DC 20420, or visit your local VA office.

Federal Housing Administration Loans

Like the VA loans described above, FHA-backed loans are made through a bank or other lending institution and guaranteed by the government. There are similar difficulties in finding amenable lenders because of the low interest rates attached to federally guaranteed loans. But there are banks still making FHA-backed loans . . . and you don't have to be a veteran to get one. The red tape is extensive. The house will be inspected and assessed, and the FHA must approve its location and structural soundness before your loan can be processed. This can be a big disadvantage if the seller wants to close the deal quickly. But if the owner can be persuaded to wait, you'll be able to make a low down payment and to take as many as 30 to 35 years to pay back the loan. The long term of the loan reduces monthly payments to manageable levels, making an FHA loan attractive to lower-income buyers. (But remember that the longer the term of the loan, the more money you'll pay back in interest.)

You can find out about the current terms and requirements for FHA loans by writing to the Federal Housing Authority, Department of Housing and Urban Development, 451 7th Street SW, Washington, DC 20410.

Farmers Home Administration Loans

If you want a home in a rural area, and you're older or have a low income, you should get in touch with the Farmers Home Administration. This agency can make loans with a life of 33 years and adjusts its interest rates, depending on your earnings and the size of your family. The problems you will encounter stem mostly from eligibility and availability. Although the FmHA has begun to sponsor loans in the same way that the FHA does, the loans in most areas are still made by the agency itself. Therefore, funds are limited and the requirements are detailed. To find out what kind of programs are available in the areas where you're looking, contact the local FmHA representative through the office of the Department of Agriculture nearest you, or write to the Farmers Home Administration, Department of Agriculture, Washington, DC 20250.

"New" Mortgages

The present inflationary climate has given rise to some interesting variations on mortgages:

Variable-Rate Mortgages

The interest on such a mortgage is adjusted (no more than once a year in most cases) according to a national index that reflects the going rates for loans. The adjustment can be no more than 0.5 percent each year, and the limit is usually 2.5 percent over the life of the loan.

Rollover Mortgages

The mortgage is written as a series of short-term loans. You choose the length of time between renewals, usually three, four, or five years. Each time the loan is up for renewal, the interest rate can be raised 0.5 percent, but it can't go up more than 5 percent over the course of the whole mortgage.

Graduated Payment Mortgages

The mortgage is written at a fixed rate, like a conventional mortgage, but the interest is somewhat higher than the going rate. In return for the higher interest, you get to pay the loan back in smaller installments during the early years of the loan, when you are presumably working your way to higher income levels. In later years, your payments increase on the assumption that you will then be able to afford a bigger monthly bite.

Shared Appreciation Mortgages

You find the house you want to live in and sign a partnership agreement with an investor who helps you with the down payment and/or monthly payments. Investors can be family members trying to help each other buy homes or home-sellers, developers, and traditional investors. In return the investor gets tax benefits and a share of the appreciated value of the home when it is resold. The advantage to the lender is that it allows him to invest in real estate without becoming a landlord or manager, and it can yield a handsome profit.

In general you should follow conservative fiscal policies and avoid these new mortgages. The first two types described above clearly benefit the lender more than they do the borrower. And the graduated payment mortgage makes assumptions about your future earning power that may put you in financial straits later. But if the only mortgage you can find is in one of these new formats, you should consider it; it's probably better to have a house and a less-than-advantageous mortgage than to have no house. Protect yourself by insisting on a pre-payment clause that will enable you to pay off a disadvantageous mortgage should the interest and funding market improve in the future.

Seller-Backed Mortgages

The tight money market has encouraged the development of all sorts of seller-backed financing arrangements over the last few years. For instance:

- *You can assume the standing mortgage.* Usually this means that you arrange with the bank and the seller to assume the amount remaining to be paid off on the old mortgage, the amount by which the value of the house has appreciated since the old mortgage was written, and the amount the seller has already paid off. The bank will want a higher interest rate, of course, but this process may be the simplest way to secure a mortgage.

- *The seller may accept a second mortgage.* If you are able to make a down payment of 5 percent of the price and secure a mortgage for 75 percent, you may be able to arrange for the seller to offer you a mortgage for the remaining 20 percent.

- *The seller can make an installment contract, whereby the buyer pays for the house over three or four years, instead of all at once.* This may allow you to secure a series of smaller loans at lower interest rates.

- *The seller can make the purchase easier for you by selling just the house, not the land it stands on.* This substantially reduces the cost of the property. (It also, of course, means that should you want to resell the house, you'll get less than if you also owned the land.) Usually the seller provides a long-term lease on the land the house stands on. You can protect your house by arranging to hold an option to buy. This kind of sale is most common where the land itself may be of particular value, like in Hawaii or parts of California.

- *The seller can make a "wraparound" mortgage, if the terms of the original mortgage don't forbid it.* If the original mortgage was for $30,000 at 5 percent interest, the seller writes you a new mortgage for, say, $50,000 at 10 percent interest. You pay the seller as though you were paying the bank, and the seller pays the bank the balance of his or her old mortgage. You get the title to the property, and the seller keeps the difference between what he pays the bank and what you pay him. This works if the seller is not in a hurry for the money.

- *The seller can hold onto the title to the house, while the rest of the deal proceeds as with the wraparound mortgage described above.* This is called a land contract. Usually land contracts are arranged while the buyer is looking for more permanent financing.

The seller has to wait for the money under all of these arrangements, so they are not easy to set up. But there are some tax advantages for the seller in having the payments for the house spread out over time, and this can work in your favor. In any case, both seller and buyer must have advice from a competent and experienced lawyer before getting involved with one of these financing arrangements.

CLOSING

On closing, you get together with your lawyer, the seller, his or her lawyer, and the lender, and you write checks to most of them. Following are some of the most common costs and what you should do to minimize them. Despite your economizing, expect to pay as much as $3,000 to close your purchase.

- *"Points," and the loan origination fee.* As pointed out earlier, you can avoid these costs by shopping carefully among local lenders. Or you can negotiate to have the lender absorb part of the cost.

- *Lender's appraisal and inspection fee.* As pointed out earlier, if you manage to have these evaluations done early enough—before you complete the contract—you'll only have to pay for them once.

- *Insurance prepayments to cover the property.* Make sure that you select the insurer. Don't blindly continue to carry the insurance held by the previous owner.

- *Credit bureau fee.* The amount the lender paid to check up on your credit.

- *Assumption fee.* A charge made by the lender when you take over the seller's mortgage.

- *Reserves for escrow.* Money to cover taxes and assessments. These fees should be pro-rated with the seller so that you don't pay taxes for a whole year when you've only owned the property for a few months.

- *Title search.* The cost of making certain that the title to the property is clear. You may be able to split this with the seller.

- *Title insurance.* In some places the lender requires you to get title insurance for protection against claims that a search might not uncover. You may be able to arrange to share this cost with the seller. Even when it's not required, you may want to consider paying the one-time charge for this insurance to cover yourself as the owner of the house. This is generally more important with new housing than on an older home, but discuss the matter with your attorney, since each instance is different.

- *Notary and documentation fees.* Charges for the paperwork and witnessing signatures. These fees are frequently absorbed by the lender, so shop for one that does so.

- *Lender's legal fees.* Be sure to ask about these charges as you shop for financing; they vary widely from bank to bank and are a good place to save.
- *Recording and transfer charges.* Unavoidable fees assessed by the locality for all real estate transactions.
- *Adjustments.* Payments to the seller for taxes, fees, and services that he or she may have paid for in advance.
- *Interest.* The pro-rated interest on the amount of time you held your new mortgage before you made your first mortgage payment.
- *Pest inspections and survey.* You can probably get the seller to pay for these, or part of them.

This list may look like it represents a lot of money—and it does. Find out from each prospective lender what the attorney's fees, points, application fees, and origination fees add up to, and keep these closing costs in mind throughout your search for financing.

CONDOMINIUMS, COOPERATIVES, AND OTHER HOUSING OPTIONS

CONDOS

A condominium is a building or development in which you own your living space and hold the lobbies, elevators, grounds, etc., in common with the other residents. There are urban condominiums and suburban versions, too. Some are apartment houses; some are detached units on relatively spacious parcels of land. At best, a condo offers you the psychological and financial advantages of owning real estate with the conveniences of renting:

- You get the same financial advantage from your condo as you would from traditional home ownership: The tax deductions and appreciation on the property are the same.
- You may get facilities (pool, tennis courts, health club, clubhouse) that you wouldn't find in a traditional single-family house.
- Your maintenance needs, landscaping, and security arrangements are all taken care of.
- You pay taxes only on your own property, so if another owner in your condo defaults, you're immune from additional costs. This is not the case with cooperatives.

As with all new housing developments, a new condominium may not attract enough buyers to finance all the advertised facilities; the maintenance costs may be underestimated, or any of a wide array of abuses may be lurking in the future.

To protect yourself from these pitfalls:

- *Make sure the developer is reputable;* check with mortgage loan officers at the local banks, the Better Business Bureau, and the real estate board in your community. The tax assessor will know about the developer's other condominiums in the area. If possible, visit one of those condos and ask the residents if they're happy with the property, the management, and their whole investment. You can check out the contractor in the same way. Also, check with the zoning authorities and town clerk to find out if there are any problems with the development.

- *Make sure the contract shows you that your deposit is held in escrow.* That way you won't lose your money if the condominium fails before you move in.

- *Avoid buying into a condo where facilities are only planned.* The tennis courts, pool, etc., should be on the site, not on the drawing board. Some states require the developer to have all facilities in place before selling any units. If your state does not, it's up to you to protect yourself.

- *Consider the size of the development when assessing the facilities.* The lovely pool becomes less lovely if you have to sign up for a once-a-month 15-minute dip.

- *Make sure the condominium owners' association holds title to the land and facilities.* Many developers are maintaining ownership of these properties and leasing them to the ownership. This means you could be in line to pay steadily escalating prices for the pool or the lease of the land your unit stands on. The same warning holds if the purchase contract locks you into a long-term management agreement with the developer or one of his or her companies.

- *Insist that the developer provide your lawyer (who should be well experienced with condominium law) with the budget, the sales contract, the condominium agreement, and any by-laws.* Don't accept any excuses. And don't buy housing, particularly a condominium or coop, without your lawyer's OK.

- *Find our about the condominium's rules.* You may discover that you can't sell your property unless the buyer is approved by the home owners' association, or that children are not allowed except for limited visits, or that you can't have a pet.

COOPS

Cooperatives are owned by a corporation composed of the building's residents. When you buy into a coop you are buying stock in the corporation, and your share of stock depends on the size of your apartment. You also pay a proportional share of the maintenance costs, the mortgage, and the taxes on the entire property. (The last two costs are tax-deductible.) The advantages of the coop are similar to those of the condominium, but the coop is generally less desirable than the condo for the following reasons:

- If one shareholder can't keep up the payments, the others must pick up the defaulted share.
- You must pay in cash for the property.
- If you plan to sell, the buyer must be approved by the other shareholders.
- It is harder to find financing for coops. You may find it impossible to finance more than 50 percent of your cost, and a much smaller percentage is all that many lenders will consider. And your interest rate will probably be several points higher than that for a traditional housing unit or for a condominium.

The main factor to keep in mind with coops and condos is that owning either will put you in close contact with your neighbors. If you can't abide by rules that you haven't made, if you find it hard to negotiate with others, and if you expect your home to be your castle, then stick with conventional home ownership.

DEVELOPMENTS

If you're in the market for a new home, one built within the past 10 years or so, or for a home with no previous owners, you're probably in the market for a tract house of some sort. The landscape in these developments is generally barren, leaving houses fully exposed to each other; you have to wait years for new plantings to provide any privacy. More importantly, the newer the development, the less real information you have, which can mean real problems:

- The houses may be cheaply constructed.
- The houses may have been put up on landfill that hasn't settled properly. They may be constructed on floodplains, or in areas with other natural problems that the developer "expects" some government intervention or project will solve. There are developments in Texas that have been flooded every year since their construction. The owners

are stuck, unable to sell their houses, and their story is repeated in other developments across the country.

- If you buy your house on the basis of a model, you may find that the specifications somehow change when it comes to your home, or that the floor plan is altered. In New Jersey, a developer sold to some people on the basis of a model, took their down payments of $7,000 each, and left town with no forwarding address.

To avoid a disaster of this magnitude, you must research your developer carefully:

- Start with the loan officer at the local banks, then go on to the Better Business Bureau, the Chamber of Commerce, and the suppliers the developer deals with.
- Find out how long the developer has been in business and visit the other homes he or she's put up—the older the better.
- Find out whether the builder will give you a Home Owner's Warranty and whether he or she is a member of the National Association of Home Builders.
- Finally, make sure that you have a lawyer look over all of the contracts involved with the home purchase.

MOBILE HOMES

If you are in the market for a new home that costs less than $20,000, you're in the market for a mobile home. Mobile homes account for almost all new housing in that price bracket—and for almost half of all new housing in this country. They are usually about half the price of conventional homes with the same floor space. A mobile home can cost as little as $6,000 or as much as your budget and imagination can accommodate. And there are many additional advantages:

- It is easier to get a loan for a mobile home, even if it is relatively expensive, than to get a mortgage for a conventional home.
- Mobile homes, of course, can be moved. Even older trailers can go where you're going in a pinch.
- Mobile homes can be sold fairly easily.
- In general, mobile homes are built for easy maintenance.

On the other hand, there are serious disadvantages to mobile homes:

- Most banks consider a mobile home to be more like a car or a TV set than a house. That means the bank won't give you a mortgage to buy one—instead, you'll have to pay cash or take out a conventional high-interest loan. There are VA and FHA programs to insure mobile home mortgages, but you will have a hard time finding a lending institution willing to make such a loan to you.

- Unlike conventional houses, mobile homes don't appreciate in value as time goes by. Instead, they depreciate like cars. Their value may drop by as much as 50 percent in five years.

- Mobile homes have had a bad safety record, ranging from problems caused by inadequate fire exits to a tendency to take off in high winds. This means that the insurance premiums on mobile homes are about double those for a regular house. Safety regulations for modern mobile homes have improved their record, but special anchoring is still a prudent idea.

- Despite the fact that you own the trailer, you will have to pay to park it and hook it up to facilities. Your other option is to find a community where there are no zoning restrictions on mobile homes and pay to have utilities installed.

- If you do rent space in a trailer park, you'll have to follow that park's rules, which may include such annoying restrictions as having to cover the crawlspace under your trailer with special skirtings that the park provides—at a special price. You may also find that there are restrictions on the age of your trailer, the number of children you can have, your pets, your radio or television habits, the length of time a visitor can stay, even restrictions on your age.

If the idea of mobile home living appeals to you, write to the American Mobile Home Association, P.O. Box 710, Golden, CO 80401. They'll help you with general information and refer you to people who can help if you have specific questions.

BUILDING YOUR OWN HOME

In the short run, building your home is inevitably more expensive than buying a ready-made home. But if you can afford the additional costs, your long-run gains can be significant.

- You can fit the size, layout, and design of your home to your family's immediate needs and even plan for future expansion.

- You can incorporate the most energy-efficient design features, appliances, and energy-using systems into your house right from the start.
- You have aesthetic control over the materials used in the house, so you'll be able to find the best-looking, best-value materials with the maintenance features you need.
- You have the greatest possible satisfaction with your home because it's been built for you right from the start.

On the other hand, you'll have a long involvement with the house which will demand a high proportion of your time and your energy, as well as your money.

- You can select a site only after investigating zoning regulations, drainage, the availability of public services, financing, title research, and surveys of the land.
- You'll have to research plans or find an architect.
- You'll have to look for a contractor and then carefully investigate the quality of the work he or she does.

In short, you'll have to decide how much the unique features of the home you'll build for yourself are worth in terms of time, effort, aggravation, and anxiety about costs.

If you decide to build, remember these important tips:

- *Make sure your architect is a member of the American Institute of Architects in Washington.* That will provide you with some assurance that he or she meets professional standards.
- *Make sure your contractor offers an NAHB (National Association of Home Builders) Home Owners' Warranty.* This home protection plan covers your house for 10 years and assures that your contractor is willing to stand behind the workmanship and materials. For additional assurance, consult the Federal Housing Authority's "DSI" list. It's a national list of the contractors whose work has failed to meet the FHA's standards for work or practices. You can get it yourself from the Housing and Urban Development Printing Office, 451 7th St., SW, Washington, DC 20410.

You can cut your costs substantially by getting a prefabricated or partially prefabricated house. The house, or parts of the house, can be assembled in sections at the factory, then shipped to your site. You can combine custom-built sections with rooms or groups of rooms that have been prefabricated.

MOVING

Can there be any more conflicting set of emotions than the combination of exhilaration and depression that usually accompanies a permanent move? In the face of all this, it's hard to get a grip on the work that has to be done, and hard to choose the best ways of getting yourself moved. If you're living in an apartment, you may be able to handle your move with a rented truck and a few friends, but moving out of quarters with more than a few rooms requires more courage and endurance than most people want to muster up. Deciding on a commercial mover is not an easy process, and doesn't solve all of your problems, either. Here are some timetables and hints to help you through.

TIMETABLES

Two Months Before

- *Take inventory.* Make separate lists of the items you want to sell, to throw away, and to give away. (Call the Salvation Army to take away things that have good use left in them . . . or your church or Goodwill, if you can drop the items off.)

- *Process your inventory.* Have an apartment or garage sale, throw out the worthless items, and have the Salvation Army or some such group take away the more useful things you haven't sold but don't want to keep. In the latter case, if you make an evaluation and keep the list of items donated, at least part of your contribution will be tax-deductible.

- *Get a change of address kit from the Post Office.* Use the forms to notify magazines, credit card companies, banks, and other correspondents. It takes six to eight weeks to get your address changed with most big organizations. Enclose a label from your current mail with your change of address to help the keypunchers get all the right information. This is also your opportunity to arrange with the Post Office to have your mail forwarded as of your moving date.

- *Begin to use up foods in your freezer and the non-perishables and canned goods in your pantry.* It's smarter to eat them than to move them.

- *Your mover must provide you with a copy of "Summary of Information for Shippers of Household Goods,"* but if you want to bone up on the information in it before you begin to get estimates, write to ICC, Household Goods Branch, Washington, DC 20423 for a free copy.

- *Begin to check up on the available movers.* Have their representatives come in to make an estimate. See the sections on choosing and dealing with movers later in the chapter.

One Month Before

- *Find out if your local utilities will disconnect your major appliances if you're taking them with you.* Movers won't unhook your gas stove or any electric appliances that are wired directly into main switches—or the TV aerial. If your utilities don't provide this service, you'll need to make other arrangements. No matter who's going to do it, this is the time to make the appointment. (Think twice about moving major appliances anyway. It's better to sell them independently or as part of the house or apartment.)

One Week Before

- *Pack your unseasonal clothes and the books you really can't do without.* Have the other books taken away by your favorite charity; give them to a school or senior citizen's club; even let the kids have a street sale. The point is not to move any more books than you have to.

- *Decide what you must pack yourself.* This includes anything fragile, rare, personal, old, or tiny. As will be pointed out later, however, especially valuable items should be packed by the movers so they are responsible in case of any damage. Make sure that you have the containers you'll need. Movers prefer cartons with flaps so the boxes can be sealed. Liquor stores are a good source for these; most supermarkets cut off the tops of cardboard boxes. Make sure the cartons are a manageable size, especially if you'll be doing your own moving. Buy new garbage pails and kitchen trash pails. You'll probably need new ones at your new place, and they come in handy to pack things like clothes, plates, and small breakables. Don't forget that laundry baskets, hampers, kitchen buckets, and other such things make excellent containers for moving.

- *Notify your utilities that you're moving and want your services cut off.* Follow up your phone call with a letter. Tell them on the phone that you want written confirmation of your termination. Otherwise, you may be slapped, even years from now, with an outrageous bill for services in a house you vacated years ago.

- *Make plans for the first few days in your new home.* Know where people are going to sleep and eat. And plan for foul-ups, especially late delivery of your household effects.

- *Make a moving plan.* Assign a code letter to each room of the new house and label all of your big items to indicate the room to which each should be moved.

- *Keep a list of which items you've packed in which boxes and of which boxes and pieces of furniture should end up in each room.* Put a list of contents on all the boxes. This will help you take a quick inventory upon your arrival and to organize yourself, if you're moving a household of more than one or two rooms, in the first few days after you move.

- *Make sure that you know exactly what fixtures, fittings, and appliances are going to be left in your new home.* All of this should have been carefully spelled out in the contract to buy. Now is the time to double-check, especially if you're renting. You don't want to arrive to find bare wires hanging from the ceiling, no doorknobs, and no clothes rods in the closets.

- *Double-check to make sure that the utilities, including the water, are going to be turned on in the new house when you arrive.* You and the previous owner or tenant might arrange to have the account transferred to your name rather than terminated. This is also the time to double-check on the appointments you made to have your own appliances disconnected if you're taking them with you.

The Big Day

- *Pack an emergency bag.* You'll need toothbrushes, toothpaste, soap, face cloths and towels, toilet paper, knives, forks, and spoons; Band-Aids, antiseptic, aspirin, hangers, a flashlight, extra lightbulbs, a spare set of house keys to both homes, and copies of all your lists. It's a good idea to have a list of phone numbers for the utilities and services in your new home. Put this bag in your car, if you're taking it, or in your bathroom, or someplace where there won't be much traffic. Make sure there's a "Do Not Move" sign on it; it won't do much good on the truck with the movers.

- *Simplify your life by arranging with a friend or neighbor to take the kids for the day.* Put your pets in the bathroom or in some such holding pen. They won't disturb the movers and the excitement won't disturb them.

- *Keep a set of keys to both houses in your pocketbook . . . or pin them to a pocket.* Give another set to the foreman. If worse comes to worst, you'll still have a spare set in the emergency bag.

- *Keep plenty of drinks around.* Don't let the movers whisk off the kettle and coffee pot and paper cups until everything else is on the truck.

- *Take your time when you sign the lists the foreman will stick under your nose.* He may claim that he has another job to get to, or try to rush you in some other way; those things are his problem. Your problem is to make certain that the lists reflect every item you've packed. One acquaintance found that an IBM Selectric had somehow never made it onto the list—or onto the truck. If anything is missing or broken, those lists are your first step in settling the dispute, so make sure you understand the movers' codes and that you agree on the condition of the goods.

- *If you're moving during the winter and your old home is going to stand vacant for a few days or longer, make sure you drain tanks and pipes after the water has been turned off. Turn off the heater, too.* Then be sure to leave a note about what you've done. Then dust off your hands, lock the door and move on.

At the New House

- *Get there before the movers do.* Label all the rooms according to your floor plans and lists.

- *Check to make sure that the utilities are working.* If you have trouble, you'll find the numbers in your utility bag. Stay calm when you complain and make sure to get everybody's name. Don't hesitate to ask for a supervisor or department manager, but stay calm. If you used a real estate agent to find your home, that agent may be able to handle your initial utility problems.

- *Introduce yourself to the neighbors . . . if you haven't met them already.* They can be an immediate help if you have questions about your new neighborhood.

CHOOSING A MOVER

- *If you are moving within your own state or city, the best way to choose a mover is to ask among your neighbors and to check with the Better Business Bureau.* Check with your state's government information office to find out whether there are any kinds of regulations governing in-state movers and whether there's any rating of the various companies. (Chances are not good in either instance.)

- *If you're moving out of state, your mover will be regulated by the Interstate Commerce Commission, the ICC.* There are local offices in Atlanta, Boston, Chicago, Fort Worth, Los Angeles, Miami, New York, Philadelphia, and San Francisco. All of these offices have computer terminals that allow you to call for up-to-date information on all 2,500 interstate movers. This will let you know how often they get the shipments to their destinations on time, how often their estimates are under the actual cost of the move, how often their customers complain.

- *Have the movers whose reputations seem good look at your house.* Remember that the estimate isn't binding, since the move is charged by weight. This is why reputation is so important. Make sure that you show the mover everything, from the old trunk in the attic and band saw in the basement to the garden hose out back, the kids' sleds in the garage, and the filing cabinet in the den. Don't assume that you'll be able to get rid of things; let the mover include everything, and you'll get a more accurate estimate.

DEALING WITH MOVERS

- *Go over your floor plans with the foreman of the moving crew.* Give instructions to him only. Aside from double-checking on the stereo and other expensive and fragile items, keep a low profile. It's hard to be on hand and yet stay out of things, but that's the wisest approach.

- *Some veterans of several moves swear that it's wise to budget a generous tip.* Give half of it in advance to the crew, and hint that the other half will be there at the end of the day if all goes well. Figure $10 per person per day, with an additional $10 for the foreman. On interstate moves, however, tipping is illegal. It may also be illegal in your state. Get it straight by asking about tips when you're getting estimates.

- *Go to the weighing of your goods or send someone you can trust.* The weight should include the van, driver, dollies and moving equipment as well as your goods. It should not include four or five 200-pound moving men.

- *If you suspect some sort of shenanigans, you can insist on a reweighing.* The mover *must* do it. He may charge you $20 or $30 but if the reweighing comes in more than 120 pounds lower than the original weighing or 25 percent more than the estimate, you don't have to pay the reweighing fee.

- *If there isn't a weigh scale, the mover may charge you at a rate of seven pounds to the square foot.* This works to your advantage only if you're moving books and paper.

- *Be sure to get copies of both weigh tickets.* There's one for the "tare," the empty weight of the truck and equipment. There's another for the gross—the weight of the truck loaded with your goods. Your copies should match the originals.

- *If your goods are shipped with other people's, ask for the vehicle load manifest, which indicates what percentage of the entire load is chargeable to you.* The driver must show this to you, and he must carry it with him. Check the tare, gross, and net of your goods on the manifest against these figures on your weigh tickets and bill of lading. These numbers must match the corresponding numbers on the vehicle load manifest. If there's an inconsistency, report it to the ICC unless the mover corrects the figures right away.

- *The mover must list all your goods and their condition.* It is crucial that you examine the inventory carefully and see that it accurately describes your goods' condition. Keep a list of anything that gets broken or damaged while being packed, packed with the wrong room's furnishings, or otherwise misplaced. Read the movers' code and then go over the inventory. Have the foreman change the notation on any item you disagree with. If the foreman won't make the change, you've still got your own note on the original.

- *Be sure to get a bill of lading.* It states the delivery place, where to reach you, and the terms of liability for loss or damage.

- *If you have antiques or any other especially valuable goods to be moved, list them on the bill of lading yourself.* Movers deny liability for these items if they aren't specified and listed on the bill of lading.

- *Check the terms of payment.* You'll usually have to pay in cash or certified check or money order. If the charges exceed the estimate by more than 10 percent, you can pay the estimate plus 10 percent, then pay the balance within 15 days. (Have two separate certified checks drawn to cover this possibility . . . one for the estimate, one for the estimate plus 10 percent. Keep enough cash on hand to cover the difference between these two sums.) This is the time to demand a reweigh if the figures seem inordinately high to you.

- *When your goods are unloaded, examine them carefully!* Note each and every problem—items missing, damaged goods, etc. Your claim will be based on the notes you have made on the inventory upon both loading *and* unloading.

TIPS IF YOU'RE MOVING INTERSTATE

- *Send your books and other dense non-breakables by common carrier.* You'll save a good deal if you ship this kind of thing via train or bus, rather than having the very dense weight added to that of your furniture and other household goods.

- *Do your own packing of clothes, linens, and other bulky, non-fragile things.* You can get containers from the moving company, or you can use containers you've found. But let the movers pack anything fragile, big, or expensive. They're not liable for things they didn't pack, so let them put the hall mirror in a container, and let them put the best china in a crate.

- *Don't pack anything you don't like, or that's readily replaceable*—like the bricks you've been using for your bookshelves. And don't take clothes that are unsuitable for a new climate.

SOURCES

GENERAL INFORMATION FOR HOME BUYERS

The Homebuyer's Guide for the 80's by Richard W. O'Neill is a complete, working guide to finding and buying the right home, from start to finish, with the alternatives. Available from Grosset and Dunlap, 51 Madison Ave., New York, NY 10010. $7.95.

Home for Sale by Owner (The Only Complete Home Selling Kit) by Gerald M. Steiner deals with the tricks of the real estate trade and both buying and selling a house. It's a primer that includes forms and describes procedures and stumbling blocks involved in selling your own home—and it's almost as useful to buyers as to sellers. E.P. Dutton, 2 Park Ave., New York, NY 10016. $7.95.

How to Inspect a House (formerly *Don't Go Buy Appearances*) by George C. Hoffman gives you an idea of how to evaluate a prospective house's condition (and therefore how much to offer). Available from Delta Books, 245 E. 47th St., New York, NY 10017. $4.95.

HOUSING ALTERNATIVES

Renting

"For Rent: A Consumer's Guide to Rental Housing." Cornell University, Distribution Center, 7 Research Park, Ithaca, NY 14850. $1.25.

Older Homes

Old Houses (A Rebuilder's Manual) by George Nash. If what you can afford is an old "fixer-upper," then this is the book you'll need to do the work. Written with the remodeler, not the builder of a new house, in mind. Prentice-Hall, Box 500, Englewood Cliffs, NJ 07632. $12.95.

"Urban Homesteading"

Urban Homesteading by James Hughes and Kenneth Bleakly. How to find, finance, and rehabilitate an abandoned inner-city house. Center for Urban Policy Research, Rutgers University, Building 4051, Kilmer Campus, New Brunswick, NJ 08903. $15.00

A Place in the Country

Finding and Buying Your House in the Country by Les Sher. By a lawyer who knows his way around easements, contracts, zoning escrow and stuff like that. Solid advice. Macmillan Books, Order Dept., Front and Brown Streets, Riverside, NJ 08075. $7.95.

Coops and Condos

"Advising People about Cooperatives" is available for $.45 from the Superintendent of Documents, U.S. Government Printing Office, Washington, DC 20402.

"The Condominium Buyer's Guide" costs $1.00 and is available from the National Association of Home Builders, 15th and M Streets, NW, Washington, DC 20005.

"Cooperative Housing and Condominiums: Home Ownership with a Difference" is available for $1.25 from the Distribution Center, Dept. FHO, 7 Research Park, Cornell University, Ithaca, NY 14850.

"Questions about Condominiums" is a free booklet available from the U.S. Department of Housing and Urban Development, Washington, DC 20410.

Sharing

Shared Houses, Shared Lives by Eric Raimy. Can't afford your own home? Teaming up with another family or individual can often make it possible. Perfect for these hard times. Available from Houghton-Mifflin Co., Wayside Road, Burlington, MA 01803. $6.50.

Prefab and Mobile Homes

"Continental Housing: Here Today, Home Tomorrow," a booklet about manufactured housing, is available from Continental Homes of New England, Daniel Webster Hwy., South, Nashua, NH 13060. $2.00.

Manufactured Housing Institute, 1745 Jefferson Davis Hwy., Suite 511, Arlington, VA 22202 will supply information about prefab housing and mobile homes if you send them a postcard.

BUILDING YOUR OWN HOME

General Information

L.M. Bruinier & Associates, Inc., 1304 S.W. Bertha Blvd., Portland, OR 97219 offers a catalog of 350 new homes for $1.50.

"How to Build a House Using Self-Help Housing Techniques" (HUD-345-1A) is available from the Superintendent of Documents, U.S. Government Printing Office, Washington, DC 20402. $1.40.

Illustrated Housebuilding ($4.95) and *Illustrated Interior Carpentry* ($5.95) by Graham Blackburn. Just right. A totally inexperienced person could build a house with these two volumes. Overlook Press, c/o Viking Press, 299 Murray Hill Parkway, East Rutherford, NJ 07073.

Kit Houses by Mail by Brad McDole and Chris Jerome. A selection of kit homes with some realistic information about their true costs. This is pricey, but if you need an introduction to this kind of shelter, this is it. Grosset &

Dunlap, Inc., Stonesong Press, 51 Madison Ave., New York, NY 10010. $14.95.

National Construction Estimator. If you're a builder or an owner-builder, this is a tool to determine costs, time, and whether it's cheaper to do it yourself or contract the job. Easy to use and indispensable. Craftsman Book Co., 542 Stevens Ave., Solana Beach, CA 92075.

"100 Affordable Homes," a book of house designs, is available from Homes for Living, Inc., 107-40 Queens Blvd., Forest Hills, NY 11375. $1.50.

The Owner-Builder and the Code (The Politics of Building Your Own Home) by K. Kern, T. Kogon, and R. Thalon. Case histories and strategies for getting your house built the way you want it. Owner-Builder Publications, P.O. Box 817, North Fork, CA 93643.

The Owner-Built Home (A How To Do It Book) by Ken Kern. Good advice on low-cost building techniques from countries that can't afford U.S.-style waste. Perfect now that we can't either. Charles Scribner's Sons, Vreeland Ave., Totowa, NJ 07512. $9.20.

"Regional Guidelines for Building Passive Energy Conserving Homes" is available from the Superintendent of Documents, U.S. Government Printing Office, Washington, DC 20402.

"Selecting and Financing a Home" (147 H) can be ordered from the Superintendent of Documents, U.S. Government Printing Office, Washington, DC 20402.

Earth-Sheltered Homes

Earth-Sheltered Housing Design. A manual of *proven* techniques from the University of Minnesota. 80,000 copies have been sold so far—so maybe you *won't* be the first on your block. Van Nostrand Reinhold, 7625 Empire Drive, Florence, KY 41042. $10.95.

Underground Houses: How to Build a Low-Cost Home by Robert L. Roy. A reasonable price for good, experienced advice on this new housing trend. Sterling Publishing, 2 Park Ave., New York, NY 10016. $5.95.

HOME ENERGY

HOME ENERGY

It's in our homes that we consume the lion's share of energy, and there that we can make the greatest impact with conservation and economy measures.

This chapter covers energy audits and energy tax credits, heating, lighting, water, air conditioning, and appliances. At the end of the chapter is a listing of energy conservation products—everything from weatherstripping to air deflectors and water restrictors, with information on their use, cost, installation, and energy-saving potential.

HOME ENERGY AUDITS AND TAX CREDITS

HOME ENERGY AUDITS

Most local utility companies will offer home energy audits free of charge or for a small fee ($10 to $15). These are evaluations from basement to roof that will tell you how and where your home is wasting energy. You'll be told if you need insulation for your ceiling, foundation, walls, or floor (over an unheated garage, basement, or crawl space); storm windows or storm doors; caulking and weatherstripping; new or relocated thermostats; or other modifications.

Some utilities go several steps farther. Some will provide estimates for recommended improvements and for the payback period for each improvement. Some will arrange for qualified contractors to do the work, offer a low-cost financing plan (often for those measures that will pay for themselves in energy cost savings in seven years or less), and inspect and certify the improvements made so you can get a tax break and increase the resale value of your property. Call your utility and inquire about the extent of their services. It can only pay off for you.

ENERGY TAX CREDITS

- *Sooner or later, energy conservation products pay for themselves in cheaper fuel bills, but you can derive further savings by claiming a federal tax credit* *on 15 percent of the first $2,000 you spend on such products installed in your principal residence—whether you own or rent.* Almost any energy conservation product (see pp. 122–136) and any purchase or installation recommended in a utility's home energy audit—with the exception of a complete new furnace or boiler—will qualify. The tax credit covers purchases made between April 1977 and January 1986. There's even a provision for wind energy for residential purposes. Use IRS form 5695 to apply. For more information, see IRS Publication 903, "Energy Credits for Individuals," available at U.S. Internal Revenue Service offices.

- *Though installing solar cooling or heating in your home can be costly, the fuel is free, and the maintenance is almost nonexistent.* You can also qualify for special income-tax credits. The tax credits for solar energy installations have been doubled to 40 percent, which means you can now deduct $4,000 instead of $2,000 on the first $10,000 spent. In addition, there are 25 states now granting state income-tax credits or deductions. For more information, call the National Solar Heating and Cooling Information Center toll free: (800) 523-2929; (in Pennsylvania) (800) 462-4983; (in Alaska and Hawaii) (800) 523-4700.

HEATING YOUR HOME

THE CHOICES IN HEATING SYSTEMS

Six fuels are used to generate heat in American homes. Their prices vary from one area to another, but in general, they rank as follows from the most expensive downwards:

Electricity

Even though electricity is converted directly into heat with 100 percent efficiency, electric heating isn't usually efficient. Its efficiency is determined by the fuel used to generate it—whether it's oil, coal, falling water, or nuclear power. An oil-fired generator at a power plant, for example, has a production efficiency of 35 percent to 40 percent, so the electric heating systems in the area serviced by that power plant actually operate at a much lower efficiency rate than heating units that burn oil for heat.

Electric resistance heating is prohibitively expensive, barely feasible even in extremely well-insulated houses. Don't buy promises from your utility that a new plant will soon lower your electricity costs or that as a larger-volume consumer, you'll get a discount rate. The advantages of electric resistance heating are that it's very inexpensive to install and that it can be controlled by individual thermostats or switches in each room.

An electric heat pump can reduce your electric heating bill dramatically, however, and the rising cost of fossil fuels has made it a viable alternative.

Heat pumps, which operate on the same cycle as a refrigerator, take outside air and raise its temperature before pumping it into the house. For air conditioning, the cycle is reversed. Heat pumps do lose their heating efficiency at temperatures below freezing and are often used in conjunction with an oil or gas burner at those times. They also come equipped with heat coils that it can give them a boost. A kilowatt of power produces about three kilowatts of indoor heat. This is three times more efficient than electric resistance heating.

Oil

The price of oil is constantly rising, and the quantity available is limited. Oil systems require storage tanks on your property. These tanks occupy space and can run dry. Oil furnaces also use electricity to run their circulating fans, so if you're in a rural area or any locale where you lose power frequently, your unit will shut down just as frequently.

Liquified Petroleum Gas

LP gas, like oil, requires its own tank on the premises. But some gas systems have an advantage over oil systems in that they are unaffected by electrical blackouts.

Piped-In Natural Gas

So far, this is the least expensive of the conventional fuels, though its price will continue to rise.

Wood

Wood is plentiful enough if you're not a city-dweller, and it can be quite efficient in a wood-burning stove, though not in the typical American fireplace.

If it is at all possible for you to consider a wood-burning stove, here's a way to compare its operating cost to systems that burn other fuels. One cord of wood (a pile 8' × 4' × 4') costs in the vicinity of $75 to $100, depending on where you live. This produces roughly as much heat as 146 gallons of heating oil, 17,400 cubic feet of gas, 3,300 kilowatt hours of electricity, and just under one ton of coal. This is a pretty strong argument for wood, even if you're not in a position to cut some or all of your own wood.

Don't buy a stove made of cast-iron sections screwed or bolted together. They leak a lot of air and can send as much as 80 percent of the heat they produce up the chimney. Instead, find an airtight model that regulates oxygen intake to sustain the fire and make the wood burn longer—all night, in fact. Check seams, the fit of the door, and the air inlet efficiency. If you're unfamiliar with wood-burning stoves, check *Consumer Reports*, the *Whole Earth Catalog*, and the like.

One of the cheapest woodburning set-ups can be made from—of all things—an oil barrel. Sotz Corporation (13600 N. Station Road, Columbia Station, OH 44028) produces a kit of stove parts and hardware for $59.90 postpaid. You supply two 55-gallon steel drums and may need some car-muffler cement. *Consumer Reports* gives this stove assembly (the Sotz S55HD) a splendid rating. It was more efficient than any wood burner CR tested—in fact, 65 percent better—and it operated exceptionally well with both small and enormous loads of wood. If you don't mind its looks, it can make quite a fine heater.

Solar Heat

The high cost of installing a solar system offsets any immediate savings. You may also require a back-up fuel. But since the cost of traditional fuels is rising almost continuously and their future availability is uncertain, solar heat—both passive and active—is well worth researching and considering.

To gauge the prices of various fuels in your locale accurately, get the prices of a gallon of heating oil, a therm of natural or LP gas, and a kilowatt hour of electricity, then multiply the cost of the electricity by 33 and that of the gas and oil by 1.4.

No heating fuel (with the exception of solar and electrical heating) is cleaner or safer than another *if* you maintain and service your heating unit properly.

MAINTAINING YOUR FURNACE

General Furnace Tips

- *Have the furnace serviced during the summer, so if any serious deficiency is found, you'll have time to find the best bargain on a new unit.* Most people in the market for a new furnace don't have the luxury of shopping leisurely; the old units usually give up the ghost during a cold spell and must be replaced immediately. But you can get a better price for a furnace in the summer. Also, heating contractors are always available then, and charge less for their services than in the winter.

- *Dust of any kind can affect furnace performance.* If the exhaust from your clothes dryer empties into the furnace area, install an outlet filter so lint won't get into the furnace. And make sure that sawdust released into the air from the workshop doesn't interfere with the furnace's operation.

- *Both gas and oil furnaces must have a good supply of air to enable the flame to burn efficiently.* And improper combustion as a result of inadequate ventilation or a poorly maintained or malfunctioning furnace can produce lethal carbon monoxide. The furnace room should *not* be airtight. If your furnace can't get the proper venting, an air passage should be installed.

- *Air filters on forced-air furnaces, like those on an air conditioner, must be cleaned at least once a month, otherwise air flow is impaired, less heat is transferred, and more fuel is used.* A clogged filter can reduce heat output by up to 70 percent. If a flashlight beam won't shine through the filter, clean or replace it.

- *Consider investing in a two-speed blower.* It will operate on low when the furnace is normally off, keeping room temperatures more even by circulating the air (and not letting all the hot air end up near the ceiling). Ceiling fans (p. 103) do the same thing.

Your Oil Furnace

Things You Can Check Yourself

- *Check the flame.* If it's dirty or producing smoke, your burner needs an adjustment. Call a serviceman.

- *Is there any buildup of soot?* There will probably be a small amount in the firebox, created when the burner starts up and the fuel is improperly mixed with air. But if there is a substantial amount, your furnace is wasting precious fuel.

- *Check the chimney and the barometric damper.* The damper is located on the pipe leading from the furnace to the chimney. It emits cool air to help with combustion while retaining warm air in the furnace. To do so, it has to open and shut freely. If it sticks, oil it, then check later when the furnace is operating to make sure it swings freely. While you're checking the damper, blow cigarette or candle smoke to see if it's sucked through and up the chimney. If it isn't, the chimney might be plugged. Have it checked.

Things the Serviceman Should Check

Be sure that your serviceman does the following:

- *Check the temperature of the stack.* If it's too high (and it can run up to 700–800°), heat is being wasted when it goes up the chimney. A simple remedy is to increase the speed of the circulating fan. You can also try a smaller nozzle (it's the nozzle that shoots a fine spray of oil droplets mixed with air into the furnace). Furnaces that were manufactured in less energy-conscious times are equipped with nozzles that can easily be reduced 20 percent in size, increasing fuel economy without decreasing the comfort level of your home.

- *Check the stack gas.* A good serviceman should be equipped with a smoke density measuring device that can determine the soot level and the carbon dioxide level, both of which assist in evaluating the furnace's thermal efficiency.

- *Make sure there's no soot in the heat exchanger, firepot, and pipes.* They should be totally free of soot when he finishes.

- *Check that the draft—the draw of air into the firebox—is right for a fuel-efficient flame.* About 2,000 cubic feet of air are needed to burn a single gallon of fuel oil.

Your Natural Gas Furnace

- *Natural gas tends to burn rather cleanly; as with any boiler or furnace, however, it's highly important that the gas burners be properly vented for the most thorough and efficient combustion.* Check that you're getting an even flame, without smoke. It should be blue, with no sign of yellow. If there is yellow, you can adjust the air setting yourself. Allow at least five minutes for the furnace to heat up before beginning. Open the vents, and then shut them slowly, adjusting the yellow flame downwards until it becomes blue and gives off no smoke.

- *When the winter season ends and you have no need of your furnace, be sure to have the pilot light, if there is one, extinguished for the summer (but don't blow it out).* The pilot light consumes 10 percent of your annual gas supply.

MAINTAINING YOUR HEAT DISTRIBUTION SYSTEM

There are seven ways heat can be distributed within a house: warm air is circulated by a fan; hot water is pumped about; steam rises of its own accord; and electric resistors, wood-burning stoves, fireplaces, and solar collectors radiate heat on site. Following are maintenance or improvement tips for all but the solar collectors.

Warm Air

Most warm air systems use oil or natural gas for heat and electricity to operate a circulating fan. They draw cool air through registers in the floor, pass it over a firepot, then circulate it in ducts throughout the house.

- *When the furnace shuts down, the fan should continue to run to draw all the heat out of the burner. Make sure it does.* The temperatures at which the fan cuts in and out are adjustable. Servicemen tend to set it high, having it cut in at 175° to 200° and out at 140° to 150°. You'll get more heating efficiency from a cut-in at 120° and a cut-out at 100°. Hot air will be circulated sooner and longer.

- *Lubricate the fan's motor at least two or three times during the winter season.* Your instruction manual will tell you where and when.

- *When you oil the motor, check the belt tension.* There should be 1/4″ to 1/2″ play midway between the pulleys. If there isn't, you're wasting electricity and wearing down a belt. There is a variable-diameter pulley on the motor that can be adjusted; try to set the belt so the fan will operate at its highest speed.
- *Keep the filters clean.* Once a month, please.

Hot Water

If a house isn't heated by circulating warm air, then it's usually heated by circulating hot water. Water has to be heated to 180° before it is pumped through baseboard radiators. Then it is returned to a burner for reheating. An expansion of heated water and a flow-control valve stops the circulation when the pump is not working. These systems operate on either oil or natural gas.

- *When you turn on your system for the first time in the fall, bleed air from each of the radiators.* If you don't, air trapped in the radiators will stop the water flow and the radiators can stay cold. With the heating system turned on, simply open the radiator's vent screw at one end until hot water spurts out, catching the water in a cup or a rag. Then replace the screw tightly.
- *The expansion tank has to have air space within to facilitate the expansion of water.* And the relief valve that prevents excessive pressure buildups should also be checked periodically. Consult your owner's manual for specific maintenance instructions.
- *Check the manufacturer's specifications to see if the water-level gauge on the boiler is marked at the proper level.*

Steam Heat

While a hot water system circulates water at 180° through a house, a steam heat system, usually found in older homes, boils water at 212°. The steam produced then rises through pipes and distributes its heat from iron radiators. As the water cools, it condenses and flows naturally back down to the boiler for reheating. These systems are usually powered by an oil furnace.

- *These systems must be flushed out at least monthly.* Open the flush valve and let the boiler drain until the water runs clear.
- *Make sure to maintain the water in the boiler at the level recommended by the manufacturer.* Too much water reduces the unit's efficiency; with too little, the unit won't operate.
- *The age of some of these systems makes leaks inevitable.* Repair them immediately; otherwise, you'll lose steam, heat, and pressure.

- *Feel radiators to make sure they're giving off heat.* If any are cold, check air valves on the radiator or any vents on the steam main.

Electric Heat

This is the one heating system that is practically maintenance-free. There are little things you can do, however, to insure the greatest efficiency.

- *Clean your heater with a vacuum cleaner periodically throughout the heating season.* Dust and dirt that accumulate on the coils can hinder efficiency and waste electricity.
- *Wall-mounted electric convectors should be aimed to direct a maximum amount of warm air into the room.* Make sure deflectors are installed if this flow is blocked by anything.
- *Always make sure baseboard units are not blocked in any way; heat deflectors cannot be used on these.*
- *Many new homes are equipped with radiant heating coils running through ceilings and floors. Spot check to make sure that the heat from these surfaces is even; otherwise you could have a broken cable, which is dangerous.*

Woodburning Stoves

The Shakers, a religious group whose members were renowned for their craftsmanship, had the right idea when it came to installing stove pipes. They ran them a few feet below the ceiling all the way to the other side of the room before sending them outside. They got additional warmth from the pipes, thereby increasing the efficiency of their stoves. Try this yourself.

Fireplaces

Getting the Most from Them

- *When using a fireplace without glass doors, you should close the doors to the room.* Otherwise the draft caused by the fire will pull heated air from other rooms and up the chimney. If there are no doors you can close, turn the furnace thermostat down to 52° so the furnace won't be producing even more hot air to be drawn up the chimney.
- *Make sure the damper fits tightly; take a flashlight and check.* Close it as soon as a fire dies out, and keep it closed whenever the fireplace is not in use.
- *An unused fireplace should be sealed off, preferably with boards across the front.* If you like the look of an open fireplace, the chimney can be plugged or the flue closed, if you have one. Substantial amounts of heated or cooled air can be lost up an open chimney.

- *Before you light the first fire of the winter, make sure nothing is blocking the chimney.* Hold a small mirror in the flue opening. Can you see the sky's reflection? If so, you're OK.

- *Hot and cold air vents in the fireplace can save heated air that would otherwise go up the chimney.* Cold floor air is drawn through bottom vents, heated as it rises, then either emitted through a top outlet into the same room or ducted into another area of the house.

- *If you're building, remember that a chimney placed in the middle of the house spreads its warmth to surrounding rooms.*

Firewood

- *Wood is always cheaper by the cord than by the bundle.*

- *Cords come in two sizes:* standard, 8′ × 4′ × 4′; and face (or short) cord, 8′ × 4′ × 1′ or 2′. A face cord looks like a cord from the front, but its price should be only one-fourth that of a full cord if it's one foot deep, or one-half that of a full cord if it's two feet deep.

- *If you buy a "truckload" you can get clipped.* There's no way of knowing just how much wood you're getting, and a half-ton pickup truck certainly can't carry a cord, which weighs around two tons.

- *The U.S. Forest Service offers free firewood from public land; up to 20 cords is yours for the chopping.* Eleven states don't have national forests, and supplies are scarcer in the east, but if you'd like to take advantage of this free offer, you can always plan a camping trip or stop by a forest on the way home from a vacation. Your local U.S. Department of Agriculture Cooperative Extension Service will direct you. You can also call the National Forest Service nearest you or write to the USDA Forest Service, Information Office, Box 2417, Washington, DC 20013.

- *Burning freshly cut wood deposits flammable creosote in your chimney.* Always make sure that the wood you burn has been cut and split for at least six months. The best way is to chop green wood yourself and stack it six months before you use it. You can save money this way since green wood is cheaper.

- *To recognize seasoned wood, check the ends.* Cracks should emanate from the center and they should be dark with age.

- *You get more heat and almost twice as much burning time from hardwoods such as oak, maple, ash, or hickory than you do from softwoods such as butternut, pine, hemlock, and the like.*

- *Keeping a couple of days' supply of wood indoors makes for a cleaner, easier burning fire.* Any wood stored outside should be covered to keep off rain and snow, and it should be kept off the ground to prevent decay.

- *Newspaper logs are a source of free heat.* You can roll your own from all the newspapers you'd normally throw out or recycle. Instead of buying an expensive rolling machine, you can wrap papers around a broomstick. Roll small thicknesses together to approximate log size and secure the logs with wire. There are three possible approaches:

  — The tightest logs are made by wetting the paper and then rolling it. But then you have to wait a month or two for them to dry.
  — You can forget the wetting and, instead, roll the logs dry and as tightly as possible.
  — Or you can make a small log first, tie it with wire, and soak it in charcoal lighter or kerosene (**never** gasoline). Then cover it with more tightly rolled newspaper and secure the entire log with wire. This makes for a steady-burning log that will last two to four hours and will work well along with unsoaked logs.

- *Kindling can be made by folding a few sheets of newspapers on the diagonal and knotting them in the middle.* Note: Because colored newsprint has usually been coated, it doesn't work as well as black and white. Send it off to the recyclers.

MORE TIPS TO CUT YOUR HEAT BILLS

- *Each one-degree drop in your thermostat setting means about a 3 percent savings on your fuel bill.* Dress warmer and get used to keeping your house as cool as possible. To get accustomed to a cooler house, don't turn the temperature down radically, do it gradually—one degree every day or so until you work your way down to an economical level. During the winter the thermostat should be set at 65° during the day and 60° at night.

- *Many older thermostats cannot be turned down any lower than 60°.* This is wasteful, especially while you're away on a trip. Consider replacing such a thermostat, and while you're at it, why not spring for one with an automatic setback? (see p. 131).

- *The well-mounted thermostat should be: on an inside wall; protected from drafts so it won't keep the furnace running when the rest of your home is warm; and away from heat-producing appliances like TVs or lamps, so they won't shut the unit off when the rest of your home is cold.*

- *It is most economical to keep the temperature inside relatively stable during the winter (unless you're going to be away for more than four hours). During the summer, this is not the case.* It's always wasteful to leave an air conditioner on when you leave the house, since a room can be recooled in less than half an hour. Heating takes more time and energy. So set the thermostat back to 55° only if you're going to be away for more than four hours.

- *A lot of heat is wasted by improper distribution of heat throughout the house.* Adjust air flow registers or radiators to supply the proper amount of heat for each room. Close down dampers in rooms that are hotter; open them in cooler ones. A balance means efficient heating.

- *If the temperature can be adjusted, keep it cooler in the laundry room, bathroom, and kitchen.* These rooms get warm when they're used anyway. A radiant heat lamp in the bathroom can be a good idea. It can be turned on when a warmer bathroom is necessary. Use it with a time switch (see p. 137).

- *Close upstairs bedroom doors or shut off heating outlets there during the day; open the doors or reactivate the heaters again in the evening.* It's wasteful to heat rooms when they're not being used.

- *Closing off rooms during the winter is an energy-saver.* And rooms like workshops and game rooms that are used infrequently should be heated only when in use. In the game room, if there's any exercise equipment or physical activity going on, remember that increased body heat from the physical activity offsets the need for a highly heated room.

- *Even in rooms you're closing off, it's a good idea to seal the windows and the doors to minimize heat loss.* To prevent mildew, keep closed-off rooms as dry as possible (sealing the windows helps here by minimizing condensation on the inside of the window glass). Allow sunlight to shine in and air them out occasionally on dry, sunny days.

- *Many kitchens and bathrooms have exhaust fans that remove steam and odors. They also remove heat in the winter and air-conditioned air in the summer.* In fact, an exhaust fan can suck all the heat or air conditioning from a house in one hour. In some bathrooms the fan is turned on by the same switch that controls the light, and is therefore often on when it's not needed. Have the two functions on separate switches, and think about a timer switch for the fan so it can't be left running (see p. 137). Keep the filters on these fans clean (especially in the kitchen, where a filter clogs quickly) so that bad air can be removed much faster.

- *Keep the door on the clothes dryer shut, or heated or cooled air will escape through the dryer exhaust.*

- *Don't place furniture against cold, outside walls.* You'll be colder using it and more tempted to turn up the thermostat.

- *Chairs, drapes, cabinets, and the like should not block radiators or air ducts.* Radiators need a wide berth, but you can invest in inexpensive heat deflectors for ducts (see p. 129).

- *The original purpose of the footstool was to keep feet comfortably above the cool floor drafts.* It can still make a difference; you'll be more comfortable with your lowered thermostat.

- *Wearing heavy socks, bedroom shoes, or lightweight footwear will enable you to keep the thermostat lower without feeling chilly.*

- *Keep throws, afghans, or lap rugs handy on the sofa or on the arms of comfortable chairs for use while reading or watching TV.*

- *An electric blanket costs about $.04 a night to operate and enables you to turn the thermostat way down and reduce home-energy costs 30 percent.* Keep controls away from open windows or heaters, as these can affect blanket operation. And consider dual controls if there are two of you in one bed (and don't get the controls mixed up).

- *Another way to stay warmer in bed is to use non-electric pads that reflect body heat.* Made of reflective-coated polyurethane with a laminated polyfoam backing, these reflect body heat back between the sheets. Use them as you would a regular bed pad. These are available in many department stores for a reasonable $8 to $12.

- *The color of your roof and house can make a difference in energy efficiency.* If you live in an area that has hard winters, darker colors (especially for the roof) will absorb heat. Light colors reflect heat, so if keeping cool is your objective, keep it light.

- *If you have an outside entrance that can be altered to create a small foyer with double doors, do it.* Not only is this a handy place to leave winter gear, but it also cuts heat loss substantially when people enter and leave the house.

- *Window coverings are highly important in all air-conditioned or heated homes.* Pulling the drapes in winter minimizes drafts and cuts heat loss by as much as 30 percent. In summer, drapes can save your air conditioner up to 50 percent of its work by stopping the sunlight from shining in and heating the room. Drapes should be hung so that when they're open they don't interfere with sunlight and ventilation. A lined drape works better as an insulator. Shades can also serve the same function as drapes. To make window shades really work for you, it's a good idea to have two per window—one white, the other dark. Pull down the white shade in the summer to reflect heat; use the darker one in winter to absorb the heat and radiate it into the room. (See also window shades, p. 131.)

- *Window screens can block as much as 40 percent of the sun's warmth.* Remove them in the fall.

- *Consider adding a window on the south side of your house.* By letting in the sun it can save upwards of 30 gallons of oil per season if it is sealed properly and the drapes are pulled at night.

- *If you've got a ceiling in bad condition, instead of plastering and painting it, try acoustical ceiling tiles.* They will not only cushion the room for sound, but add insulation. The same goes for walls, especially outside ones. Panel walls, especially outside ones, with wood or cork, and seal them beforehand with tar paper, plastic sheeting, or some solid material to cut drafts. Wall hangings, rugs, quilts, and the like will work nicely as insulation, too.

- *Dust, grime, and dirt on radiators insulate and block heat transfer.* So do metallic paint and glossy light colors. Always paint in matte and satin finishes and dark colors: these will radiate heat better. Radiators should be painted while they're warm so the paint will be baked on.

- *Boxes built around radiators prevent transfer of heat.* Cover radiators with grillwork if you feel they're unsightly, but leave the tops uncovered so the heat can rise.

- *If you're entertaining a large group, turn down the thermostat before your guests arrive.* Their collective body heat will warm the place up. A human body produces as much heat as a 175-watt heater, which is why the old-fashioned canopied beds with curtains worked so well.

- *Even little things like assembling the kids at the front door and opening it once to let them all out can save fuel.* The same goes for letting guests out. Say your good-byes either inside or out, not at the open door. Be strict with your pets as well; don't let them in and out every half-hour.

- *Even without a solar energy system, heavy heat-absorbing objects such as flower pots or an indoor windowbox will radiate the heat they've absorbed during the day.* For that reason, don't cover a concrete floor, even stone or brick fixtures or a dark wall. One of the components of solar energy systems is the heat collector, which often consists of rocks, 50-gallon barrels of water, a bed of sand, or any other material that can absorb heat and radiate it into the house when the sun has gone down.

- *A heated garage is a waste of money.* If your car won't start, use a hair dryer (see p. 219) or buy a better battery or a set of jumper cables (which no car should be without anyway).

AIR CONDITIONING

KEEPING COOL WITHOUT AIR CONDITIONING

Starting with Yourself

- *Wear lightweight clothing and try not to rush about.*
- *Chores that require some physical effort—like housework—should be done during the cooler periods of the day.*
- *Midday naps can comfortably get you through the hot part of the day and give you extra hours at night before you get tired.* And if your bedroom is hot, you might consider sleeping in a cooler part of the house.
- *Cold drinks always do a lot to keep you cool, but go easy on sugared, syrupy soft drinks.* Drink juices or plain iced water; these fluids are better for you and more thirst-quenching.
- *Eating cold meals keeps you cooler both while you eat and while you prepare the food.* Saves energy, too.
- *Quick showers or swims keep you refreshed.* If you hop in when you come home from work, you may be cooled down enough so that there's no need for the air conditioning.

Fans

Fans cost a fraction of the amount it costs to operate an air conditioner, and the results can be quite pleasant. Keeping air moving, even if it's warm air, is the secret to staying comfortable in the summertime.

Ventilating Fans

These fans either bring air from the outside in or expel the air already inside the house (thereby creating suction, which brings in air from the outside). They're especially handy after sunset, when the air outside cools down much faster than the air inside. Window fans are the classic example.

Attic fans are the most effective of them all. Permanently mounted in the ceiling of the top story of a home, they suck air through windows and doors and blow it out enlarged vents in the attic. If they're large enough, they can create a cool draft throughout the house. Larger attic fans require professional installation. Nutone puts out a small but powerful unit for smaller homes that fits between 24" ceiling joists and can be installed by one person after an opening has been cut in the ceiling. Its louvers are also weather-stripped and close snugly when the fan is not running. This should be a feature of any fan you buy, or heat will escape in the winter.

Circulating Fans

These move air around a room or rooms within the house. They are most useful when the air inside a house is cooler than that outside (which can be accomplished by opening windows to receive the cool night air, then closing them in the morning).

Ceiling fans deserve their renewed popularity. They use no more electricity than a 15-watt light bulb and they keep air moving throughout a room, unlike other circulating fans that tend to aim moving air wherever they're pointed. The result can be a 10° to 12° reduction in room temperature. In winter they can cut a heating bill by as much as 20 percent; heated air rises and the ceiling fan circulates it back downwards, where it gets to you. Ceiling fans are especially good if you're stuck with cathedral ceilings (which can be cooler in the summer) and need all that heat on the ceiling forced downwards. The oldest manufacturer of ceiling fans is Hunter Fan Co., 2500 Frisco Ave., P.O. Box 14775, Memphis, TN 38114.

Portable fans are always handy to cool small areas. But they won't do much good unless they're of the oscillating variety.

Around the House

- *Heat rises, so by opening attic or upstairs windows, you let it escape.* When you open windows, it's important to open them at the top so the heat that has risen can escape. Also, opening windows on different sides of the house creates cross-currents that can make things more comfortable.

- *Insulation helps in summer as well.* Weatherstripping and insulation keep heat out in the summer, just as they keep it in during the winter.

- *Make sure the attic is ventilated.* The sun can easily heat the unventilated attic of a dark-roofed house to 130°. This in turn heats the house itself, even if it's insulated.

- *Open windows at night to let in the cool air, then close them early in the morning to trap that cool air.* Block out the sun by drawing drapes or pulling down shades on any windows that might admit sunlight.

- *If humidity is a problem, try a dehumidifier during those times when you have the windows down.*

- *Awnings can shade windows from the harsh sun and admit light and breeze.* They're worth considering—the amount of heat admitted through windows can be reduced by as much as 80 percent, which can lower the temperature by up to 15°. *Note:* When installing awnings, try to place them at a height that won't block the sun's low-angled rays in the winter.

- *Rolling up rugs in the summer makes things seem cooler while giving the rugs a break.*

- *Painting the roof of your house with aluminum paint can lower the temperature by up to 10°.* The metal coating reflects the sun's rays instead of absorbing them.

- *One-third of your summer heat comes from appliances—lights, dishwashers, dryers, color TVs, etc.* Use them only when you need them and during the cool part of the day.

THE EFFICIENT AIR CONDITIONER

Buying Tips

You must consider two things when selecting an air conditioner:

1) *The right size.* A unit that is too small has to work harder to cool you off; one that is too big will lower the temperature quickly, then click off. Often it won't have been on long enough to remove humidity from the air, so you might be cool but still uncomfortable.

    The Electric Energy Association has devised the following formula to help you pick the right-sized air conditioner:

$$\frac{\text{WHILE}}{60} = \text{BTU}$$

    Here's a breakdown:
    W: width of the room (in feet)
    H: height of the room (in feet)
    I: insulation (if room is well-insulated, use the number 10; if it's poorly insulated, on a top floor, or has a lot of windows, use 18)
    L: length of the room (in feet)
    E: exposure (if the room's longest outside wall faces north, use 16; east, 17; south, 18; west, 20)
    BTU: (British Thermal Units): the measure of cooling capacity (heat dispersion) by which air conditioners are rated

    If the formula gives a BTU number that is not available, choose the closest smaller one.

2) *The Energy Efficiency Rating*—By law, appliances are given an EER number. The higher it is, the better. EERs usually run between 7 and 12. Always buy high-efficiency air conditioners, even if they cost a little more than other models with the same cooling capacity (BTU). You'll save the extra investment in lower power bills.

    The EER is obtained by dividing the number of BTUs by the wattage.

An EER of 10 or over is very good; 8 or 9 is good. The Federal Trade Commission requires that any unit manufactured after May 19, 1980 display the yellow and black EER label (see illustration). This informs you how the appliance's EER compares with the least and most efficient models of the same capacity, and how much the unit will cost to operate annually, so that you can see how buying a unit with a higher EER will pay off.

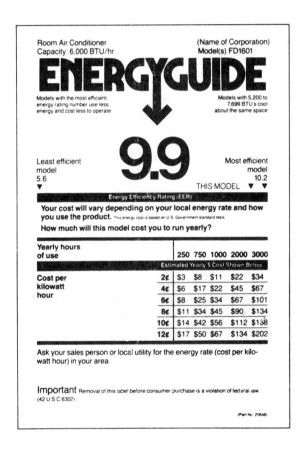

Using Air Conditioners

Some utilities, like Con Edison in the New York metropolitan area, raise their rates between May 15 and October 15 and lower them during the seven-month winter billing period. This, of course, is done for two reasons: It raises the utility's profits by a huge amount, and it encourages the consumer to economize, especially on air conditioning. In order to keep your air conditioner running as efficiently as possible, we suggest the following:

- *The most efficient way to use an air conditioner is to use it only when you really need to.* Think twice before you turn it on.

- *If at all possible, place any window air conditioners on the shady side of the house, preferably the north.* They won't have to work as hard.

- *If you have an attic fan, use it either in place of your air conditioner or to get rid of overheated air in the house before turning on the air conditioner in the evening.*

- *Each additional degree of cooling means 5 percent more electricity used.* The federal government requests that you keep your thermostat no lower than 78°, which is comfortable enough. And by installing a thermometer outdoors, you can see when the outside temperature is 78° or less and open the windows.

- *Since window units usually have only vague markings like "colder" or "coldest," it's up to you to calibrate your unit by actual degrees.* Place a thermometer in a central location in the room. Start the unit on its lowest setting and let it run until the room is at a uniform temperature. Raise the thermostat in steps until you reach 78° and mark whatever setting your air conditioner reads. That's what you should always use. Setting a temperature control at its coldest setting will *not* get a room cooler faster. It only gets the room colder than you need to have it.

- *Use a higher setting on the hottest of days to keep cold air circulating; on humid days, a low setting removes more moisture, making you comfortable with less cooling.*

- *Air conditioners cool air by removing humidity.* Don't put it back in the air by keeping a bathroom, laundry room, or kitchen door open when these rooms are being used. And while the doors are shut, open windows there to release the moisture you've built up.

- *Activities that create moisture and heat should be performed in the cooler morning or evening hours so as not to put an extra load on the air conditioner.*

- *An air conditioner has a fresh air vent. It can come in handy if there are smokers in the room, but otherwise keep it closed.* Fresh summer air is generally humid and hot; your air conditioner can work better without it.

- *If no one's home, don't cool the house.* Turn off the air conditioning when you leave and buy a timer, if you like, to turn it on shortly before you return (see p. 137).

- *Because cool air is heavier than warm air, it settles on the floor and can flow into open hot air registers, under doors, even into fireplaces with open dampers.* Seal these outlets as best you can.

- *Don't let the sun shine in.* Use drapes or shades (see p. 131) or reflective window film (see p. 000).

- *Light bulbs and appliances give off a lot of heat that can counter the work of an air conditioner.* Turn off the TV, radio, lights, or anything else that is adding to both your air conditioning load and your electricity bill. For every dollar you save by using them less, you save an additional $.50 in air conditioning.

- *Round-the-clock usage can freeze up a unit.* If your air conditioner stops cooling and sounds different, turn it off for a few hours and let it thaw.

- *Always keep closet and cabinet doors closed while the air conditioner is on.* This also applies in winter when the heat's on.

Maintenance

- *Keep the filters clear or the unit will get clogged, and more electricity will be required to turn the fan.* The filter is located behind the removable front panel and can be vacuumed, washed, or shaken clean. Clean the filter *at least* once a month. When vacuuming, also vacuum any other accessible parts of the unit.

- *The blower and the electric motor should be lubricated.* Follow the manufacturer's recommendations in your instruction manual.

- *Clogged condenser coils and fins (the metal grill or spines on the outside of the unit) can reduce a unit's efficiency.* Again, consult your owner's manual for cleaning instructions.

- *In preparation for winter, remove the air conditioner and seal the window.* If that isn't possible, seal the unit on both sides to protect it from the weather and keep it from letting cold air into the room. Air conditioner covers are available for $2.00 to $8.00 at most home supply stores. They are made of tough plastic that you can secure around the outside of the unit. Be sure to measure your air conditioner before you head out to buy a cover. You can also use your own plastic and heavy tape.

GENERAL WATER-SAVING TIPS

The average person uses over 130 gallons of water per day. Here are some ways to cut down.

THE TOILET

The conventional flush toilet is a colossal water-waster. The tank holds five to seven gallons of water, and most people flush down over 30 gallons daily.

Forty-five percent of the water used in the average American residence goes for flushing. The days before water shortages gave birth to this type of waste. Now it must be curbed:

- *For starters, flush less—only when it's essential.*
- *Fill plastic containers with water, seal them, and place them in the toilet tank to displace water.* That way less water is used when you flush. (Note: Don't use bricks—they can damage the tank and flushing apparatus.)
- *Don't use the toilet as an ashtray or wastebasket.*
- *Make sure your toilet doesn't leak; it can waste more than 50 gallons of water a day.* Place a little food coloring in the toilet tank. If it seeps down to the bowl, you have a leak.
- *Consider a water-saving toilet.* There are 3.5-gallon models available from the larger American manufacturers. The IFO Cascade, a three-liter toilet from Sweden, is 77 percent more efficient than these. Send $3.00 for information to Western Builders Co-op, 2150 Pine Drive, Prescott, AZ 86301.

OTHER TIPS

- *When brushing your teeth, use a glassful of water.* It works just as well as letting the tap run at the rate of three gallons per minute.
- *Avoid running the tap for a cold drink of water.* Chill a full pitcher of water and keep it in the refrigerator.
- *Reuse water from showers, baths, or the dishwasher rinse cycle for watering plants.* Mildly soapy water is fine for them, but don't use greasy water from pots and pans.
- *Report water wastage.* Most utilities have hot lines you can call to report open hydrants, leaking water mains, and the like. Be civic-minded— it only takes a minute.

FIXING LEAKS

Faucet Leaks

A minor faucet drip can leak 5,000 gallons of water per year, and getting someone to come and fix it can be costly. Doing it yourself is a snap—all it takes is a little common sense and a wrench, a pair of pliers, a screwdriver, and a replacement washer (a box of assorted sizes will cost you less than $2). Here's how:

1) Make sure that the water supply to the faucet is cut off. You'll usually find the valve controlling the water supply in the cabinet beneath or behind the faucet.

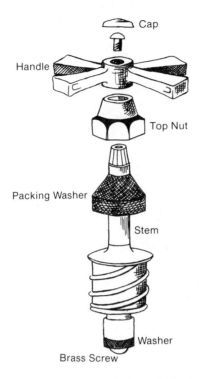

Cap

Handle

Top Nut

Packing Washer

Stem

Washer

Brass Screw

2) Close the drain so that any parts you might drop into the sink or tub won't go down.

3) The culprit is going to be the washer (at the bottom of the accompanying illustration). It will, nine times out of ten, be worn and need replacing, so you have to work your way down to it. Following along on the illustration:

4) Pry off the cap, then remove the screw and handle.

5) Next comes the top nut. This is where you need the wrench, though pliers might work, depending on how tightly it's screwed on. Unscrew it counter-clockwise and remove.

6) The packing washer should remain on the stem; leave it there.

7) Replace the faucet handle and unscrew it as if you were turning off the water. The stem assembly will come right out.

8) At the bottom is the washer, which will probably be pressed flat and have grooves cut into it. Remove it by unscrewing the brass screw and replace it with a new one. Washers usually have a number on the underside so that you'll know which size to use.

9) Reassemble—everything goes clockwise this time. If the faucet was leaking around the tap nut, add some packing there.

10) Turn on the water and pat yourself on the back.

Pipe Leaks

Pipe leaks can be repaired by wrapping the pipe tightly with heavy twine. There are also epoxies and putties that can be applied to a pipe from the outside to save you a call to a plumber. In most cases the pipes should be dry and clean before application of these compounds. The repairs will last indefinitely.

THE YARD

- *Buy nozzles for your garden hoses.* Those with automatic release triggers are best. Water is supplied when you pull and shut off when you release. These are especially helpful when you're washing your car; the days of letting the hose run while you wash must be considered a thing of the past.

- *Another waste of water-bill dollars is watering the lawn.* If you ever hold off watering and the grass gets a little brown, you'll notice how it returns to a nice, healthy green after a rain. As long as the seed bed is reasonably deep, dry periods won't hurt the yard.

  If you must water your yard, at least don't overdo it. An inch of water per week is plenty. Place an empty coffee or soup can on the grass near the sprinkler, and make sure it doesn't collect more than an inch of water.

HEATING WATER

The hot water heater, one of the major energy-consumers in the American house, uses about five times more energy than the oven. 23 percent of the electric bill in an electrically heated home and 41 percent of the bill in a home heated otherwise is consumed by the hot water heater. It's that silent appliance that most people don't turn on or off, and it gobbles power to keep hot water ready for you at the turn of a faucet, even when you're sleeping or away on vacation. The average person uses about 15 gallons of hot water a day or 450 gallons a month or 5,400 gallons a year. A family of four spends about $25 a month ($300 a year) to heat its water electrically.

There are three areas where hot water is used in the home: the kitchen, bathroom, and laundry room. Following are tips on how to economize in each one of these, preceded by general hints on how to make the hot water heater itself more energy-efficient.

MAKING YOUR HOT WATER HEATER MORE EFFICIENT

- *The hot water heater should always be as close as possible to the appliances that use hot water, not stuck away in a place like the garage.* The farther away it is, the more electricity it uses. For every 20 feet your hot water pipes could be shortened, you'd save enough heated water *in one month* for 10 showers. Ten to 15 percent of the power a hot water heater consumes is used to heat water that goes cold in the pipes when you turn off a faucet or the dishwasher shuts off.

- *If you have a choice, keep in mind that heating with electricity costs over 2.5 times more than heating with gas.*

- *There are three items, all discussed in the Energy Conservation Products section, that can slash your hot water costs, and they can pay for themselves in a matter of months:*

  — *Hot water pipe insulation* to maintain the temperature of hot water in pipes leading from hot water heater to water taps;

  — *A heavy-duty timer* to turn the hot water heater off when you're asleep at night or out of the house during the day;

  — *A hot water heater blanket* to prevent heat loss from within the tank.

- *Lower your water heater thermostat.* For every ten degrees you lower it, you can save more than 6 percent in water heating energy, and you simultaneously extend the life of your hot water heater because corrosion is increased by higher temperatures. If you have a dishwasher you need to have your hot water heater set at 140°; otherwise you can easily get by with it set at 110° to 120°. Some new hot water heaters have built-in boosters to elevate water temperature for the dishwasher. If you're fortunate enough to have one, then you can set the thermostat at 110°.

  If your water heater has no degree calibration and simply reads low, medium, etc., use a thermometer to test the water temperature until you get the setting you want. Then mark it on the hot water heater dial.

- *When you have a serviceman in to check your furnace have him check the hot water heater, especially if it's a gas heater.* It also has flames, barometric dampers, and stacks that require proper adjustment to be fuel-efficient. A well-maintained hot water heater can least 10 to 15 years.

- *Near the bottom of the hot water heater is a small tap—by draining a pan of water from the heater every month or two you remove scale, sediment, rust, and mineral (lime) deposits that settle on the bottom and reduce heat transfer.* You can tell by the amount of sediment you get just how often you should do this.

- *Ask your plumber about putting a water holding tank in your attic.* Attics are always hot in the summer (sometimes upwards of 130°), and water in the tank will be heated before it runs into the hot water tank. If your attic roof is insulated (though it shouldn't be), an attic holding tank can work in winter as well because the attic will be warm.

- *An awkward but extremely efficient way to get free hot water is this: leave your garden hose filled with water in the summer sun.* When you need to do the dishes, wash some clothes, or take a bath, run the hose indoors and use the hot water in the hose. The longer it is, the more it will store.

- *A word about leaky faucets: FIX THEM!* They mean money down the drain, especially if it's hot water that's leaking. It's hot water faucets that tend to leak because the intense heat of the hot water deteriorates the washers inside the faucet faster. Most people don't consider a pinhole leak very significant, but it can cost you 6.5 gallons of water an hour, 156 gallons a day, and 56,940 gallons a year. If it's hot water, it can cost you almost $225 in heating alone. See pages 108–110 to find out how to repair a leaky faucet.

- *Many household cleaning products work better in cold water—try it first.*

- *The general rule of thumb should be this: when you reach for any hot water tap, stop!* Ask yourself, "Is this hot water really necessary here? Will cold water do?" It often will.

- *Consider a solar or heat pump hot water heating system.* Though both of these require a conventional back-up system, they can save you money by cutting fuel costs substantially and earn you a tax break (see p. 90 for income tax credits on solar units). Heat pumps are exempt from sales tax in some states, including Florida and California, but won't get you a state income tax break as yet.

    The solar hot water heating system can cost anywhere from $1,200 to $4,500 installed and take anywhere from three to 10 years to pay for itself at current oil and electrical rates. You'll appreciate its value when you consider that energy costs will continue to rise and that it's virtually maintenance-free. On the other hand, the heat pump water system costs only $800 to $900 and can pay for itself in three years. With all the talk about solar, this is the overlooked money and energy saver. A heat pump water heater works on the same principle as a heat pump air conditioner (see pp. 90–91). It may need booster coils if the temperature drops to extreme lows in your area.

MORE TIPS FOR SAVING HOT WATER

The Bathroom

Seventy-five percent of the water used in an American residence goes down the bathroom drain—and around half of it is hot. Here are some ways to cut it down:

- *A water-saver shower head can mean annual savings of 24,000 gallons of water and fuel costs of $100 a year for a family of four.* It cuts the shower flow from a wasteful five to 10 gallons of water per minute to two or three gallons per minute, still a generous amount. There are more than 20 manufacturers of water-saver shower heads. Make sure that the head you're considering delivers no more than three gallons per minute. Some also come equipped with throttles and valves so you can shut the shower down to a trickle while you soap up, thereby increasing your savings even more. A lever adjusts the quality of the spray on the most expensive heads. Cost: $5 to $20.

- *Water restrictors eliminate waste in the shower even more simply.* A water restrictor is a stainless steel disc with a small hole in the center. It

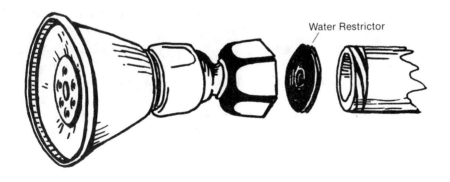

Water Restrictor

can limit the flow of water by up to 60 percent. It can be inserted simply by unscrewing the shower head. Cost: Free by writing to Con Edison, Consumer Affairs, Room 1625-S, 4 Irving Place, New York NY 10003.

- *Showers generally consume less water than baths (eight to 12 gallons as compared to 10 to 15 gallons).* For easy proof, put the plug into the bathtub, then take your shower. You'll see how much less water you use. But remember that long showers are taboo.

- *People waste water bathing by turning on the hot water and letting the water run until it's hot before putting in the plug.* Put in the plug first; when the hot water arrives, it will easily heat up the cold water you've already got in the tub.

- *If you've got a single water tap on your bathroom sink, invest in a rubber stopper if your metal drain plug doesn't work.* By plugging the drain you'll save water by getting the water temperature you want in the sink instead of waiting for it to come out of the tap. Do this for everything from washing your face to shaving. A family of four that fills the basin instead of letting the water run can save 45 gallons of water a day.

- *You use as much energy in* two days *shaving with a razor blade while letting the hot water run as you would in a* year *shaving with an electric shaver.* Six gallons of hot water can easily run down an open drain during the five minutes it takes to shave. If you prefer a blade, put some water in the plugged sink; don't run it. You should plug the sink while washing as well as while shaving.

- *Faucet aerators cut the flow of water from any faucet and mix air with it to save two or three gallons per minute, or from 40 percent to 60 percent of the water you'd normally use.* You have less splashing but retain good water intensity. The aerators are chrome-plated brass fittings that can be screwed onto faucets that have either inside or outside faucet threads. Adaptors are available for unthreaded taps. Cost: A most reasonable $.88 to $1.40.

The Kitchen

The dishwasher is the top consumer of hot water in the kitchen, but can be more economical than doing the dishes by hand. That takes 27 to 33 gallons of hot water compared to the dishwasher's 19.25.

Here are a few tips to follow in washing dishes and using the kitchen sink:

- *Always run a full load; the dishwasher uses the same amount of hot water whether it's partially loaded or full.* Smaller households need use the dishwasher only once every two or three evenings. If every family with a dishwasher used it just one time less per week, we'd save 9,000 barrels of oil each day, enough to heat 140,000 homes during the winter.

- *Load according to the manufacturer's instructions; you'll be able to get more in.*

- *Measure the detergent carefully.* Follow the manufacturer's instructions and adjust the recommended amount to the hardness or softness of the water.

- *Clean the filters on your dishwasher frequently.* An inhibited water flow can put a strain on the motor.

- *Rinse dishes right after meals in a sinkful of cold tap water so the food won't set.* Soak any pans or dishes that have food encrusted on them.

- *When you have a soup pot or large pan that needs to be filled with water so it can soak, place in the sink and then wash or rinse other dishes over it until it fills up.* Let it soak and wash later.

- *Don't use the rinse-hold cycle on the dishwasher.* It unnecessarily consumes three to seven gallons of hot water. If the dishes have been rinsed in cold water, they'll get completely clean in the regular cycle.

- *Don't buy a dishwasher with a plate warmer or drying cycle unless you can cut it off.* This is a real energy waster. Turning off the drying cycle can save 45 percent of the energy consumed by the dishwasher. If you're already stuck and don't have a switch to cut off the heating element, use a kitchen timer to see how long it takes to get to the drying cycle. Then whenever you start the dishwasher, set the timer. When it goes off, simply stop the dishwasher and open the door. Everything inside will dry quickly and spotlessly. And the humidity and heat will make the room more comfortable in the winter.

- *Don't use hot water to wash debris into the garbage disposal.* Cold water is cheaper and congeals fats, oils, and greases into solids which will easily wash down your sink.

- *When rinsing dishes you've washed by hand, rinse them in a panful of hot water.* Or, if you have a double sink, rinse them in the other side. But plug the sink up; don't run the water.

- *A handy way not to overuse dishwashing detergent and hot water when washing by hand is to mix a solution of detergent and water in a small container.* Wet the dishes, then use a dishwashing brush to dip in the soap solution and scrub the dishes. Then rinse.

- *In the winter the hot water you use to make pasta, boil corn or eggs, or wash the dishes should be retained in the sink for the heat and humidity it can provide.* The same goes for water in the bathtub.

The Laundry

- *Wash clothes in cold or warm water whenever possible.* And it usually is possible. If every American used cold water for laundry, we'd save 100,000 barrels of oil a day, enough to heat 1,600,000 homes for a winter.

- *Always use the water level control on your washer to adjust for small loads.* If you don't have one, always wash full loads.

- *Treating stains when they are fresh and pre-soaking especially dirty clothes prevents your having to run them through a wash cycle more than once.*

APPLIANCES

Over one billion appliances are at work in homes throughout the country at an annual cost to the American public of over $10.5 billion. To spend less and cut repair costs, read on.

BUYING TIPS

- *Always check* Consumer Reports *(available in your local library).* They have objectively tested and rated practically everything. They also conduct surveys among their two million subscribers and publish "Frequency of Repair Records" that should really be the determining factor in choosing an appliance to buy.

- *The EER, Energy Efficiency Rating, is an extremely important factor (see pages 104–105).* New government rulings require that all major appliances carry an EER label, which tells how much the appliance will cost to run for a year of average use.

- *Servicemen know which brands are the most repair-prone and which are the most trouble-free.* Whenever you have to have an appliance fixed, ask the repairman about other appliances and brands he's worked on and which are best.

- *Try to be accurate in determining your needs.* Don't buy an appliance that's too small; it'll have to strain and won't last as long. And don't buy one that's too large; it'll use more power than necessary.

- *Complicated gadgetry eventually breaks down; there are simply more moving parts to stop moving.* Stick to no-frills appliances.

- *Don't buy an appliance unless experience has shown that you really need it.* No impulse shopping!

- *Buying small appliances like toaster ovens that have thermostats will save energy and money.*

- *Always investigate the warranty or guarantee and make sure you understand it.* A longer-term warranty and a manufacturer's confidence in a product usually go hand in hand.

- *Be sure to find out who can do repairs under the warranty.* An authorized repair facility near you is a big plus, not only because of convenience, but because local dealers and repair people have local reputations to uphold.

- *Free home trials can be a trap.* Make sure that the "receipt" you're signing isn't a purchase contract.

- *"Reconditioned" or "rebuilt" appliances, if they are reconditioned or rebuilt by the original manufacturer, can be a deal.* But new appliances on sale are often nearly as cheap, and buying new means you'll get accessories, instruction booklets, and other niceties.

- *Once you have narrowed your choices, start shopping around.* Prices will vary from store to store. Manufacturers usually suggest a retail price, but what you eventually pay is up to you.

- *Wholesale prices or special discount prices don't always provide the deal you imagine.* Know whether the price includes free delivery and installation, and what charges any financing entails.

- *Offering to buy a high-priced appliance with cash can give you some bargaining power.* Sometimes dealers (illegally) won't charge you sales tax on a cash sale. Paying cash also saves you from high installment interest rates.

- *Consider shopping in a nearby state or county where the sales tax is either not as high or not applicable if the appliance is shipped.* Don't travel too far, or the cost of transportation will cancel out your savings.

- *Wait for an appliance to go on sale.* With dealers such as Sears-Roebuck, you can get a sale price without having to wait too long. Sears has both mail-order and local retail outlets, and each has the same items on sale at different times. It's always worth the wait. Appliances generally go on sale twice a year—right after Christmas and in mid-summer.

- *If you're buying a "demonstrator" or "floor model," try to get a bigger discount than the dealer offers you.*

- *Consider buying a secondhand appliance only if the appliance can be repaired at a later date.* Check that out before buying.

- *Buy appliances with replaceable parts.* When you make the purchase, ask if the appliance can be broken down to components. Some appliances can be completely disassembled; all parts are removable and replaceable. This is the way appliances should be made.

TIPS FOR MAINTAINING AND REPAIRING APPLIANCES

- *It's essential to read the instruction book; if appliances were maintained and used according to the manufacturer's instructions, there would be fewer breakdowns.* Many people will unpack anything from a camera to a food processor, throw the package, warranty, and instruction book in the garbage, then scratch their heads and say, "Now how does this thing work?" Preventive maintenance goes a long way in prolonging the life of an appliance.

- *43 out of 100 service calls are unnecessary.* The problem is usually a button, dial, or switch pushed in the wrong direction; a blown fuse; a tripped circuit breaker; a loose wire in the plug; or, yes, that the appliance isn't plugged in. Do some checking before calling a repairman.

- *Always take small appliances in to the repair shop yourself.* Having a repairman come to you will cost much more.

- *There are books on servicing home equipment.* Your local Cooperative Extension Service and the library have them. Try to do your own trouble shooting first, but don't get in over your head. If you have to call a serviceman, it's best to show him an appliance that needs to be fixed, not a pile of parts that need to be assembled.

- *When you've tried everything, call the store's service manager, give him the make and model number of your broken appliance, and explain the problem and the trouble-shooting you've done.* Ask for any suggestions; what he recommends may save you a service call.

- *Have an idea how long your appliance should last.* If it breaks down after many years of service, it might be time to move on to a new one. From the Department of Agriculture, here are the life expectancies of some of our more popular appliances:

	Years	
Clothes dryers	14	
Freezers	15	
Ranges, electric and gas	16	
Refrigerators	16	
Sewing machines	24	
Televisions		
black and white	11	
color	7–8	(approximately)
Toasters		
manual	10	
automatic	7	

Vacuum cleaners
tank	15
upright	18
Washing machines	11

- *Appliance service contracts tend to be unnecessary and unprofitable.* If you shopped around and checked *Consumer Reports'* "Frequency of Repair" records when you bought, sent in the warranty, and followed the manufacturer's use and maintenance instructions, you should be pretty well protected. And a service call, *if* you do need it, will probably cost less than a service contract.

- *Once part of an appliance—such as the gasket on a pressure cooker, the top of a blender, or the pot of a coffee maker—breaks or is lost, many people retire the appliance. Don't!* It's easy to get a replacement part: Drop a postcard to the manufacturer and request the part needed. The manufacturer's address should be on the appliance and in the instruction manual. Be sure to give the complete model number and a description of the appliance. Or phone (toll-free if possible) the manufacturer's branch nearest you, ask for the parts department, and place your order. You can also try the authorized factory representative. Whether you write or phone, you will be given an order number and the cost of the part, including postage and handling. Remit by mail and wait. Some manufacturers are remarkably prompt; others, not so prompt. But you'll have saved an appliance.

- *When you do have a service call for a malfunctioning appliance, make sure you know exactly what was wrong and what repairs were made.* Make a note of this, along with date and cost (preferably on the back of the bill you're given). If the same thing goes wrong again, you'll know immediately that you have a valid complaint, and complaining is what you should do.

- *If you get a lemon, and the supplier and manufacturer ignore your complaints, raise hell!* They're usually banking on your giving up the fight. Don't. First there's your Better Business Bureau. Next is the industry's consumer protection agency, the Major Appliance Consumer Action Panel (MACAP), 20 North Wacker Drive, Chicago, IL 60606. Call collect: (312) 236-3165.

USING APPLIANCES

- *When at all possible, use appliances during off-peak periods—usually before 10:00 a.m. and after 10:00 p.m.* It is during peak demand periods that utility companies have to provide the most electricity—and often charge more for it. Using larger appliances like washers, dryers, air conditioners, and hot water heaters (when rigged with a switch, see page 137) at off-peak periods reduces pressure on the utility and can help cut both your and their expenditures, because they won't have to supply as much power during rush hours.

- *An instant-on television uses electricity continually to remain in a state of readiness.* Convenient, but wasteful. Either hook up a switch on the electrical cord or unplug the set when it's not in use.

- *A full bag or a stopped-up hose strains a vacuum cleaner's motor and wastes energy.* Keep tabs on both.

- *Reuse vacuum cleaner bags.* Cut off the bottom, empty, fold, staple, and it's ready to go again. The next time you empty it, use a staple remover to take out the staples so that it can be restapled and reused indefinitely.

- *An old-fashioned, hand-operated carpet sweeper is an economical way to keep your floors clean.* Dampening the brushes of your sweeper will double its efficiency.

LIGHTING

Our familiar incandescent bulbs produce light by heating a tiny filament. But the output is 90 percent heat and 10 percent light, and the heat is usually wasted because it's generated in the wrong place (on the ceiling) or at the wrong time (in summer or in rooms that are already sufficiently heated).

Fluorescent bulbs are dramatically more energy-efficient; a 30-watt fluorescent bulb puts out more light than a 100-watt incandescent bulb. Many people think of fluorescents as sources of cold, hard light, but they're available in warm tones as well. And fluorescents last up to 10 times longer than incandescents, so the higher price you pay for the fluorescent bulb means savings in the long run. If you use an incandescent bulb over six hours a day, replacing it with a fluorescent bulb can save about $15.00 a year.

There are lightweight fluorescent fixtures that can simply be installed and plugged into a wall socket. But buy the fixtures with removable bulbs. Some manufacturers (like GE) have a unit that is completely disposable—when the bulb goes, you dispose, wastefully, of the entire unit.

An extremely simple way to convert from incandescent to fluorescent is to purchase the new circular fluorescent fixtures that screw into incandescent bulb sockets like regular light bulbs. No adapter is needed. The circles range in diameter from 7" to 11.5". You can use them in lamps, too, as long as the fluorescent bulb isn't too wide to fit inside the lamp shade. The cost ranges from $3.00 to $30.00.

Other tips:

- *A dimmed light uses less electricity and provides more pleasant illumination than a brightly burning bulb.* Buy dimmers; what seems like a luxury item is in fact an energy-saver. Most dimmers can be adjusted to any level, although some have switches with only one or two settings. Dimmers should not be used on any motor-driven appliance; damage can result from limiting the current. There are three types available, costing from $4.50 to $16.00.
  — *Wall dimmers.* These replace wall switches and control whatever the switch did.
  — *Tabletop dimmers.* Simply plug a lamp or two into the dimmer box and the dimmer box into the wall.
  — *Cord dimmers.* These can easily be hooked up to lampcords and are just as efficient and much more compact than the tabletop models.
- *Of all the incandescent light bulbs, the plain old general service bulb is most efficient.* Long-life bulbs are inefficient energy users; eye-saving bulbs are more expensive; and krypton-filled outdooor lamps, while energy-efficient, cost three times as much as general service bulbs.
- *In selecting a room color, bear in mind that darker walls and ceilings absorb light while lighter colors reflect it.* And sunlight streaming through a window can illuminate a lighter room better than it can a darker one.
- *Locating lamps in corners permits them to give off much more light by providing another wall for reflection.*
- *A kerosene lamp is useful not only during blackouts, but also at mealtime or any other intimate occasion when a warm light is preferable to the bright glare of electric lights.*
- *Three-way light bulbs should be used whenever possible.* They may cost more, but they regulate brightness to save electricity and they last three times longer.
- *It is always more economical to turn off an incandescent light when you leave the room.* The electric surge needed to light an incandescent bulb is equal to only one or two seconds of light time. Turn off fluorescents only if you'll be out of the room for more than two hours.
- *A switch that controls several light fixtures at once wastes energy.* Control every bulb with a separate switch.
- *If you think two bulbs are better than one, think again.* A 100-watt bulb will give more light than two 60-watts (1740 lumens vs. 1720 lumens).
- *Dust on light bulbs lowers their illumination level by as much as 10 percent.* Keep them clean.

- *When illumination is required only for effect, for transit through an area, or to illuminate a rarely frequented area, use bulbs of lower wattage.* Forty watts will do for closets, garage, attic, and basement.

- *For work areas—desk, kitchen, sewing area, or hobby area—use good localized lighting from lamps, not an overhead fixture that floods the entire room with light.* You'll see better and more economically. Indirect lighting looks best anyway; a living room, for example, looks much better illuminated by table lamps than it does when illuminated by an overhead light.

- *The old myth that watching TV without a light is bad for your eyes has been disproved.* When the TV is on, turn lights off or down to their lowest levels. This reduces glare, saves energy, and reduces the heat level in the room during the summer.

- *A proper lampshade:*
  — is white or off-white;
  — conceals the bulb—whether you're standing or sitting;
  — is dense enough only to keep the light from glaring through;
  — reflects the light both up and down;
  — has a bottom that provides a wide spread.

- *Those fancy gaslights outside a home may look great, but one of them can burn more than one-sixth of the average home's monthly gas consumption.*

- *Check both inside and outside your house.* You're sure to find higher-wattage bulbs than you need. Using a lower wattage saves electricity. Always try a lower-wattage bulb when replacing a burned-out bulb. Or don't replace it at all.

- *Light-control units or photo-electric cells are easy to install (they screw right into the socket) and by turning outside security lights on at dusk and off at dawn, they can save much more electricity than you would turning them off and on yourself.*

ENERGY CONSERVATION PRODUCTS

The methods and machinery we use in our homes were bestowed upon us during times of unlimited energy. Now this wasteful flow of energy through our homes means big bucks wasted and threatens our limited resources. Buying any of the following energy conservation products can save anywhere from a few dollars to a few hundred dollars per year. They're available from hardware stores, home centers, and the like, unless otherwise mentioned.

SEALERS

Caulking

This elastic, adhesive material is squeezed from a tube into gaps and seams where different types and sizes of building materials meet, or where pipes and wires enter your house. It can be oil-based (which lasts one year) or acrylic latex (which lasts 10 years) or silicone (which lasts 20 years and is pliable, capable of stretching with expansions and contractions of the materials it's sealing). Caulk also comes in many colors, so it will blend in with the color of your house.

Caulking stops heat loss. You may dismiss these tiny escape outlets as inconsequential, but they aren't. Combined, they could be the equivalent of a one-square-foot hole through which expensive heated and cooled air escapes. Cost: $.45 to $2.50 per 11 oz. caulking cartridge; $1.50 to $3.50 for a caulking gun.

A word about storing caulk: Because it has a tendency to dry out over time, melt some candle wax or paraffin into the tip of the caulk tube or cartridge. A tight seal that's easy to remove will be formed.

where should you apply caulk?

1. (= A) Around door and window frames and at corners of house.
2. (= B) Between house framing and foundation.
3. (= C) Between house siding and sheathing.

Weatherstripping for Doors

A crack just one-eighth of an inch wide around an average door is as large as a hole in your wall about 4" × 6"—it's just like missing a window pane. If you can slip a quarter underneath a door, you're losing valuable heat. Weatherstrip your doors properly and you can save at least $25.00 per outside door in fuel costs.

There are various types of weatherstripping. Generally plastic, foam, or spring metal that is squeezed by the door when it's closed is used on the top and sides; flexible plastic or rubber door sweeps are attached to the bottom of the door with screws or nails, or threshold installations are screwed into the floor. Outside doors see a lot of action—the average door is easily opened and closed 1,000 or more times per year—so the job should be done to last.

The garage door (the one you use for the car) also needs weatherstripping. Make sure that weatherstripping is installed along the side and that a rubber seal is placed across the bottom. And because the garage gets quite cold, if there is a door leading into the house, it, too, should be weatherstripped. Or consider adding a storm door; in the summer you can remove the glass for extra ventilation. A pull-down stairway leading into the attic should also be sealed (as well as insulated).

Even a mail chute can leak a lot of heat. Weatherstrip it if necessary. If it has springs, make sure they close the chute tightly. A large keyhole on an old door can also let heat escape—seal it.

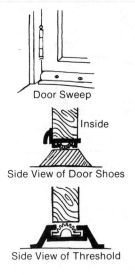

Door Sweep

Inside

Side View of Door Shoes

Side View of Threshold

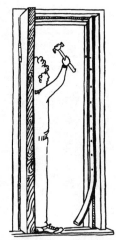

Weather Stripping for Doors

Cost: Door sides and tops—$1.00 to $4.00; door sweeps—$1.60 to $3.20; door thresholds—$3.00 to $7.30; kits that include these various types of weatherstripping—$3.00 to $6.00.

Weatherstripping for Windows

On a windy day, up to 25 percent of your heat is lost through windows and doors. You can gauge heat loss with two devices: 1) Make a draft gauge from a single piece of plastic wrap or very light tissue paper fastened across the bottom of a coat hanger. Hold this closely in front of window or door— drafts will make it flutter. Or use a lit candle in the same way. Any motion of either of these means low-efficiency heating. And if you've noticed that breezes move the curtains, you're really in bad shape. By weatherstripping your windows you can lop a sizable chunk off your fuel costs.

Weatherstripping comes in a variety of materials—metal and felt, spring metal, rubber and vinyl strips, adhesive foam, sponge rubber tape, and vinyl tubing.

When applying weatherstripping, pay special attention to windows facing west (these catch prevailing breezes) and windows facing north (these are exposed to the coldest air). If you have any windows that you never open, seal them permanently and install a permanent storm window on the inside or outside. For windows you use, make sure the weatherstripping material allows the windows to slide open and shut freely while sealing it well when

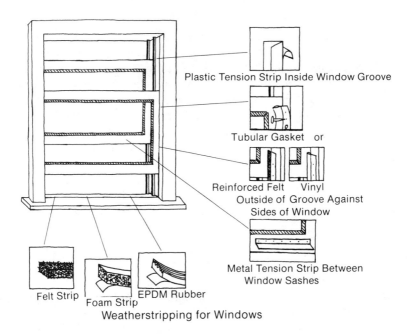

Plastic Tension Strip Inside Window Groove

Tubular Gasket or

Reinforced Felt Vinyl
Outside of Groove Against
Sides of Window

Metal Tension Strip Between
Window Sashes

Felt Strip
Foam Strip
EPDM Rubber

Weatherstripping for Windows

it's closed. And while weatherstripping, be sure to apply it around the attic fan, if you have one. The same goes for the edges of a window air conditioning unit, where it meets the window frame. Sealing this perimeter means maximum summer cooling and winter heat retention.

Especially in winter, some air infiltration from outside is necessary—both you and your furnace need fresh air. But the levels of air from the outside permitted inside most American households are excessive. An indicator that you have the right amount of weatherstripping, caulking, and insulation is the sporadic appearance of a light mist on your windows or on the downwind side of your house.

Cost: $.45 to $7.00 per window.

Miscellaneous Sealers

- Draft blockers are compact, plastic foam cut-outs that can be placed under electric switches or outlet plates. It has been estimated that as much as 8 percent of the heat lost in a typical home goes through the wall switches and sockets. Not only are there cracks here, but the metal plates and circuit boxes conduct heat away from the inside of the house.
  Cost: $1.50 to $3.00 for a packet of eight.

- Inside covers for kitchen exhaust fans are magnetically attached to seal the fans when they're not turned on. Most exhaust fans come equipped with outside vent covers, but cold air can easily penetrate them, making an inside cover a necessity as well.
  Cost: $2.00 to $2.50. Frost King makes both 8-inch and 10-inch models.

- Door and window draft guards are thermal-lined tubes, 24 to 44 inches in length and two to three inches in diameter, that are filled with sand or some other loose insulating material. Also called doggle draft guards and draft dodgers, they're floppy and can be laid snugly against cracks to stop the flow of air. Draft guards are excellent for doors and windows that are used during the winter and cannot be sealed. If you like to open your window at night, place a draft guard at the base of the bedroom door to prevent heat loss in the rest of the house. When not in use, hang it out of the way on the door knob.
  Cost: $3.00 to $7.00. Also available by mail order from Energy Savers, P.O. Box 99, New Rochelle, NY 10804 or Sunset House, 339 Sunset Building, Beverly Hills, CA 90215.

INSULATION

Walls, Floors, Windows, and Doors

Heat, like water, tends to seek its own level. In the winter it escapes outside; in summer, the flow is reversed and warm air tries to equalize with the cool air inside the house. All you can do is slow the flow, and insulation is what does it. Three inches of insulation in the ceiling can cut your fuel bill by 35 percent; two inches under the flooring can lop off 15 percent; and two inches in the walls, another 10 percent, for a total of 60 percent. This alone should convince you it's worthwhile.

Buy insulation with two criteria in mind:

1) *R-value,* which is an insulation efficiency rating—the higher the better. To select the proper R-value, ask your local utility company or any insulation contractor or building materials dealer what's best. Because heat rises, you need a higher R-value for attic floors than for exterior walls, the basement ceiling, or the crawl space under the house. To be assured of an accurate R-value, look for NAHB (National Association of Homebuilders) ratings. The NAHB does its own testing.

2) *Type—you have four to pick from:*
   - *Blanket and batt* is manufactured in widths of 16 inches and 24 inches to fit between the standard-sized framing joists and studs of most American homes. This type is excellent for attic floors or basement ceilings. It comes in rolls that you simply unroll into the space to be insulated. It's made of fibers of glass, rock, or slag. You're assured of a constant R-value, since the thickness is always uniform. If your home has a lot of irregular spaces or was built before standardized house construction, you can still use batt-type insulation by cutting pieces to fit.

   - *Loose-fill type* is sold by the bag and manufactured in pellet, fibrous, or granular form. It's made of everything from expanded mica (zonolite or vermiculite) to shredded paper treated with boric acid (to make it fire-resistant). Loose-fills have to be carefully leveled to a specific thickness, and the do-it-yourselfer can often be inaccurate. It leaves few air gaps, however, because it can be packed into place. If used in vertical walls, it can settle over the years and leave a non-insulated gap at the top. Also, unlike batt-type, it has no vapor barrier; you have to lay your own (see below).

   - *Rigid-foam plastic insulation* is made from polyurethane or polystyrene. Panels are sold in different sizes and thicknesses. It has three advantages: It has a high insulation value, in spite of its minimal thickness and weight; it's sound absorbent; and a vapor barrier of foil lining is attached. The big disadvantage is that it's a fire hazard. If used in exposed or semi-exposed spaces, it's highly combustible, and it produces poisonous and explosive gases while burning. Rigid-foam plastic insulation should not be used where it might be exposed to open flame inside the home.

   - *Foamed-in-place plastic insulation* is usually made of urea-formaldehyde or polyurethane. It must be pumped into walls by a professional contractor in a liquid form; then it hardens into something like sty-rofoam. This, too, is combustible and can produce noxious fumes. And some people claim it's poisonous, so if it doesn't harden properly it can cause problems. It's been banned in one state and lawsuits concerning it are pending in others. The U.S. Customer Product Safety Commission has toll-free hotlines for urea-formaldehyde foam-insulating problems: It's (800) 638-8326; in Maryland, (800) 492-8363; in Alaska, Hawaii, Puerto Rico, and the Virgin Islands, (800) 638-8337.

More Hints about Insulation

- *Any insulation you install* must *have a vapor barrier applied to the warm (heated) side; otherwise, warm, moisture-laden air coming into contact with the cold surface of the insulation in the attic will condense into dew that, over time, can cause serious damage beneath the insulation.* Vapor barriers stop this moisture from forming between the cold and warm surfaces. The batt and blanket and rigid types of insulation are manufactured with a foil vapor barrier attached. When using loose-fills you have to lay your own, then pour the insulation over it. Common vapor barrier materials are aluminum foil, aluminum paint, polyethylene film, varnish and rubber-base paints, and urethanes.

- *If your eyes start burning or your head aches and you're always tired, you might have overinsulated your home so that impurities in the air cannot escape.*

- *Always wear a mask when working with insulation, especially fiberglass— particles released into the air and inhaled can have adverse long- and short-term effects on your health.*

- *Save your receipts and check to see if you are entitled to a tax credit because you insulated.* The receipts can also come in handy when you're selling your house; they serve as proof that it's insulated to a specific R-value, and good insulation is a fine selling point.

- *Don't seal the louvers in the attic or in the crawl space under the house.* These are necessary for ventilation and to prevent moisture buildup. Also, don't insulate the ceiling or walls of the attic; insulate the floor, or moisture may be trapped in the attic, causing wood to rot, and heat savings elsewhere in the house will be lost in the attic.

- *One quick way to determine whether your house needs extra insulation is to walk outside on a very gray, sunless winter day after a snow and take a look at the exterior of the house.* Is snow melting on the roof or on the ground and shrubs around the house? If so, heat is escaping and you're in-sulation-deficient.

- *Hand pack insulation around chimney, electrical conduits or wiring, and vent pipes coming up through the attic floor.* To find gaps, turn off the attic light and look for light coming through holes and cracks from underneath.

- *Forgetting to insulate any of the following reduces your benefits:*

  — *The trap door to the attic.* Staple insulation directly to the back of it.

  — *Attic flooring or catwalks.* If you have to remove the planking to get underneath, do so.

  — *Under eaves and above outer walls.* Insulation is extremely important here, but be sure not to block any vents under the eaves. A piece of scrap wood or cardboard jammed between the rafters and slightly above the insulation will keep vents unplugged efficiently.

  — *Cellar windows.* These are especially susceptible to the cold. Seal them well, with either polyethylene covering or boards and insulation.

  — *The "sill plate" (the plank atop your foundation).* Any cracks between it and the foundation should be sealed. Stuff insulation in and seal with caulk.

  — *The garage.* Without proper insulation, a garage will draw heat from the house. Garage walls adjoining the house should be insulated, and if you have a floor over the garage, make sure the garage ceiling is insulated.

Appliances, Pipes, and Ducts

- *Hot water heaters are not made with enough insulation, and heat loss there can cost you upwards of $25.00 annually.* A good insulating jacket around the water heater can reduce the loss by 80 percent and save 10 percent of the fuel the heater normally uses. If you can feel any heat on the tank exterior, especially above the middle, you should insulate. Kits of water-heater insulation include holding tape so that you can get a tight fit around the tank. You can also use six-inch fiberglass ceiling insulation, taped well.
  Cost: $8.00 to $28.00.

- *Duct insulation should be applied to all ductwork running through your house, especially that in unheated attics or basements.* Some brands have self-adhesive strips for easy application; others have to be installed with duct tape. Before applying, check the ducts for any air leaks and patch them with duct tape. A foil backing on your insulation is the vapor barrier and should be installed against the duct.

  Ducts with two or three inches of insulation can save as much as 15 percent of the operating expense for your forced-air furnace, heat pump, or central air conditioner.

Cost: $.18 to $1.35 per square foot for insulation; $1.50 to $6.00 for duct tape from 30 to 180 feet in length.

- *A big waste of energy and water is hot water that cools down while sitting in the pipes.* When you turn on the hot tap, you have to wait until the pipes empty out and the freshly heated water appears. For every ten feet of hot water pipe you insulate, you save enough hot water per month to do three full-cycle loads in a dishwasher. There are three main types of insulating for pipes:
  - *Snap-on.* Make absolutely sure you buy insulation of the correct diameter to fit your pipes or copper tubing.
  - *Thick self-adhering tape.*
  - *A roll of fiberglass with a separate plastic outer wrapping.* Cost: $.05 to $.85 per foot.

STORM WINDOWS, SHUTTERS, AND SHADES

In the winter, window glass, which is only about one-eighth inch thick, needs some insulation. Otherwise it conducts heat away from inside your home.

Inside Storm Window Kits

An inexpensive, do-it-yourself, energy-saving alternative is an inside storm window kit. Each kit contains plastic sheets to cover windows and some means of sealing and holding the sheets in place. The dead air trapped between the plastic and the window glass is an excellent insulator and stops the loss of heat.

These kits all do the same thing, but prices vary greatly, according to the thickness of the plastic sheets and the way they are attached to the window frame. Thicker plastic resists tearing and is easier to clean. And the more expensive kits have aluminum channels that fit into place and facilitate easy installation and removal of the plastic.

Other tips:

- *You can also buy thin four-mil plastic sheeting and tape it up yourself, saving the price of a kit.*
- *Many indoor kits work outdoors as well, if you prefer to put the plastic there.*
- *Remember, it's dead air space that does the trick, and to have dead air there must be no cracks and leaks in your windows and window frames.* Caulk first if necessary.

Cost: $1.00 or less to $12.00 per window.

Outside Storm Windows

Outside storm windows perform virtually the same function as those installed inside; the difference is that outside windows are permanently attached and need not be removed during the warm months. Most models have three tracks—one for a screen and two for upper and lower panes of glass.

Some shopping around is necessary. Cheaper versions don't have rigid frames and won't fit closely against the window frame, thereby defeating their purpose. Others don't have weatherstripping throughout to insure air-tightness; still others don't have tight-fitting sashes that lock firmly in position and sit closely together in their tracks. Beyond these considerations, make sure any storm window you're considering has two small "weep-holes" about one-eighth inch in diameter at the bottom. They allow rain water that penetrates the screen to run from the window sill.

If you have them installed by a contractor, make sure the ones you ordered are delivered (instead of cheaper ones). Check the work before the contractor leaves (panes of glass can be broken during installation), and get contracts, etc., in writing.

Cost: For better quality, $35.00 and up per window, depending on the size of the window.

Shutters and Shades

Along with curtains and inside storm windows, shutters and shades can stop heat loss through windows.

There are several indoor shutter kits that do good insulating jobs, and the cheaper ones work about as well as the more expensive ones. Prices range from $30.00 to slightly over $200.00. Roller shades can also be expensive and have to be correctly installed to do any good. They are made of everything from hollow plastic slats to metalized plastic and fiber batting sandwiched between fabric covers. Prices here can run approximately $100.00 per window. If that frightens you, remember that even regular window shades provide a surprising amount of insulation.

To work really well, window shades and shutters have to be closed manually when the sun goes down to prevent heat loss from the house, and they must be open when the sun comes up to receive the sun's radiant energy. Storm windows—inside or out—perform both functions, preventing heat loss and absorbing sunlight. For decorative window insulation that provides privacy as well, however, shades, shutters, and draperies can work quite satisfactorily. These are also excellent for larger sash windows or even sky-lights.

There are two new technological developments in window shades that warrant mention:

- A shade with an aluminized surface that absorbs and reflects heat back into the house. If the shades fit snugly an inch from the win-dowpane, with no more than one-quarter inch clearance all around the window frame, heat savings in the room can amount to 45 percent.

- A window quilt will also reduce heat loss by as much as 40 percent to 50 percent in the winter and will cut summer heat absorption by 60 percent to 70 percent. Composed of a quilted five-layer sandwich of polyester insulation fabric with an aluminized vapor barrier, these window quilts run in plastic tracks so that air cannot escape at top, bottom, or around the edges. They come in various colors and can be custom-made by Appropriate Technology Corporation, P.O. Box 975, Brattleboro, VT 15301.

Other Devices

- *Sun screens* are attached to the outside of a window and deflect sunlight before it enters the room, making for a cooler interior in the summer. Their closely woven fiberglass weave also allows a view to the outside. Sun screens can also be attached to shade rollers and used indoors, but with this arrangement, some of the sun's heat enters the house. In winter, sun screens should be removed from windows that receive sunlight so the sun can be allowed to do some supplemental heating by shining inside. For more information, including a sample, write to Phifer Wire Products, P.O. Box 1700, Tuscaloosa, AL 35401.

- *Reflective film for windows* is thin plastic that can be applied directly onto glass windowpanes or onto sliding glass doors. The normal heat loss from window glass in winter can be reduced between 10 percent and 40 percent, and about 75 percent of the summer sun is screened out, reducing the amount of work your air conditioner has to do. The film also helps to prevent your drapes, furniture, and carpet from fading in the sun without your having to roll down shades or pull drapes. Another benefit is the daytime privacy the reflective window film provides.

  This film is available in a variety of tints—silver, bronze, gold, and smoke. Each differs in how well it reflects solar rays, so be sure to inspect samples before you choose what you want. Check the instructions and be careful when applying; this film has a tendency to bubble when applied to windows.

  Cost: $1.00 to $1.54 per square foot.

HEATING AND COOLING AIDS

Automatic Setback Thermostat

There are two times your wall thermostat should be set down: when you're asleep and when you're not at home. Ignoring a thermostat can result in a tremendous amount of waste. It's so easy to set, but we forget that down in the basement a furnace is slaving away, guzzling gallons of heating oil. Timers with double or single setbacks can help you. The single setback automatically lowers the temperature at night. If your house is regularly empty during the day, the double setback can lower the temperature then, too. The savings amount to around 12 percent of your annual fuel cost, making it well worth the investment.

Professional installation is usually required here, though Rhodes, Inc., does manufacture its Heat Watcher, a unit that does not require professional installment. It consists of a timer and a small one-watt heater that you place near your thermostat and plug into the wall. A timer activates the tiny heater, which activates the thermostat, which turns down the furnace.

About the fanciest of these devices is a new digital automatic thermostat. You can program it for varying weekday and weekend schedules. The time of day, day of week, and set temperature are all displayed for easy monitoring.

Cost: Thermostats sell for $40.00 to $150.00; they can cost up to $200.00 when professionally installed.

Air Deflectors for Registers (Vents)

The contractor who installs any forced-air heating system has no way of knowing how efficiently placed the vents will be once the occupants furnish their house. Vents often end up blowing behind drapes or a piece of furniture, or even up against the ceiling. And because the heat or air conditioning is misdirected, it takes more fuel than is necessary to maintain the desired room

temperature. Deflectors are simple, adjustable metal or plastic devices that magnetically snap onto any register. They range from 10 inches to 20 inches wide, and you can make them even longer with extensions. They allow you to direct heated or cooled air into the room for maximum temperature control and energy savings.

Cost: $1.50 to $4.00 each.

Heat Reflectors for Radiators

Radiators are located against walls—usually outside walls at that—which therefore receive an unnecessary share of the heat. A heat reflector placed behind a radiator reflects radiant heat back into the room, where it belongs. These panels are usually sold in 32″ × 40″ sheets that are about one-quarter inch thick, but they can be cut to size. They're composed of rigid plastic foam covered on one side with metal foil. The foam insulates and the foil (positioned towards the room) reflects heat. These can be especially helpful in older, radiator-equipped apartment buildings where heat levels are not always high enough. They are available by mail order from R.F.P., Inc., 26 Howe Place, Yonkers, NY 10708.

You can make your own by buying foam core board from an art supplier or insulation board from a lumber yard and taping aluminum foil over it.

Cost: $3.00 to $6.00 per radiator.

Radiator Thermostats

Once installed on a radiator, a thermostat regulates the amount of heat the radiator puts out. Some models even set back the room temperature at night. This reduces wear and tear on you and the valve; you won't be constantly turning the radiator on and off. It also saves energy; people usually raise windows to cool an overheated room, or, if no one's there, the room stays overheated.

Initial costs may delay your savings—these usually have to be professionally installed—but in the long run they're a good investment.

Cost: $14.00 to $100.00.

Furnace Improvement Accessories

Using an oil burner for 15 years takes as much fuel as driving a car 500,000 miles. A lot of technology and energy-saving features have been developed recently that can cut fuel costs and increase heat output.

- *Flame-retention burners.* These self-contained units can generate a higher flame temperature in a smaller combustion space. The result is more usable heat from fuel oil, which is ignited right at the end of the burner head instead of being spewed into a cold firebox where it is ignited and, more often than not, doesn't fully burn. Flame-retention burners require no firebox, which is an advantage because fireboxes on conventional units have to be warmed up before the furnace can start heating the house.

Cost: $250.00 to $350.00, including installation.

- *Blue-flame burners.* A blue flame is the most efficient flame of all; any yellow in a flame shows that impurities or too much air is present. This burner mixes air and oil so well that a blue flame always results. It is available, however, only as part of a complete unit, not as a replacement part. This could change at any time, though. Available from Blueray Systems, Inc., Mineola, NY 11501.

- *Automatic flue dampers.* When the furnace is off, the draft through it pulls warm air up the chimney. A flue damper—a circular metal plate fitted inside the flue pipe—can reduce fuel use by 20 percent by closing the flue when the furnace is off. Savings depend on the type of furnace and are generally greater with hot-water or steam-heat systems than with forced air.

Cost: $100.00 to $400.00, without installation.

- *Flue heat recovery devices.* With an oil furnace, about 75 percent of the heat produced actually heats the house. The remaining 25 percent goes up the chimney along with the smoke and combustion exhaust. These devices recover some of that excess heat. They can be difficult to install and may violate building code regulations in some areas. They also don't provide substantial savings unless the temperature of the flue gases is 450° or more. Furthermore, it's impractical to move this recovered heat more than 20 feet from the furnace, and you won't reap any savings unless the heat is directed into an area that is monitored by your thermostat. But under the right conditions they can be quite a worthwhile investment.

Cost: $90.00 to $200.00.

- *Electric-spark ignition systems.* Pilot lights, especially those on gas-fired heating systems, waste extraordinary amounts of fuel while the furnace is not operating. Electric-spark ignition eliminates this waste completely. When the thermostat clicks the furnace on, an electric spark ignites the pilot, which, in turn, ignites the main burner. It can pay for itself in less than a season.

Price: $200.00 to $250.00, including installation.

Fireplace Systems

A fireplace is actually likely to steal more heat than it delivers; the draft up the chimney draws warmth from the room along with warmth from the fire. Heat loss is at its greatest as a fire dies down. Here are several devices that can be employed to give you both the pleasure and the efficiency you ought to be getting from your fireplace.

- *Glass door fire screens.* Adjustable vents or dampers are located at the bottom of these glass doors. Like sun passing through a windowpane, radiant energy from a fire passes through closed glass doors and warms the room. Vents keep the draw of room heat to a minimum. When you leave the room, the dampers can be closed completely, thus preventing cold outside air from coming in.

- *Hollow-tube grates.* Combining glass doors with a tubular grate makes for the most efficient fireplace you can own. Such a grate is used in place of andirons and is composed of a set of C-shaped pipes whose open ends face into the room near floor level. Logs rest on the tubes, which curve up the back of the firebox and back over the logs to face into the room. The heat from the fire creates a draft—cool air enters the tubes on the bottom, is heated, and emerges at the top. Some models use an electric motor to increase circulation.

- *Fire board.* Any piece of solid material such as Masonite or fireproof asbestos can be used to cover the fireplace and stop the flow of warm air up the chimney once the fire gets low. There are also canvas curtains on the market that can be drawn over the front of the fireplace, but check just how fireproof these are before using them.

- *Chimney top damper.* Installed at the *top* of your chimney, this cast-aluminum damper protects against heat loss and keeps out birds, squirrels, rain, and snow. Furthermore, since warm air remains inside the chimney, your fireplace will draw immediately—rather than smoking when you start a fire. These are ideal for old houses without fireplace dampers, or even for new houses whose dampers may have become warped by intense heat. They are opened and closed manually by a stainless steel cable that drops down the chimney. Spring loading keeps the damper open normally; it cannot close accidentally when a fire is going.
Cost: $65.00 to $90.00.

Thermosiphoning Air Panels

Referred to as TAP, this system consists of corrugated metal roofing panels that are painted black to absorb heat and faced with glass to keep the heat from escaping. These panels are mounted to a wooden box on a sunny wall of the house and are connected to the interior by air vents. The sun-heated air inside the panels can help heat the house.

Cost: As little as $150.00 if you install it yourself.

Heat Saver for Clother Dryers

About 20,000 BTUs of heat, laden with humidity, are vented out of the average American home every time a load of clothes is dried. In winter, this heat and humidity can be retained indoors by a dryer heat saver that can be attached to the dryer's exhaust hose or pipe. A standard furnace filter, along with the lint filter inside the dryer, keep lint out of the house, and a valve lets you vent the air inside (in winter) or outside (in summer).

Cost: Around $45.00.

TIMERS

Timers for Large Appliances

Heavy-duty timers can limit energy use by large appliances. If a room air conditioner in a household where everybody is away during the day is plugged into a timer, for example, the air conditioner will shut off in the morning and turn on again shortly before anyone returns in the evening (so the house will already be cool).

Most hot water is consumed in the morning and in the evening for bathing, shaving, and dishwashing. But the hot water heater keeps heating water all day and all night. A wired-in timer will shut the unit off during the day while you're away and during the night while you're asleep.

Specially made pool timers can control two or more pool appliances at once—the filter pumps, heaters, and automatic cleaning equipment. But watch it here; a timer connected to a pool heater can automatically heat a pool for the family when no one's around, and the waste involved can be appalling.

Cost: $15.00 to $60.00.

Spring-Wound Switch Timers

These are designed to replace conventional light switches. They shut off the power after a given amount of time. These are excellent for power-squandering items like bathroom and kitchen exhaust fans or radiant heat bulbs in bathrooms. They'll produce savings on hall or stairwell lights that you need just long enough to pass through, and will shut off lights that kids would otherwise leave on. The switches themselves use no electricity; they operate on a compressed coiled spring. You can choose timers that register anywhere from several minutes to many hours.

Cost: $10.00 to $12.50.

Electric Timers for Lamps and Small Appliances

These timers plug into wall sockets, and appliances or lights are plugged into them to be turned on and off automatically. The timer's 24-hour clock can shut on and off whenever you want, one or more times a day. Some can control more than one appliance. Not only can they pay for themselves in less than a year, but they can protect you by turning lights on and off when you're away. And they can make life easy; you can set one to turn on the coffee maker so the coffee's ready when you get up. Be sure to purchase a timer that's right for your wattage needs.

Cost: $6.00 to $15.00.

SOURCES

ALTERNATE ENERGY SOURCES

The Conservation and Renewable Energy Inquiry and Referral Service. The one place to go if you want information about renewable resources, including solar, wind power, and alcohol fuels is CAREIRS. It will give you basic information about alternate energy sources, and if you need more than the basics, they'll refer you to the people you need. Write to them at Renewable Energy Information, P.O. Box 1607, Rockville, MD 20850, or use one of their toll-free numbers: the continental United States, the Virgin Islands, and Puerto Rico—(800) 523-2929; Pennsylvania—(800) 462-4983; Alaska and Hawaii—(800) 537-4700.

Harnessing the Wind for Home Energy by Dermot McGuigan. The basic primer about wind power, with a good bibliography. Garden Way Publishing, Charlotte, VT 05545. $4.95.

How to Buy Solar Energy Without Getting Burnt by Malcolm Wells and Irwin Spetgang. Comments from 100 owners of solar homes, plus model contracts for solar installations. Rodale Press, 33 E. Minor St., Emmaus, PA 18049. $6.95.

Is Solar Water Heating Right for You? Available from the Superintendent of Documents, U.S. Government Printing Office, Washington, DC 20402. Free.

The Passive Solar Energy Book by Edward Mazria. For those who are totally committed to solar, the best energy source available. A fine, useful book with great explanations and extensive reference charts—even the government uses it as a reference for tax rebates. A classic. Rodale Press, 33 E. Minor St., Emmaus, PA 18049. $24.95.

Save Energy, Save Dollars. This modestly priced booklet is one you can read easily, understand the first time through, and begin to use right away. Cornell University Distribution Center, 7 Research Park, Ithaca, NY 14853. $2.50.

The Solar Age Information Directory. If solar energy interests you, this is the best single information source. This 40-page pamphlet produced by *Solar Age* magazine lists sources of information, support, tools, plans, educational materials, and publications about solar energy across the country. This is a best bet for newcomers and experienced solar agers. Write to: *Solar Age*, Church Hill, Harrisville, NH 13450.

Solar Energy and Your Home. One of the many useful publications available from the National Solar Energy Heating and Cooling Center, P.O. Box 1607, Rockville, MD 20850.

Solar Heating and Cooling, edited by Holly Antonili. One of the best overviews of the options, especially for the price. Sunset Books, Lane Publishing Company, Menlo Park, CA 94025. $3.95.

The Solar Home Book: Heating, Cooling and Designing with the Sun by Bruce Anderson and Michael Riordan. Although published in 1976, this is still a good source for the uninformed. Available from Brick House Publishing, 3 Main St., Andover, MA 01810. $9.50.

Wood Heat by John Vivian. No assumptions are made here about what you already know. Everything is covered, from how to stack your fire wood and light it to cooking on a wood stove. Rodale Press, 33 E. Minor St., Emmaus, PA 18049. $7.95.

CONSERVATION

Al Ubell's Energy-Saving Guide for Homeowners by Alvin Ubell and George Merlis. Solid, easy-to-follow advice on how to raise your E.Q. (Energy Quotient), according to the Household Hints and Safety Reporter for ABC Television's "Good Morning America." A Jeffrey Weiss book, Warner Books Edition, 75 Rockefeller Plaza, New York NY 10019. $4.95.

The Department of Energy, Technical Information Center, P.O. Box 62, Oak Ridge, TN 37830 supplies a variety of pamphlets on home conservation. No catalog is available. Write to them stating your needs and they'll send you what they have . . . free.

Energy Management Checklist for the Home. Write to the Superintendent of Documents, U.S. Government Printing Office, Washington, DC 20402. $.75.

Home Energy Savers' Workbook (FEA/D-77/117). The Superintendent of Documents, U.S. Government Printing Office, Washington, DC 20402. $1.00.

Making the Most of Your Energy Dollars. Available from the Superintendent of Documents, U.S. Government Printing Office, Washington, DC 20402. $.70.

Questions and Answers on Home Insulation. Write to the Superintendent of Documents, U.S. Government Printing Office, Washington, DC 20402. $1.10.

The Thomas Alva Edison Foundation offers books that will help your children understand why insulation is important, how much energy it takes to heat water, and how much hot water normal household tasks consume.

Be ready for strange boxes in your refrigerator and footsteps in the attic—but maybe they'll start turning off the lights. Booklets are $.50 each; three are $1.00. Bulk rates are available for classes and groups. Write to the foundation at Cambridge Office Plaza, Suite 141, 18280 West 10 Mile Road, Southfield, MI 48075.

Water Conservation Checklist for the Home (PA-1192). The Superintendent of Documents, U.S. Government Printing Office, Washington, DC 20402. $.70.

Your Guide to Free Energy Information by Arthur Liebers is a 128-page paperback sourcebook of reliable and free energy conservation information organizing hundreds of brochures, pamphlets, folders, and fliers. It gives a brief description of each, with addresses and phone numbers. Well worth the price. From Delair Publishing Co., Inc., 420 Lexington Ave., New York, NY 10170. $2.95 postpaid.

Your local utility. Don't overlook the information and services relating to conservation and energy resources available from your local utility. Most electric companies have a library of free pamphlets, and if you're lucky, they'll also have energy auditors who will evaluate your home's energy profile. Be prepared for a combination of sound advice and self-excusing propaganda. Contact the customer service department or public information department.

APPLIANCES

A Consumer's Guide to Portable Appliances. Write to the Edison Electric Institute, 1111 19th St., NW, Washington, DC 20036. Free.

Consumer's Resource Handbook. For information on how to deal with consumer problems with your appliances, write to the Consumer Information Center, Dept. 44, Pueblo, CO 81009. Ask for item #619J. Free.

How to Avoid Unnecessary Service Calls on Your Electrical Appliances. The Edison Electric Institute, 1111 19th St., NW, Washington, DC 20036. Free.

How to Use Your Electric Range for All It's Worth. Available from the Edison Electric Institute, 1111 19th St., NW, Washington, DC 20036. Free.

You Fix It: Small Appliances by R. Emerson Harris et al. What to do when your toaster won't toast. Arco Publishing, 219 Park Ave. S., New York, NY 10003. $4.95.

HOME
MAINTENANCE

SOURCES 186

HOME
MAINTENANCE

HOUSECLEANING AND HOUSEHOLD MAINTENANCE

Literally every cleaning job in the house, as well as many maintenance chores, can be performed by using cheap, common household chemicals or goods. For instance, you can substitute equal parts of water and household ammonia for expensive cleaning solutions. Or use club soda to clean and polish at the same time. You don't need special copper cleaners; use a spray bottle filled with vinegar and salt instead. The list is endless; you can make everything from oven cleaner to furniture polish, and save hundreds of dollars annually.

This chapter is filled with tips on maintaining, cleaning, and painting your home. But the heart of the chapter is the section of charts giving recipes for making your own potions and instructions for using them to save by doing it yourself.

FURNITURE

Buying Furniture

- *Always buy furniture on sale for at least a 20 percent reduction or on clearance for up to 50 percent off.*
- *Instead of paying a lot for furniture you don't use, buy cheaper, more utilitarian pieces and use them.* Many families keep living and dining rooms off-limits to their kids. These rooms are usually heated and air-conditioned all year. It's both a waste of energy and a waste of space not to use these rooms. If you already have furniture the kids aren't allowed to use, try investing in slipcovers to absorb wear and tear. Remove these when the kids grow up, or when company comes.
- *Used furniture is always cheaper and frequently sturdier than new furniture.* Always pay a visit to the local thrift or secondhand store when you're shopping for a piece of furniture. The cost of a well-constructed used

(Continued on page 172)

HOMEMADE HOUSEHOLD CLEANING AND MAINTENANCE PRODUCTS

Home Cleaning

Kitchen

General Cleaning

Defrosting Aid	Shortening or non-stick spray	Rub inside of the freezer compartment when you've finished defrosting. Ice will slip right off the next time you defrost.
Dishwasher Detergent Booster	A few tbsp. vinegar	Save money by using the cheapest brand of dishwashing detergent and adding vinegar. Cuts grease, leaves dishes sparkling.
Drain Opener	1/2 cup baking soda, boiling water	Pour some boiling water down the drain, then baking soda, followed by more boiling water.
	1 cup salt, 1 cup baking soda, boiling water	Pour dry ingredients down drain, then boiling water. Should unclog drain.
	1/2 cup baking soda, 1/2 cup vinegar	Use with bathroom plunger instead of a commercial drain cleaner.
Electric Coffee-Maker Cleaner	50 percent solution of vinegar and water	Run liquid through a couple of times to remove all scale and buildup.
Garbage Disposal Freshener	Rind of orange, grapefruit, or lemon	Feed into the disposal.
Grease Cutter	Vinegar	Works well on enamel surfaces—stovetops, refrigerators, walls painted with enamel paint. Also works well when added to mop bucket.

Porcelain Sink Cleaner	Detergent, 1/4 cup chlorine bleach, water	Spread detergent around, plug sink and run a few inches of warm water into it, add bleach, rub, let stand 10 to 15 minutes, re-rub, rinse.
Porcelain Sink Cleaner (Heavily Stained)	Paste of 2 tbsp. baking powder and hydrogen peroxide	Apply paste to sink with a rag and leave overnight.
Cookware *(Also see "Metals," page 148.)*		
Aluminum Cookware	1 qt. water, 2 tbsp. vinegar or cream of tartar	To clean inside, boil solution 10 to 15 minutes, then wash and dry.
	Lemon halves dipped in salt	To clean outside, rub until tarnish disappears, rinse and dry.
Burnt Cookware Cleaner	Baking soda and water	Sprinkle affected area generously with baking soda and add just enough water to moisten. Let stand several hours.
	Dry laundry detergent	While cookware is still hot, sprinkle liberally with detergent; let sit, covered with newspaper or paper towels, for several hours. Works well on encrusted broiler pans.
Enamelware (Stained)	Baking soda and water	Leave in solution overnight.
Nonstick Cookware (Stained)	2 tbsp. baking soda, 1/2 cup vinegar (or 1/4 cup household bleach), 1 cup water, salad oil	Bring mixture of baking soda, vinegar, and water to a boil; boil for 10 minutes; use salad oil to reseason pan.

Glassware and China

China Cleaner (Restore Original Luster)	Lemon juice and salt	Rub with sponge dipped in lemon juice and sprinkled with salt.
Crystal/Glassware Cleaner	1 cup white vinegar, 3 cups warm water	Wash with soapy water, rinse in vinegar/water solution, then air dry (or use a lint-free towel if you're in a hurry).
Decanter/Narrow-Neck Vase Cleaner	Sand and white vinegar	Pour mixture in, let it sit half an hour, swirl, then shake, let soak another half-hour, repeat. Continue no longer than 4 hours.
Tea and Other Stain Remover	2 qts. water, 1/2 cup bleach	Soak china overnight in solution, then wash in hot soapy water.
	1 tsp. denture cleanser, boiling water	Pour water into teapot or other china container, add powder, soak overnight.
	Baking soda or Borax	Cover darkened area with powder and scour.

Oven

Oven Cleaner	Salt	When anything spills inside the oven, sprinkle salt on it for easy removal when the oven has cooled down.
	1 tbsp. caustic soda, 1 cup hot water, 1 tbsp. flour	Dissolve soda in hot water, set aside; make paste with flour and a little water, and add to soda and hot water solution. Can be bottled for later use. Use rubber gloves and avoid fumes when applying.
	1 dish of full-strength ammonia, large pan of boiling water	In warm oven, place dish of ammonia on top shelf and large pan of boiling water on bottom. Let sit overnight, then air out and wash with soap and water.

Oven Cleaner (continued)	1/2 oz. baking soda, 1 cup warm water	Wipe solution over inside of oven (may streak). Continue to use oven; whenever you clean it will be a breeze. Reapply after cleaning.
	1 cup dishwashing soap and hot water	Lay oven parts on towel in bathtub. Draw enough hot water to cover and add soap. Let soak while you clean rest of oven.

Metals

MULTIPURPOSE CLEANERS

Aluminum, Brass, or Copper Cleaner	Lemon halves dipped in salt	Apply, rub until tarnish disappears, rinse and dry.
Brass, Copper, Bronze Sealer	Cellulose clear lacquer	Seals these metals so they don't need cleaning; dries in 10 minutes. Won't work on cookware; will on all other utensils.

SILVER

Cleaner	1 qt. water, 1 tbsp. baking soda, 1 tbsp. salt	Bring mixture to boil in aluminum pot, drop silverware in a few pieces at a time, boil 3 to 5 minutes, let dry on terrycloth, then buff.
	2 tbsp. baking soda per qt. of boiling water, piece of aluminum foil	Crush foil, place in glass baking dish along with silver, arranged so none will touch. Fill dish with boiling water, sprinkle baking soda in, let soak 5 minutes (no longer than 10 minutes), then dry.
Egg Tarnish Remover	Salt and lemon juice	Rub silver.

Polishing Rag	1 tbsp. ammonia, 1 tbsp. powdered whitener, 2 cups boiling water	Steep mixture for 15 minutes, then soak terrycloth towel in it. Let towel drip dry (don't wring) and use to dry your silver. (Whitener available from hardware store.)
Tarnish Retarder	Alum	Place in silverware drawer.

OTHER METALS

Brass Cleaner	Paste of vinegar, salt, and white flour	Apply heavy coat, let dry, rinse with warm water and dry.
	Equal parts vinegar and water	Soak for an hour or more, scrub with brush, rinse, dry.
Brass Tarnish Retarder	Olive oil	Moisten cloth, rub, then buff lightly.
Bronze Cleaner	Paraffin oil	Moisten cloth, rub, then buff lightly.
Chrome Cleaner	2 parts kerosene, 1 part rubbing alcohol	Apply, then buff.
	Regular paste wax, peanut butter, white flour, or ammonia	Use any of these as you would polish.
Copper Cleaner	1/2 cup white vinegar, 1/4 cup table salt, 1/4 cup commercial cleanser	Apply with fine steel wool if copper is heavily tarnished; otherwise, application with a damp sponge is fine. Rinse with hot water and dry.
	Vinegar and 3 tbsp. salt	Fill spray bottle and coat copper heavily. Leave 10 to 15 minutes, rub clean with cloth.

Copper Cleaner (continued)	Catsup or Worcestershire sauce	Rub until tarnish disappears.
	Sour milk	Good for copper-bottomed pots and pans. Place pot in flat dish and soak copper bottom for 1 hour, then clean.
Pewter Cleaner	Cabbage leaves	Rub until tarnish disappears.
	Thick paste of wood ash from fireplace mixed with water	Apply with damp sponge, rinse, dry.
Stainless Steel Cleaner	Fine steel wool	Rub (doesn't scratch), then rinse and dry.
	2 tbsp. bleach, hot water	Fill dishpan, add bleach, soak several hours or until clean, then wash in soapy water.
	Dishrag and soap	After washing dishes, wring excess water from rag, rub over bar of soap, then wipe stainless steel stove hoods, counter moldings, even countertops and tiles. Polish with dry cloth.
	Vinegar	Removes dullness.
Plastics		
Cap, Dish, and Thermos Bottle Cleaner	Baking soda and water	Scour or soak.
	Denture cleanser tablets and hot water	Soak for 1 hour.
Odor Remover	Crumpled newspaper	Cover plastic container or thermos and leave overnight.

Counter and Table Tops

Formica Polish	Club soda	Wipe down, buff.
Plastic Polish	Toothpaste or Turtle Wax	Apply, let dry, buff.

Bathroom

Bathroom Fixtures	Kerosene	For the best shine possible, use an old cloth that has been dipped in kerosene. Leaves no odor.
Ceramic Tile	1/2 cup ammonia, 1/2 cup light vinegar, 1/4 cup washing soda, 1 gal. warm water	For light cleaning.
	Paste of baking soda and bleach	For stained ceramic. Scrub stains away.
Porcelain (Old, Stained)	Naphtha soap, hot water, 1/2 cup mineral spirits	Shave bar of naphtha soap into bucket of hot water and add mineral spirits. Stir; brush vigorously on stain.
Porcelain (Yellowed)	Salt and turpentine	Scrub with mixture, rinse.
Shower Door/Mirror Cleaner	White vinegar, club soda, or rubbing alcohol (more expensive)	Apply with sponge. Vinegar also removes hard-water stains from windows.
Steam Stopper (Mirrors)	Glycerine	Apply light film to prevent steam from fogging mirrors.

Stain Remover	Cut lemon or paste of lemon juice and Borax	Light stains on porcelain can be removed with cut lemon; dark stains and rust, with paste of Borax and lemon juice.
Tub and Sink Cleanser	Paste of peroxide and cream of tartar	Scrub vigorously, rinse thoroughly. For stubborn stains, apply paste and add a drop or two of household ammonia and let sit for 2 hours.

Carpets

General Cleaners

Dry Cleaner/Brightener	Salt or salt and cornmeal	Sprinkle over rug. Wait an hour or more and vacuum. Cornmeal works especially well on stained rugs. Rub into trouble spots.
Liquid Cleaner	Plain ammonia and warm water	Apply with sponge.
	Soapy detergent, 1 tbsp. ammonia, warm water	Churn up to get as much froth as possible. Use suds as cleanser. Spread over carpet, let dry, and vacuum.
Stain Remover	Add 1 tsp. white vinegar to above	Apply to stain with sponge, working from outside in (as you should do with all stains). Rub until stain disappears; then rinse with cold water.
	Shaving cream or club soda	Lifts off stain.
	2 tbsp. detergent, 3 tbsp. vinegar, 1 qt. warm water	For old stains. Work into stain; blot with paper towel.

Specific Spot Removers

Candle Wax	Blotter and an iron	Place blotter on top of wax and apply warm iron. The blotter absorbs the wax. You can also use a brown paper bag instead of a blotter. (Also see "Gum," below.)
Egg (Raw)	Salt	Cover dropped egg with salt and leave it for 15 minutes; sweep it up and away.
Glue	Vinegar	Soak spot until glue is loosened.
Gum	Ice cubes, spot remover	Ice makes gum brittle so that it will break away. Stain remover takes care of any remaining stain. Also works for candle wax.
Ink (Ballpoint)	Hairspray, water, and vinegar	Soak spot with hairspray; let dry; then brush gently with vinegar and water solution.
Mud	Salt	Sprinkle salt on mud, leave at least quarter hour, and remove with vacuum cleaner.
Paint, Tar, Oil, or Polish	Eucalyptus oil	Apply to soften old stains. Sometimes this treatment should be followed with an application of dry cleaning fluid.
Red Wine	White wine	Saturate stain and rinse.

Floors

Wood

Faded and Spotted Floor Cleaner	Brown shoe polish	Wax and shine spots.

Quick Shine	Wax paper	Attach wax paper to mop; the dirt sticks to wax paper. Spruces up existing wax.
Scratch Remover	Fine (soapless) steel wool and paste wax	Rub scratches until they disappear. Also removes tar spots.
Squeak Stopper	Talcum powder, liquid wax, liquid soap, or thinned glue	When swept or applied between cracks, lubricates wood planks rubbing against each other.
Varnished Floor Cleaner	Cold tea	Apply like liquid cleaner.
Linoleum, Asphalt, and Vinyl Tile		
Heel Mark Remover	Kerosene or turpentine	Works on wood as well.
Linoleum Cleaner	Milk	Wipe up spills and splashes with milk. Unlike water, it protects wax shine.
Linoleum Polish (Nonslip)	Hot water, 1 pt. rubbing alcohol, 3 oz. brown shellac	Mix ingredients in a jar set in hot water. Stir until completely dissolved; then seal tightly. After washing and drying linoleum, brush on polish and let dry.
White Spot Remover (Asphalt Tile)	Baby oil	Apply and rub.

Walls

Painted-Wall Cleaners

Enamel-Painted Wall Cleaner	1/2 cup kerosene per gal. of warm water	Apply with cloth.
Stain Remover	Artgum eraser	Anything that can be erased from paper can be erased from a painted wall and from wood or fabric as well.
Wall Wash	1/2 cup ammonia, 1/4 cup white vinegar, 1/4 cup washing soda, 1 gal. warm water	Wash wall from bottom up; otherwise water dripping down on unwashed area forms streaks that are difficult to remove.

Wood

Brown-Stained Wood Walls	Equal parts warm water and lemon oil	Restores finish while removing dirt.
Woodwork Cleaner	Starch and warm water	Apply with sponge; let dry; rub with soft, clean cloth.

Wallpaper

Crayon Remover	Fine grade steel wool or baking soda	Apply baking soda to damp cloth, remove mark with gentle rubbing, or try steel wool, again rubbing lightly. Can also treat a grease stain. See next listing.
Grease or Wax Remover	Artgum eraser, rye bread, talcum powder, or dry Borax powder	Rub any of these on stains.

155

Grease or Wax Remover (cont.)	Paste of Fullers Earth and carbon tetrachloride	Apply; let dry; brush off.
	Paste of cornstarch and water	Apply; let dry; brush off.
	Blotting paper and an iron	Apply blotter to spot and press with warm iron. The grease melts and the paper absorbs it. Note: Both paste methods above and this method may have to be repeated until stain disappears.

Glass

Crystal Chandelier Cleaner	Glass container filled with 3 parts water, 1 part denatured alcohol	Spread dropcloth or newspaper. Dunk each pendant in solution and let drip dry. Wipe down any parts that can't be immersed.
	Ammonia and water	Wear cotton work gloves. Dip fingers in solution and rub crystal.
Picture Glass Cleaner	White bread	Rub glass until clean. *Leaves protective coat as well.*
Scratch Remover	Toothpaste	Rub glass gently until scratch disappears.
Tabletop Cleaner	Lemon juice	Rub in; dry with paper towels; shine with newspaper.
Window Cleaner	Equal parts of kerosene, water, rubbing alcohol	Mix ingredients and shake well. Rub on glass; let dry; polish off. Stores well and works well.
	2 cups kerosene, 1 gal. warm water	Also protects windows; rain water will bead off.

Window Wipe	3 tbsp. ammonia, 1 tbsp. white vinegar, water	Fill spray container; use like Windex.
	Newspaper	Because it's lint-free, newspaper works well, and it is cheaper than paper towels.

Stone

Brick or Fireplace Cleaner	Vinegar	Scrub down brick; then sponge with water.
	Artgum eraser, 1/2 cup trisodium phosphate per gal. of water	Eraser removes smoke stains from porous rock. What's left can be dissolved with the solution.
	1/4 cup (4 oz.) naphtha soap, 1 qt. hot water, 8 oz. powdered pumice, 1/2 cup ammonia	Heat water and naphtha until naphtha dissolves. Cook, adding pumice and ammonia. Apply to fireplace with paintbrush. Leave on at least half an hour; then using a scrub brush, scrub the bricks with warm water and rinse well.
Marble Cleaner	1/2 lemon dipped in salt or Borax	Rub lightly over entire surface, concentrating on stains; let stand 5 to 10 minutes; wash down with mild soap and water solution; dry.
	Paste of water and baking soda	Scour; let stand a short while; rinse with warm water.
Slate or Quarry Tile Cleaner	Warm water, detergent, mineral oil	Clean with water and detergent; polish with a small amount of oil on a rag.

Soot Reducer	Salt	Throw in burning fire occasionally. Can reduce soot by two-thirds.

Furniture

Wood Furniture (General)

Cigarette Burn Remover	Mayonnaise	Rub in; let stand 20 minutes; wipe off.
	Rottenstone (available at hardware stores) and salad oil	Rub only into burned spot, following the grain of the wood. Wipe with a cloth dipped in oil; then buff and polish.
	Wax stick	Carefully scrape off charred wood. Heat a knife blade so that it will soften the wax; apply the wax to the damaged area and then smooth it with your finger.
Dirt and Grease Remover	1 cup kerosene, 1/2 cup water	Test first. Wipe furniture down; dry immediately with another cloth.
Furniture Polish	Equal parts *boiled* linseed oil, turpentine, white vinegar	Mix ingredients; stir and shake well. Apply with soft cloth and wipe dry; polish with another cloth. (Boiled linseed oil can be purchased at hardware store; boiling your own won't produce the same thing.)
	1 cup turpentine, 2 cups linseed oil, 1 cup water	This one takes a bit more rubbing but produces an equally good shine.

	1 cup turpentine, 1 cup linseed oil, 1/2 cup rubbing alcohol, 1/2 cup vinegar	Also works on leather.
	3 parts olive oil, 1 part white vinegar	Gives a high shine.
Furniture Polish Remover	Equal parts lemon oil and turpentine	Wipe furniture down; dry immediately with another cloth.
	1/2 cup white vinegar, 1/2 cup water	
	Equal parts turpentine, olive oil, warm water	
Paper Remover (Stuck to Wood Surfaces)	Salad oil	Gradually saturate paper, a few drops at a time; let sit; rub off with cloth.
Scratch Remover (Small Scratches)	White petroleum jelly	Cover scratch with petroleum jelly and leave it for 24 hours. Then rub in, wipe off excess, and buff.
Scratch Remover (Larger Scratches)	Crayon, wax stick, beeswax, or shoe polish (liquid or paste)	If scratch is bad, gently rub down with fine steel wool before touching up or refinishing. Then cover with appropriate color; keep applying until scratch disappears. (Shoe polish works best on glossy surfaces.)
Varnished Furniture Cleaner	Cool tea or 1 cup white vinegar, 1 gal. warm water	

White Liquid-Mark Remover	Paste of butter, margarine, or mayonnaise mixed with cigarette ashes	Rub into spot with damp cloth; buff; then wax.
	Toothpaste, with or without baking soda	Use baking soda for heavier stains.
	Oil (olive, cooking, lemon) or petroleum jelly and mild abrasive (salt, ashes, pumice, or soda)	Let paste stand for 5 minutes. Buff; then wax.
	Coat of petroleum jelly or cooking oil	Leave on 24 hours; remove.

Specific Woods

Ebony	Black eyebrow pencil	Use to touch up scratches.
Mahogany	Brown paste wax (also dark brown crayon)	Apply to touch up scratches.
Mahogany (Red)	Iodine	Apply with small artist's brush.
Maple	Equal parts linseed oil and turpentine	Apply with cotton swab; let dry; buff.
Teak	Equal parts linseed oil and turpentine	Before applying solution, lightly rub with very fine steel wool.

Walnut	Piece of fresh, unsalted walnut or pecan meat	Break off piece of nut; rub freshly exposed surface on furniture.
	Boiled linseed oil	Use as furniture polish.
Wicker		
Moisturizer	Lemon oil	Apply weekly or whenever possible to keep wicker from drying out.
Tightener	Hot, soapy water	If wicker furniture is wobbly, wash it outdoors with hot, soapy water and let dry.
	Hot water with vinegar	The hot water tightens the cane; the vinegar freshens it. (Also for cane seats.)
Whitener	Warm water and salt solution	Keeps wicker from yellowing.
Upholstery		
Cleaner	1/2 to 1 cup mild detergent, 2 cups boiling water	Let mixture cool; it will form a jelly-like substance. Whip to foam with handmixer, apply.
Grease Spills	Salt	Salt absorbs the grease, but it must be applied immediately.
Smudge Remover	Artgum eraser	Erase slight smudges from cotton upholstery.
Stain Remover	Shaving cream	Spray on. Lifts off most stains and smudges.
Stain Remover (Fresh Stain)	Cornstarch, Fullers Earth, or talcum	Cover stain, rub in, and leave until stain is absorbed. Brush off; wipe down area with damp cloth.

Wrought Iron and Other Metal Furniture

Rust Remover — Turpentine — Scrub down rust spots with turpentine using very fine steel wool.

Leather Furniture

GENERAL

Cleaner — Stale beer — Wipe down leather; buff.

— Mild solution of chlorine bleach and water

— Well beaten egg white — First rub furniture down with damp cloth. Follow with cloth dipped in egg white. When dry, polish with soft, clean cloth.

— 1 part white vinegar or water, 2 parts linseed oil — Shake well before using. Use water solution for cleaner leather. Also moisturizes leather and keeps it from cracking.

Mildew Remover — Denatured alcohol

Preservative — Milk

Stain Remover — Rubber cement — Apply thick coat over stain. Peel off when almost dry.

LEATHER SEATS

Seat Cleaner — 1/2 lemon — Rub lemon over seat; then polish.

LEATHER TABLETOPS

Indentation Remover/Leather Protector	Lemon oil	Apply lemon oil twice a day for a week to indentation; use monthly to make impervious to indentations and marks.
Wax Remover	1/4 cup white vinegar, 1/2 cup water	Apply with rag.
Vinyl and Plastic		
Cleaner	1 tbsp. washing soda, 1 qt. water	Wipe down with solution.
	Baking soda or white vinegar, mild dishwashing soap	Sprinkle baking soda or pour vinegar on terrycloth or similar material and apply. Then wipe down with mild dishwashing soap. (Never use oil on vinyl; it hardens it irrevocably.)

Deodorizers

Bathroom Odor Absorber	Activated charcoal	Place near toilet bowl. Replace every 4 to 6 weeks.
Carpet Deodorizer	Soda water, or Alka-Seltzer or baking soda with water	Rub into areas soiled by pet or baby accidents.
Closet Damp Chaser	Charcoal briquets	To absorb and prevent dampness, put briquets in a coffee can and punch holes in plastic cover (or leave uncovered).
	1 doz. pieces of chalk	Tie together and hang in closet.
Closet Deodorizer	Old nylon stocking filled with cedar chips	Hang in musty closet. Absorbs odor and repels moths.

163

Closet Scrub	Equal parts lemon juice and rubbing alcohol	Wipe down closet walls with sponge or rag dipped in solution.
Drawer Freshener	A few whole cloves	Place in bottom of drawer.
Drawer Sachet	Orange, lemon, lime, or apple pomander ball	Completely cover the peel of any of these fruits by sticking whole cloves into it. Mix ground cinnamon and orrisroot powder in a paper bag (a teaspoon of cinnamon and a tablespoon of orrisroot powder for smaller fruit, double for larger). Put the fruit in the bag and shake until it is covered with this fixative powder. Store in a dry place for two weeks; it will shrink and emit a spicy fragrance. Remove it from the bag, and place it in the drawer.
Fish Smell Remover (China)	1 tsp. vinegar	Add to dishwater.
Fish Smell Remover (Silver)	1 tsp. mustard	Add to dishwater.
Paint Smell Absorber	1 onion	Cut in half; place cut sides up in room.
Refrigerator Deodorizer	Box of baking soda	Open and place in refrigerator; stir occasionally to lengthen effective life. Use later for kitchen cleaning.
	Cotton ball soaked with vanilla extract, slice of white bread, or half a lemon	Change weekly.
	Teaspoon-sized ball of child's modelling clay	Change monthly.
Room Freshener	Wintergreen oil on a cotton ball	Place inconspicuously in every room; it lasts for months. Never buy aerosol room deodorizers again.

	Dried herbs, flowers, spices, and oil	Put in a covered bowl and remove cover to release fragrance. The bowl can be placed on a radiator; the heat diffuses the aroma. Freshen with a few drops of vanilla or essential oils (cedar, orange, sandlewood, musk).
Smoke and Odor Absorber	Vinegar	Keep a small bowl wherever needed—in the kitchen while frying, in a room filled with cigarette smoke (a dish of ammonia also works there). Smoke can also be cleared from a room by dampening a towel in a solution of water and vinegar and waving it around the room.

Controlling Pests

Ant Repellent	Cleaner–disinfectant (such as Pine-Sol)	Use around baseboards and window frames.
	Talcum powder, baking powder, salt, or cayenne pepper	Sprinkle around the house. Ants don't like to cross these substances.
Cockroach Poison	Boric acid	A pound can be effective for a year or more. Generously apply in moist, warm, dark places where roaches collect—behind cabinets and stove, under sink, etc. Infinitely better and cheaper than aerosols and other commercial sprays, whose effects are short-lived.
	Saucer of sour wine or any cheap brand	Roaches can't hold their liquor. They crawl onto saucer, drink a little wine, instantly get drunk, pass out in the wine, and drown. Works better than a "roach motel."
Repellent (To Keep Insects Out of Staples)	1 tsp. salt and square of cloth	Tie salt in piece of cloth and store with flour, cornstarch, sugar, etc.

Mouse Repellent	Mint or camphor balls	Sprinkle in areas of mouse activity—in trunks, under furniture, in closets, etc.
Red Ant Repellent	Green sage	Place anywhere you've seen red ants.
Slug and Snail Killer (*Garden*)	Stale beer	Leave a dish of stale beer out before sunset. The next morning it will be full of animals.

Pet Care

Dry Shampoo	Baking soda or cornmeal	Rub in thoroughly; brush out.
Flea Repellent	Salt or fresh pine needles	Sprinkle around dog or cat house. Salt can also be sprinkled on animal, rubbed in, and brushed out.
Flea Shampoo	5 cups kerosene, 1/2 cup oleic acid, 1/4 cup triethanolamine	Use as you would store-bought shampoo.
Kitty Litter Box Freshener	1 tbsp. baking soda	Before adding new litter, sprinkle on bottom of box.
Rinse	Baking soda	Add to rinse water for shinier, odor-free, and softer coat.
Shedding Retarder	Olive oil, coconut oil, or lanolin	Rub in every 10 days or so.
Skunk Odor Remover	Tomato juice, or vinegar-and-water solution	Rub in well, then rinse out.

Children

Baby Powder Substitute	Cornstarch	Spread onto diaper area. Has same protective effects.
Deodorizer	Damp cloth dipped in baking soda	Use to wipe up baby mess. No odors are left behind.
Gum Remover (From Hair)	Cold cream	Rub into hair; remove gum and excess cream with dry towel.
	Ice cube	Makes gum brittle enough to break it off.
	Peanut butter	Loosens gum. Apply with fingers and rub in. Remove with tissue.
Rubber Nipple Protector	Salt solution	Clean inside and out with solution to reduce deterioration of rubber.
Scuffed Shoes	Raw potato or rubbing alcohol	Rub shoes with potato or alcohol to make polish adhere better.
Shampoo Protector	Petroleum jelly	Apply to eyebrows and eyelids to protect baby's eyes.
Splinters	Cooking oil	Soak for a few minutes to make removal easier.
	Ice cube	Numbs area so pain is less.
Stuffed Toy Cleaner	Cornstarch	Rub in; let stand a few minutes; brush off.

Miscellaneous

Artificial (Plastic) Flower Cleaner	Large paper bag, cornmeal or salt	Put flowers in bag with salt or cornmeal; shake; abrasive will remove dust.

167

Item	Material	Instructions
Clock Cleaner (Enclosed Wall Clocks)	Cotton ball saturated with kerosene	Place in bottom of clock case for a few days. Dirt will be loosened by kerosene fumes and fall.
Decal Remover	White vinegar	Paint decal with several coats of vinegar, giving it time to soak in; then scrape off.
Gilt Frame Cleaner	Beer	Doesn't harm gilt.
Guitar Cleaner	Toothpaste	Rub onto guitar; let dry; buff.
Jewelry Cleaner	Toothpaste	Clean with soft rag and toothpaste.
Piano Key Cleaner	Toothpaste	Use well dampened rag to apply. Rub, wipe dry, and buff.
Shoe Polish Softener	1 or 2 drops of turpentine	Add to hard, dried-out shoe polish.
Steam Iron Cleaner (Inside)	Equal parts water and white vinegar	Use to remove mineral deposits from inside steam iron. Fill iron; let steam for several minutes; turn off and let sit for an hour. Empty and rinse.
Steam Iron Cleaner (Outside)	Toothpaste, or heated vinegar with salt	Apply and rub to remove brown, burned-on spots from plate of iron.
Stereo Needle Cleaner	Denatured alcohol	Apply with cotton swab. Press upward against needle, *gently wiggle*, then remove carefully.
Telephone Cleaner	Rubbing alcohol	
Windshield Washing Solvent	1 qt. rubbing alcohol, 1 cup water, 2 tbsp. liquid detergent	Won't freeze below 35°. (Also see p. 219.)

Home Repairs

Glassware and China Repair

Chip and Nick Repairer	Emery board	Smooth up damaged areas on glassware or china.
Crack Repairer (China)	Milk	Simmer the piece for half an hour. Larger cracks may require up to 45 minutes. The protein in milk seals the cracks.
Crack Sealer	Clear nail polish or melted paraffin	Paint over crack; remove excess with nail polish remover. Melted paraffin works especially well on vases.
Glass Repairer	Melted alum	Alum doesn't show, unlike some glues.
Scratch Remover	Toothpaste	Polish scratches away.

Plastering

Quick Plaster	Equal parts of powdered laundry starch and salt, with a little water	Mix a thick paste and apply.
Slower-Hardening Plaster	Few drops of white vinegar	Add vinegar to plaster compound along with water.
Spackle Substitute	Kitchen cleanser mixed with paint	Use to seal small holes and hairline cracks in walls. Doesn't have to be painted afterwards.

Spackle Substitute (*continued*)	White glue, shredded tissue paper	Mix and knead compound until putty-like and apply. (Small holes may be filled with white glue alone squirted straight from the bottle.)
	Paste of white glue and baking soda, with food color as dye	Apply to crack with finger.
	Toothpaste	Smooth with damp sponge after applying.

Paint and Varnish Removers

Paint Remover (Oil-Base Paint)	2 parts household ammonia to 1 part turpentine	Apply with stiff brush; leave on for a few minutes; wipe off with cloth.
Paint Remover (Water-Base Paint)	Boiling water and soap	Scrape off excess, hold over pot of boiling water and rub with soap.
Paint Splatter Remover	Nail polish remover	Removes splatters from clothing.
Paint Stain Remover	Equal parts turpentine and household ammonia	Removes stains from clothing.
Varnish Remover	3 tbsp. baking soda, 1 qt. water	Apply with rough cloth or stiff bristle brush.

Wood Stains

Furniture Stain	Fabric dye	Works exceptionally well on unpainted furniture.

| Picture Frame Stain | Liquid shoe polish | Apply 2 coats, then polish with paste wax. |

Miscellaneous

Oil Paint Storage	4 tbsp. mineral spirits	Prevents film from forming on top of oil paint. Add to can and cover. Do not stir until you reopen it. For other hints on storing paint, see page 174.
Rusted Nuts and Bolts	Carbonated beverage or household ammonia	Soak; then loosen.
Wallpaper Remover	Vinegar and hot water	Apply at least 2 coats with roller or sponge. Paper should peel right off.
Window Froster	4 tbsp. epsom salts diluted in 1/2 pt. warm beer	Apply with paint brush.
Window Putty Softener	Linseed oil	Brush on liquid and let soak in. Scrape putty away.

NOTE: If you haven't been convinced to make your own cleaning solutions, HHHT has one more suggestion. Buy concentrated cleaning products by the gallon from janitorial supply houses. Dilute and use them at home for big savings. Check your Yellow Pages for the supply house nearest you.

piece, including the time and money required for recovering and refinishing, can be much less than that of a new piece that won't last as long and isn't covered in a fabric that's exactly your choice. Older pieces of furniture are also likely to have more interesting designs than today's assembly-line pieces.

- *Unfinished furniture is often characterized by poor construction and low quality.* It might work well in a kid's room, but a piece of used furniture may cost less and look better.

- *Interior woodwork or furniture need not be varnished or polyurethaned.* A coating of plastic often cheapens the appearance of furniture; besides, it traps moisture, and can be bad for the wood pores. It also prevents the beautiful color changes untreated wood undergoes. Oiling a piece of furniture with tung oil is easier than varnishing; it provides protection, and the results are handsome. Use butcher block wax on freshly sanded floors for an elegant finish that won't make your floor look like it's covered with Saran Wrap. It will save you time and money.

Maintaining Furniture

- *After washing slipcovers, put them back on the furniture while they're slightly damp and let them dry in place.* This will save you having to iron them.

- *Tumble dry slipcovers without heat every few months to get the dust out.*

- *Color piping on furniture with matching indelible ink or with a felt-tip pen when it wears thin.*

- *When you have a sofa or easy chair reupholstered, cover one side of each cushion with plastic for everyday use.* Then, when company comes, flip the cushion over to the clean fabric side.

- *When wicker seats in your chairs start to sag, pour boiling water over them and let them dry in sunlight.* The cane will tighten.

- *Bolstering sagging chair springs is easy.* Turn the chair upside down, make a paper pattern (template) of the rim around the springs at the bottom, and cut a piece of plywood to size. Nail or screw the wood to the rim. This forces the springs back up, readying the chair for many more hours of sitting.

- *Furniture polish will penetrate wood better if it's warmed in a pan of hot water first.* Place the bottle in water.

RUGS AND FLOORS

- *To make rugs and carpets last longer:*
  — Keep them free of ground-in dirt that abrades and weakens the fibers.

— Rotate the position of your rugs annually.

— Put pads underneath them.

— Wool rugs need humidity; give them an occasional light spray or misting of water.

— Roll rugs diagonally; they won't buckle while being carried.

— If you store rugs standing up, wrap them around a pole to provide support and prevent buckling.

- *Old Oriental rugs are a good investment and a joy to own.* They also tend to be quite expensive; however, it's often possible to buy rugs that are dry-rotted but still in unworn condition. They're cheap. You can then have the back coated with a plastic-reinforced material and the result is a beautiful rug that's worth a lot of money but costs you very little.

- *Before the days of vacuum cleaners and carpet sweepers, people used to take their Oriental and hooked rugs, lay them face down in fresh snow, and leave them there for a day.* The dirt and grime would be gently eased out by the snow. Don't ask how.

- *For a carpet burn, glue fuzz from another part of the rug onto the spot.* Cover it with wax paper (glue will not adhere to it) and weight it down until it's dry.

- *Steam raises indented places in rugs where heavy objects have been placed.* Hold your steam iron over the spot, but don't press down on it. The steam alone will raise the nap.

- *Keep wood floors waxed so they won't wear down.* A brick wrapped in two wool socks makes an efficient floor polisher.

WALLS AND WINDOWS

Painting and Papering

- *Keep house surfaces painted.* The longer you wait, the more paint and effort (scraping, etc.) it will take to repaint.

- *Good quality materials always represent a better deal because they last longer.* It takes the same amount of time to apply a good quality paint or wallpaper as it does a cheap brand that won't last as long.

- *Choose appropriate colors to make your rooms seem what they're not.* Lighter colors make a room seem cooler, airier, larger. Darker colors make for a warmer, cozier, seemingly smaller space. Here are some more tips:
  — A darker ceiling color will make the ceiling seem lower and camouflage flaws.

— If one side of a narrow hallway is painted with a dark shade of a color and the other side with a lighter shade of the same color, the effect is to make the hallway seem wider.

● *A gallon of paint covers, on the average, 600 square feet on a first coat and 900 on a second.*

● *Figure the square footage of a radiator by measuring the front and multiplying by seven.*

● *When you finish painting or papering a room, keep a record, somewhere in the room itself, of just how much paint or wallpaper the job took.* Make a note behind a light switch plate, on the wall behind a picture—anywhere is fine so long as it's in the same place in each room so you won't have to go searching. Using those notes, you'll buy the right amount the next time around and save.

● *A good brush makes for easier painting and will last indefinitely if properly cared for.* Here are some ways to get the most out of it:

— Before painting, soak the brush in linseed oil for 12 hours. This makes it easier to clean later and prolongs its life.

— If a brush has hardened, don't throw it out; soak it in hot vinegar, then wash it in warm, sudsy water.

— Use a solution of two tablespoons salt, one cup kerosene, and one quart warm water to soak brushes stiff with paint.

— Fabric softener added to the final rinse water softens bristles.

— When brushes are clean and dry, wrap them in plastic bags and seal with masking tape.

— If a brush starts to lose its bristles, coat the base with clear nail polish or shellac to hold them in place.

— A little petroleum jelly applied to a clean paint brush acts as a preservative.

● *Save coffee cans with plastic covers to use for cleaning brushes.* When using paint thinner, put some in a can with brushes that seem clean, cover the can, and let it sit for a few days. Additional paint will settle to the bottom. Pour off the clear thinner and reuse it.

● *When paint is stored for an extended period of time, a skin usually forms over the top. Here are some ways to store it so you can be assured of being able to use it again.*

— Store the can upside down (make sure it's tightly sealed).

— Before capping a can of oil paint, add four tablespoons of mineral spirits or sprinkle it with paint thinner. Don't stir the paint until its time to reuse it.

— Cut a circular disc of aluminum foil or waxed paper and slide it into the paint can over the paint. Press out the air bubbles, and replace the lid tightly.

— Breathe—yes, breathe—into the can before sealing it. Moisture trapped in the can keeps film from forming on the paint.

— Melted paraffin over the top seals paint best of all, like it does jellies.

— Store latex paint in a warm place. Freezing ruins it.

● *It's also a good idea to paint a line on the outside of the can to mark the paint level.* This tells you how much paint you have left, as well as what color it is, and saves your having to reopen the can to find out.

● *A drop of black paint added to a can of white paint keeps it from yellowing.*

● *Figure how much wallpaper you'll need* by measuring the perimeter of the room in feet, multiplying that figure by the room height, and dividing by 30. This should give you the total number of rolls you'll need after you deduct two rolls per average-size doorway or window. Overlapping is allowed for in this formula.

● *It's very simple to repaste loose wallpaper before it becomes brittle and tears off.* Special paste is available in stores, or try Elmer's white glue.

Paint Spills

If there's lots of it, spoon up what you can, working in from the edge of the spill to prevent spreading. Mop with newspaper, then with tissues. Then follow the appropriate procedure, as outlined below.

● *Latex (water-base) paint.* Don't let it dry. Wash the surface with lots of cold water. Rubbing alcohol may remove dried paint, but don't count on it.

● *Oil-base paint.*

— On natural fibers: Sop up as much paint as possible. Soak the surface with a generous amount of paint remover or alcohol. Use turpentine if you have no paint remover. Wash with lots of cold water, then warm soapy water, then a final rinse of clear water.

— On artificial fibers and plastics, including vinyl flooring: Soak with alcohol, then wash with detergent and warm water.

● *Paint that has dried and set.* If you really want to take a chance, try a little paint thinner. This will loosen up the paint. It may also eat through the fabric or surface on which the paint was spilled. If this begins to happen, pour on lots of cold water—which you should have ready before you start. If the worst doesn't happen, treat the paint as if it were fresh. Paint thinner will definitely dissolve plastic and most adhesives, so be careful about what you're pouring it on.

Other Wall and Window Tips

- *Door stops and door checks keep doorknobs from damaging walls.*
- *Once the putty around window glass starts to go, water can seep in, damage the remaining putty, and start rotting the sash.* Repair it; it's simple.

THE BEDROOM

- *Sheets can yellow over time if they're stored in a place that's too warm.* You can wash the yellow out in a solution of 1 gallon hot water, ½ cup electric dishwasher compound, ¼ cup liquid bleach, and ¼ cup white vinegar, using *only* stainless steel, plastic, or enamel container (for 100% cotton, soak overnight in solution). Wash, adding vinegar to rinse water. Or try dyeing them if they're all cotton. (Patterned polyester and cotton blend sheets look rather ghastly after dyeing.)
- *You can extend the life of sheets that are showing signs of wear and tear by cutting them down the middle and sewing the outside edges together with a flat seam.* Hem the outside edges and you're all set. You can also make pillowcases from old sheets.
- *Starch pillowcases lightly and they'll be less vulnerable to stains from face and hair creams or oils.*

THE KITCHEN

- *Use dishrags or small hand towels instead of paper towels.* Hang them on drawers or refrigerator handles.
- *Or use newspapers instead of paper towels.* True, newspaper isn't absorbent like paper towels; but for wiping out skillets, cleaning windows or glass, and other cleaning jobs, it's ideal.
- *If you don't have a dishwasher, take a small container, put a couple of squirts of liquid dishwashing soap and some water in it, and keep it in the sink.* Dip a brush in the soapy solution to wash instead of randomly squirting and wasting detergent.

THE BATHROOM

- *If you stop to think about all the slivers of soap you throw out over the years, you'll realize that they can mount up. Here are three things to do with those bits and pieces:*
  — Press a wet sliver of soap onto a larger, new bar and let it dry. The two will meld.
  — Collect pieces in an old sock or nylon stocking. The sock works well as a scrub pad in the shower; the nylon stocking, for washing

dishes. You can also insert them in a slot you slice in a sponge. Use this sponge in the shower; it gets nice and soapy.

— Save the pieces, run them through the blender, and make liquid soap.

- *Always unwrap bars of soap right after you buy them.* They'll last longer. Let soap bars dry in a drawer to freshen the drawer and its contents.

- *To keep soap from dissolving in the water that collects around it, place it on a soap rack when it's not in use.*

- *Pressing a toilet paper roll so that it is oval instead of round prevents yards at a time from rolling off the roll.* And cheaper is not always better. Check.

- *Water seeping behind tiles around your bathtub or shower can cause a lot of trouble before you know it.* Any missing grout around bathtub and shower tiles should be replaced instantly so the water won't do real damage. The same goes for the joint between the bathtub and the walls.

EXTERIOR

General Tips

- *Cracks and holes in blacktop paving should be repaired;* otherwise water can seep into and under the adjoining pavement, freeze, expand, and create even larger cracks and holes.

- *Roof gutters should be cleaned after the leaves fall off the trees in the autumn.* An accumulation not only blocks the flow of water, which can then back up onto the roof and leak into the house; it also soaks up water and can accumulate enough weight to pull the gutter loose.

- *Downspouts should be extended to carry water at least eight feet from the house.* This can prevent your basement from flooding during a heavy rain if the ground is frozen and can't absorb or let the water run off.

- *A water leak into your home should be given immediate attention.* Make sure all surfaces are thoroughly dry, then patch them. A roof leak usually makes itself known rather quickly, but seepage through cracks where different materials meet (between doors or windows and their sidings, etc.) can cause extensive damage before you realize it. Check periodically.

Landscaping to Save Money and Energy

Cold Climates

- *Concentrate plantings on the north, east, and west sides of the house to protect against wind, the worst heat robber.* Plant rows of trees and shrubs to provide deep, thick windbreaks.

- *Put a patio or pavement on the south side of the house.* These absorb the sun's energy and extend the outdoor season by a few weeks.
- *Keep a wide swathe of the property from the southeast to the southwest free of trees and shrubs.* This lets through even the low winter sun, maximizing its energy donation.
- *To control summer heat, plant a tall, high-crowned tree close to the south wall of the house.* When it's mature, it will shade the roof without interfering with the warming southern sun in the winter.

Hot, Arid Climates

- *Concentrate your gardening indoors.* Houseplants do more to improve the indoor climate in this environment than in any other by humidifying and cooling the air. And they never break down.
- *Put low shrubs like mesquite or cactus on the east side.* They absorb heat without blocking the light.
- *Protect the western exposure with a low, densely leafed tree, high bushes, or low cactus.* These absorb heat and cut down on glare.
- *Protect the western side of your landscaping with lots of mulch (wood chips are very good) interspersed with plants.* This cuts down on glare and conserves moisture.
- *Keep patios or balconies on the north or east sides to minimize heat storage.*
- *If your budget is limited, concentrate your resources on blocking the sun on the south side of the house.* Tall trees, like the desert gum, and thickly vined trellises are very effective sun screens.

Hot, Humid Climates

- *Your goals in this kind of climate are to cut down on heat storage and maximize ventilation.* Avoid pavement in your landscaping, and use palm trees to create a high, airy canopy over the house.
- *Protect the southern exposure with trellises and vines, especially deciduous vines, which lose their leaves and let in the winter sun.*
- *Funnel the prevailing breezes with plantings of trees and bushes.* Fragrant flower trees are an especially well-planned choice, since they scent the cooling air when they are in bloom.
- *A house on a slight rise is ideal for this climate, since the elevation maximizes drainage and ventilation.*
- *Here again, if your resources are limited, concentrate on protecting the south side of the house from the noonday sun.*

Temperate Climates

- *Your goals in this kind of climate are to protect the northern exposure from winter winds and the southern exposure from summer heat.*

- *Plant small to medium-size flowering trees on the southwest and northeast to cut down on wind and sun.*

- *Protect the northern and western walls with a thick evergreen hedge.*

- *A patio and trellis on the south side provides shade in the summer and an effective heat collector in early spring and late fall.* A single row of deciduous trees and low hedges adds to these effects.

- *Create a wind wall on the north to shield against winter storms.* Work away from the house, starting with a row of tall, thick evergreens. Dense deciduous trees and bushes should be planted to the north of the evergreens to add to their effect.

Miscellaneous Landscaping Tips

- *Get your plants, bulbs, trees, and shrubs from nurseries in the same climate zone as your own.* These are likely to transplant successfully, adapt to your landscape, and grow better than stock shipped from a warmer or cooler zone. Don't expect a tree from a Georgia mail-order nursery to do well in upstate New York.

- *Collect plants from wooded areas (with permission) and from your friends.* Slips from hedges, shrubs, and even some flowering plants can be rooted and transplanted, giving you some free greenery.

- *Cut down on expensive watering by using mulch.* A generous layer of bark, leaves, sawdust, grass clippings, chopped newspaper, plastic, or even pebbles and stones keeps the ground between plants moist and weed-free. Mulch also keeps the ground warmer in the winter, protecting delicate root systems.

- *Don't buy topsoil to improve your lawn base.* Plant rye grass and turn it under when it is several inches high. Then repeat the process. With this and a little fertilizer, you'll soon have soil rich enough for a final seeding.

- *Buy the right fertilizer for your garden's needs.* Commercial fertilizers combine nitrogen, phosphorus, and potassium. A three-number code indicates the proportions. If your plants need help with their leaves, the first number should be high; if it's flowering that needs help, a high second number is best; and if the root systems need strengthening, the third number should be highest.

- *Smaller weeds are easier to pull than bigger ones, and bigger ones use nutrients in the soil that your grass or shrubbery could use.* Make it easy for yourself.

- *If you need outbuildings, like a storage shed, a wood box, or a doghouse, build them along the side of the house that needs protection from the prevailing winds.*

- *If your entrance isn't protected by a foyer, plant a thick, tall hedge perpendicular to the door on the side nearest the prevailing wind.* This helps to cut down on heat loss.

- *The best fertilizer for your garden can't be bought; it's the compost you can create out of your kitchen and garden waste.* Mix lawn clippings and leaves with your organic kitchen scraps. Turn it every few weeks, and in six months, you'll have valuable food for your garden.

- *If you need large-scale fertilizing, get your supplies at a farmers' market.* You can get well-rotted cow manure ("green" manure will ruin your plants) in large quantities for reasonable prices. Small bags of manure from hardware or garden centers are not good buys for most gardens.

MISCELLANEOUS HOUSEHOLD TIPS

HOME PLANTING

- *Many people waste money on commercially packed potting soil because they want to be sure that it's free of bugs and diseases.* All you have to do is dig up some soil from anywhere and bake it in the oven. Cover it with aluminum foil and put a meat thermometer in the middle. When the soil temperature is 180°, cook it for half an hour without letting the temperature go over 200°. Cool it for 24 hours, then use.

- *You can save money by rooting your own plants instead of buying them in the store.* Here are some things you can grow instead of throwing into the garbage:
  — Peach pits: plant them an inch deep.
  — Avocado pits: soak them in fresh water until they sprout, then transfer them to a pot.
  — Pineapple tops: place them in jar of water, fleshy part down. When roots appear, plant.
  — Parsley: sprinkle some on a moist sponge and leave it near a window until it sprouts.

- *Here are several types of plants that can be bred easily. Just snip off a branch, root it in water, then plant it in soil.*

African violets (chancy)	Pandanus
Arrowhead	Philodendron
Begonias	Pothos
English ivy	Swedish ivy
Oleander	Wandering jew

- *Other plants such as roses can be rooted by making a hole in a new potato and inserting the cutting.* The raw potato has the right amount of moisture to start the process.
- *Bugs and other pests can generally be controlled by sticking a clove of garlic into the soil.* As it grows, just push the shoots back into the soil.
- *Give your leftovers to your plants:*
  — Soapy water is fine, but avoid grease.
  — Eggshells are an excellent source of calcium for plants, especially succulents and cacti. Finely chopped banana peels also provide valuable nutrients.
  — Water in which you've boiled eggs, potatoes or corn is full of minerals. Let it cool before using, of course.
  — Flat club soda is fine.
  — A birth control pill dissolved in a quart of water sends plants bursting into bloom.
  — Unflavored gelatin makes an excellent food. Dissolve one packet in a cup of hot water and feed the mixture to plants, followed by three cups of cold water. Give it to them monthly.
- *Four boosters for ferns:*
  — Castor oil (1 tsp.) or olive oil (2 tbsp.) every three or four months
  — Tea
  — A weak ammonia solution (which contains nitrogen)
  — A raw onion in the bottom of the pot.

THE TELEPHONE

Toll-Free Numbers

Thousands of businesses—insurance companies, airlines, hotels, department stores, etc.—have toll-free numbers. Before you dial long-distance, it never hurts to check with toll-free information at (800) 555-1212 to see if the business you're phoning has a toll-free listing.

The phone company, naturally, hasn't published a listing of toll-free numbers, but Dial 800 Publishing Co., Box 995, Radio City Station, New York, NY 10019 has. For $3.49 (postpaid) they'll send you an alphabetical listing by subject entitled *Dial Free: Dial 800.* There's also the *Toll Free Digest,* available in bookstores and published by the Toll Free Digest Co., Inc., Box 800, Claverack, NY 12513. Or the *National Directory of Toll-Free Numbers* from Landmark Publishing, Box 3278, Burlington, VT 05401, $9.95.

General Long-Distance Tips

- *The time of day you call makes a big difference.* Know the discount periods:

	MON	TUES	WED	THURS	FRI	SAT	SUN
8 am to 5 pm	Full day rate						
5 pm to 11 pm	35% discount evening rate						35% disc. eve.
11 pm to 8 am	60% discount night and weekend rate						

- *Keep a three-minute egg timer by the phone so you'll know when you're talking overtime.* Don't gab; it can cost you dearly.

- *Make a list of things you want to discuss before you dial;* you can expedite your business, and you won't have to call back because you forgot something.

- *Always—repeat, always—get credit for wrong numbers or when your connection is cut off and you have to redial.* The operator will arrange for it. (The same goes for areas where you are charged message units for local calls—get credit!) Your savings can mount up.

Private Long-Distance Companies

One of the newest twists in telephone services are the companies that allow you to make long-distance calls on their lines, at rates up to 50 percent less than those charged by the phone company.

You subscribe for a monthly rate, and you will be given an access number that permits you to make your calls on the company's lines. You will also be given a personal account number that allows the company to charge you for your calls. You'll be billed at a rate much lower than the phone company's.

The hitch is that not every city is connected with every other. If you're lucky though, you'll live in a city that is served and you'll make most of your long-distance calls to other cities in the network. You'll need a touch-tone phone to use these services, but once you've gotten it, you'll probably save money with one of these systems as long as you spend more than $10.00 each month on long-distance calls.

Two of the leading companies are Sprint: (800) 521-4949 (in Michigan, (313) 645-6020) and MCI Telecommunications: (800) 243-2073.

Buy Your Own Phone

Private companies like Radio Shack sell telephones. You can save up to $70.00 annually in monthly rental fees by returning your equipment to Ma Bell and investing in your own.

BATTERIES

- *Eliminate the waste of disposable batteries;* for toys or radios that always seems to need replacement batteries, spend a little more and buy rechargeable batteries. They need recharging every month or two, even if they're not used. So don't use them in the emergency flashlight.

- *When buying a calculator or other battery-operated machine that can be purchased with a built-in rechargeable cell, choose that option.* It will pay for itself after less than a half-dozen recharges. And if you accidentally leave it on and the batteries run down, it won't be a mistake that costs you.

- *Alkaline "energizer" and "long life" batteries last about as long as regular batteries,* but they cost over one-third more. The life of any battery can be boosted by putting it in the sun or on a radiator for a few hours.

OTHER TIPS

- *When you buy anything that's defective or that you're dissatisfied with, send it back to the manufacturer.* Large corporations have public relations departments whose concern is to keep customers happy. Don't worry about the "importance" of your gripe. Even if only one of ten flashes on a flashbar doesn't fire, send the bar back to the manufacturer with a complaint. GTE Sylvania, for example, will apologize and send you two new flashbars (about a $6.00 value). And this is only one example.

- *When postage stamps stick together, put them in the freezer for half an hour; cover them with a thin piece of paper and apply a warm iron; or soak them in water, then separate.*

- *Use leftover popcorn as insulation when mailing breakables.*

- *When ballpoint pens clog up, stick them in a cigarette filter, dip them in boiling water, or hold them over a match for a few seconds.*

- *Buy a desk dispenser for cellophane tape.* After this one-time purchase, buy cellophane tape by the roll; it's cheaper.

- *Lubricate all appliances, clean their filters, and protect them from weathering.* See p. 118 on caring for appliances.

- *A worn washing machine hose can flood a house.* You can get a new one cheaply enough and install it yourself.

- *Save wear and tear on electric cords (and thereby prevent short circuits and/ or fire hazards) by pulling the plug out of the outlet instead of tugging on the cord.*

HOME RENOVATIONS

PURCHASING MATERIALS

Housing starts are at their lowest level since 1946, and competition among suppliers of building materials for the business of non-contractors is keener than ever. Even the price of lumber is said to be down. The benefits to the handyman are twofold: Obviously, lumber is cheaper; in addition, you can get advice and learn about building materials from professionals more easily than before.

Here are some tips on purchasing building materials:

- *Take in your drawings or sketch.* Often a building supplier can sell you a lesser quantity or cheaper materials than you had in mind. For instance, people frequently overestimate how much lumber and sheet-rock they'll need to build a wall. Also, doubling up 2" × 6" boards instead of using solid, more expensive 4" × 6" boards makes for stronger, easier construction. A good supplier can guide you.

- *You get more for the money if you buy in bulk.* Ask for a discount (contractors usually get 10 percent) when you buy large quantities of items like sheetrock, paint, sand, gravel, or wood chips. If you can get a lot at a cheaper price, try finding a neighbor or friend to share the excess with you. But don't buy first and then try to find the friend.

- *Small hardware stores unfortunately charge higher prices.* It's a pity because these small establishments probably deserve the business, but they have tremendous difficulty competing with the chain stores. Tell the small proprietor what the competitor is charging, and perhaps he'll meet the price.

- *Most lumber is stamped with its moisture content and "green" or "dry" as well as with its species and quality grade.* If you buy wet, green wood, chances are that when it dries it will warp. If it does, return it. Better yet, prevent this from happening by checking on what you're getting.

- *Some lumber companies get rid of warped and defective pieces of wood by sending them out with orders they take over the phone, or by slipping them in the orders of inattentive walk-in customers.* To insure yourself of high-quality wood, handpick each piece yourself. Always be neat; leave the inventory as you found it. If they won't let you pick your own, shop elsewhere.

- *Many lumber companies have scrap bins in which you just might be able to find what you want for a reduced price.* Prices are arbitrary on these loose stocks, so barter. They'd throw it out if you didn't want it.

- *Measuring accurately is one of the homeowner's biggest problems.* Lumberyard men say that a good ruler is more important than a hammer and a saw.

CONTRACTING A JOB

- *When a job is complicated enough to require several different types of tradesmen (carpenters, electricians, plumbers, etc.), go ahead and hire a contractor to coordinate them.* When only one tradesman is involved, you stand to save 10 percent by hiring the worker yourself.

- *You can calculate that an addition to your house will cost roughly $35.00 to $50.00 per square foot.* Good planning is essential at these prices.

- *When you have an indoor project, get it done during the winter.* Outdoor construction is slow then, and you can get a better price when there is less demand.

- *If you don't know of a good contractor, ask friends or inquire at local lumberyards or building-supply centers.*

- *Before committing yourself to any contractor or tradesman, get estimates from at least three different individuals.* Make a list of what needs to be done as accurately as possible to be sure that all estimates are comprehensive. A cheaper estimate does you no good if it doesn't include all the work you need done.

- *Be careful when a salesman or contractor comes to you for contracting work.* You'll often be offered deals such as this: A new driveway will be put down for $3,000 as a promotion. For each customer that you bring to the contractor he'll refund $500, so by showing your driveway to six neighbors and getting them to spring for one themselves, you can get yours free. The catch can be that the contractor makes the deal with everyone, or that he does a sloppy job on your driveway and leaves town. Good contractors don't need salesmen or promoting.

- *If you require more living space, instead of building an addition, expand into a basement, attic, breezeway, garage, porch, or other enclosed area.* It'll be cheaper.

- *Rejuvenate rather than replace.* Instead of ripping out old fixtures or cabinetry, spruce them up. And new fittings can give a new lease on life to an old bathtub, washbasin, or kitchen sink. Except where more energy-efficient products are now available, you're better off with older things; they were probably built to last.

- *When you're hiring on a small scale, volunteer your services and save some money.* Sometimes tradesmen don't want anyone interfering, so you have to be tactful; but things like driving to the lumberyard or building-supply center, wielding a paint brush, or helping sand a floor can save. Labor makes up the bulk of any home remodeling or improvement bill.

- *Have the workmen store building materials in your garage or inside your house, rather than outside.* You're the one who will have to pay if anything is stolen.

- *Withhold your final payment for some leverage.* Inspect the work carefully, test all fixtures, switches, windows, doors, etc. If you're satisfied, then pay. If you're not, don't.

SOURCES

Several organizations publish and distribute valuable booklets that are either free or reasonably priced. They include the Cornerstone Library, The National Plan Service, the U.S. Government Printing Office, the Consumer Information Center, and Cornell University. Some of the titles published by these groups are included in the following list. For a complete listing of titles, free catalogs are available.

GENERAL HOUSEHOLD MAINTENANCE

Basics of Housecleaning and Home Care (IB-69). Available from Cornell University, Distribution Center, 7 Research Park, Ithaca, NY 14853. $.60.
Bathroom Planning. National Plan Service, 435 W. Fullerton Ave., Elmhurst, IL 60126. $1.25.
Family and Rec Rooms. National Plan Service, 435 W. Fullerton Ave., Elmhurst, IL 60126. $1.25.
Finding and Keeping a Healthy Home. Superintendent of Documents, U.S. Government Printing Office, Washington, DC 20402. $1.25.
Floors, Walls and Ceilings. National Plan Service, 435 W. Fullerton Ave., Elmhurst, IL 60126. $1.50.
Home Repairs—Outside. Consumer Information Center, Pueblo, CO 81009. $1.50.
Kitchen Planning. National Plan Service, 435 W. Fullerton Ave., Elmhurst, IL 60126. $1.25
The Reader's Digest Complete Do-It-Yourself Manual. Reader's Digest Books, c/o W. W. Norton & Co., 500 Fifth Ave., New York, NY 10036. $19.95.
The Reader's Digest Complete Fix-It-Yourself Manual. Reader's Digest Books, c/o W. W. Norton & Co., 500 Fifth Ave., New York, NY 10036. $19.95.
Simple Home Repairs—Inside. Superintendent of Documents, U.S. Government Printing Office, Washington, DC 20402. $1.50.

PLUMBING

Do-It-Yourself Plumbing by Max Alth is a Popular Science book that gives you the how and why of your plumbing—both designs and repairs. Available from Harper & Row, Keystone Industrial Park, Scranton, PA 18512. $12.95.
Goodbye to the Flush Toilet: Watersaving Alternatives to Cesspools, Septic Tanks and Sewers. Why we have sewers, why we need something better, why composting toilets are the next step. From Rodale Press, 33 E. Minor, Emmaus, PA 18049. $6.95.
How to Fix a Leak and Other Household Plumbing Projects. Cornerstone Library, Simon and Schuster, 1230 Avenue of the Americas, New York, NY 10020. $.50.
Plumbing Repairs. National Plan Service, 435 W. Fullerton Ave., Elmhurst, IL 60126. $1.25.
The Toilet Book: Knowing Your Toilet and How to Fix It by Helen McKenna is a good fix-it book for those who know nothing. Available from Bookpeople, 2940 Seventh Ave., Berkeley, CA 94710. $3.00.

ELECTRICAL WORK

Electrical Wiring Basics. National Plan Service, 435 W. Fullerton Ave., Elmhurst, IL 60126. $1.25.
How to Wire Electrical Outlets, Switches and Lights. Cornerstone Library, Simon and Schuster, 1230 Avenue of the Americas, New York, NY 10020. $.50.

PAINTING AND PAPERING

How to Paint Interiors. Cornerstone Library, Simon and Schuster, 1230 Avenue of the Americas, New York, NY 10020. $.50.
How to Wallpaper. Cornerstone Library, Simon and Schuster, 1230 Avenue of the Americas, New York, NY 10020. $.50.
Paint and Painting. Superintendent of Documents, U.S. Government Printing Office, Washington, DC 20402. $.85.
Painting: Inside and Out. Consumer Information Center, Pueblo, CO 81009. $1.50.
Painting and Wallpapering. National Plan Service, 435 W. Fullerton Ave., Elmhurst, IL 60126. $1.25.

BUILDING AND CARPENTRY

Basic Home Carpentry. National Plan Service, 435 W. Fullerton Ave., Elmhurst, IL 60126. $1.25.
Home Projects You Can Build. National Plan Service, 435 W. Fullerton Ave., Elmhurst, IL 60126. $1.25.
How to Build a Deck. Cornerstone Library, Simon and Schuster, 1230 Avenue of the Americas, New York, NY 10020. $.50.
Power Hand Tools. Consumer Information Center, Pueblo, CO 81009. $1.50.

FURNITURE

Bookshelves and Storage. National Plan Service, 435 W. Fullerton Ave., Elmhurst, IL 60126. $1.25.

How to Redo Your Kitchen Cabinets and Counter Tops. Cornerstone Library, Simon and Schuster, 1230 Avenue of the Americas, New York, NY 10020. $.50.

Recipe for Furniture Care. National Association of Furniture Manufacturers, 8401 Connecticut Ave., Suite 911, Washington, DC 20015. $.50.

Repairing and Refinishing Furniture. National Plan Service, 435 W. Fullerton Ave., Elmhurst, IL 60126. $1.25.

FIREPLACES

Fireplaces. National Plan Service, 435 W. Fullerton Ave., Elmhurst, IL 60126. $1.25.

Fireplaces and Chimneys. Superintendent of Documents, U. S. Government Printing Office, Washington, DC 20402. $1.25.

INSULATING

Insulating Your Home. National Plan Service, 435 W. Fullerton Ave., Elmhurst, IL 60126. $1.25.

REMODELING

Remodeling a House: Will It Be Worthwhile? Consumer Information Center, Pueblo, CO 81009. $1.50.

LANDSCAPING

Drainage Around the Home (1B14). Cornell University, Distribution Center, 7 Research Park, Ithaca, NY 14850. $.60.

Landscape Design. Cornell University, Distribution Center, 7 Research Park, Ithaca, NY 14850. $1.25.

Landscaping and Fencing. National Plan Service, 435 W. Fullerton Ave., Elmhurst, IL 60126. $1.25.

Landscaping Around the House: Get Help, Plan Carefully. Superintendent of Documents, U.S. Government Printing Office, Washington, DC 20402. $1.25.

Patios and Decks. National Plan Service, 435 W. Fullerton Ave., Elmhurst, IL 60126. $1.25.

Plants, People and Environmental Quality: A Study of Plants and Their Environmental Function by Gary Robinette. A valuable source of information on plants and their value to us and our environment. Available from the U.S. Department of Interior, National Park Service, Washington, DC 20240.

PESTS

The Bug Book: Harmless Insect Controls by Helen and John Philbrick is a practical guide to nontoxic ways to combat home and garden pests. Garden Way Publishers, Charlotte, VT 05545. $3.95.

Cockroaches: How to Control Them (#430). Available from the U.S. Department of Agriculture, Science and Educational Administration, Hyattsville, MD 02780. $1.00.

Controlling Household Pests. Superintendent of Documents, U.S. Government Printing Office, Washington, DC 20402. $.50.

Subterranean Termites: Their Prevention and Control in Buildings. Superintendent of Documents, U.S. Government Printing Office, Washington, DC 20402. $1.30.

THE CAR

THE CAR

BUYING A CAR: CONSIDER THE ALTERNATIVES

Cars mean freedom, independence, and status. They also mean gas, insurance, parking, depreciation, and tickets. If you live in the city and own a car, these costs amount to $.75 or more for every mile you drive your car.

So, before you buy, make a list of the uses you have in mind for your new car. See how many of them can be solved by car pooling, or even by a moped or a bicycle. In general, if you drive fewer than 10,000 miles a year, it is more economical to rent cars than to buy your own.

You may also want to consider the social costs of Americans' car habits. The leading cause of death among people between the ages of 5 and 24 is auto accidents. Add in the other social costs—air pollution and energy dependency and waste—and you may decide to stay carless.

If you must buy, there are lots of ways to save. First, consider buying a used car rather than a new one. The energy required to produce a new car is equivalent to that used in 10,000 miles of driving. So buying a used car saves us all that much energy. You also save by avoiding the steep depreciation that affects a new car, which loses up to 25 percent of its value as soon as you drive it off the lot.

Whether you're planning on buying a new car or a used one, you should know that the National Highway Traffic Safety Administration has set up a hot line for consumers. Before buying a new or used car, call, toll free, (800) 424-9393 between 7:45 a.m. and 4:15 p.m. Eastern Time to obtain free information on such important factors as safety recalls, fuel economy, crash test results, maintenance cost comparisons, and even tire quality ratings. You may also register any auto complaints you may have on this hot line.

SHOPPING FOR A NEW CAR

DO YOUR HOMEWORK

If you decide to buy a new car, be prepared to do some homework. You will make your biggest savings before you leave home.

- *Look at your list of reasons for needing a car and decide what kind of car you need.* If you don't need a lot of space, consider a subcompact. The smaller car can save you $1,000 a year in operating costs. Maintenance costs for large cars are usually 12 to 15 percent higher than for smaller cars.

- *Choose a model that's been in production for a while.* It takes years for the manufacturer to work out all the kinks in a new model (note all the recalls). It doesn't pay to be a test driver for Detroit.

- *Check to see if any of the models in the general category you've selected are "twins."* Most manufacturers make a general body type with identical working parts. They distinguish among them by adding cosmetic frills. Here's a list of some of the twins, compiled by John Stossel, Consumer Editor for WCBS-TV in New York, for his book *Shopping Smart* (G. P. Putnam's Sons, 200 Madison Ave., New York, NY 10016, $9.95).

Chrysler:

Dodge Aspen / Plymouth Volare
Dodge Diplomat / Chrysler le Baron
Plymouth Horizon / Dodge Omni
Chrysler Cordoba / Dodge Miranda
Dodge Colt Hatchback / Plymouth Champ
Dodge St. Regis / Chrysler New Yorker / Chrysler Newport / Plymouth Grand Fury
Dodge Challenger / Plymouth Sapporo

Ford:

Ford Fairmont / Mercury Zephyr
Ford Granada / Mercury Monarch

General Motors:

Olds Cutlass / Buick Century / Pontiac LeMans / Chevy Malibu
Olds Omega / Pontiac Phoenix / Chevy Citation / Buick Skylark
Olds '88 / Pontiac Catalina / Buick LeSabre / Chevy Caprice and Impala
Olds Cutlass Supreme / Buick Regal / Chevy Monte Carlo

You can save hundreds of dollars and lose nothing in quality by choosing one of the less expensive models. Oldsmobile prices, for example, are generally higher than Chevy prices, so you would pay more for an Olds Cutlass Supreme than for the equivalent Chevy Monte Carlo. Also, you may find that knowing about the twins may give you a few more dealers to consult and bargain with as you do your final shopping.

- *Once you have listed several models in order of preference, check their ratings in Consumer Reports, Motor Trend, and Car and Driver.* Compare features such as price, cost of options, gas mileage, comfort, and frequency of repair.

THE BEST TIME TO BUY

- *The car market is subject to seasonal price changes.* There are periods of high and low demand, and during the low periods prices can drop. Following is a listing of best times of the year to buy:

  Cars:

  New cars—August, September (worst months to buy are March, April, and May)
  Used cars—February, November, December
  Previous year's models—March

  Accessories:

  Tires—May, August
  Batteries—September
  Mufflers—September
  Seat covers—February, November

- *Monthly variables.* Car prices go up several times during the course of the year, so waiting until the end of the year doesn't produce much saving. And waiting will cost you a year of depreciation before you've even reached your own driveway. But you can save if you buy in the last few days of a month. Dealers set quotas for their salespeople to meet. At the end of the month, those folks are pressing to meet their quotas in order to keep their jobs or earn bonuses, and they are more eager to make the sale. This can mean a better deal for you. A spell of bad weather or a holiday season slump at the showroom can also work to your advantage by making dealers more needful of your business.

SELECTING A DEALER

- *Find your dealers through your Yellow Pages.* But choose dealers fairly close to you, because you will have to return to them for maintenance and repairs covered by your warranty.

- *Check up on the dealers you have chosen.* Ask the Better Business Bureau if any of them have a bad reputation. That simple call can save you lots of time and aggravation if you do have problems with your car later on.

GENERAL CONSIDERATIONS

- *Ignore the sticker price.* Buying a car is yet another time when you really should bargain. Get a price from one dealer, then take it to the next dealer on your list and see how much better he can do. Let them spiral the price down against each other and you may be able to save $1000.00 off the sticker price. Don't expect to negotiate, however, if you're buying a briskly selling popular car, or a luxury item like a BMW, a Porsche, or a Mercedes.

- *Gain bargaining power by calculating the dealer's cost.* The dealer mark-up ranges from about 10 percent on smaller models to 20 percent on full-size cars. Normally the best bargain that you'll come up with will be about $200 above the dealer's cost. You can find that cost by consulting Car/Puter's *New Car Yearbook* and any of the other sources listed on pages 234–235. Or, according to *Consumer Reports,* you can calculate that cost yourself. Multiply the sticker price (less options and shipping) by .88 for small cars, .83 for medium cars, and .79 for larger cars. Then obtain the dealer's cost for options by multiplying the retail cost of the options by .83 for small, .79 for medium, and .77 for large cars. The sum of these two figures plus shipping costs is the dealer's price.

- *Don't fall for options.* Dealers make big profits on them, and you spend unnecessary dollars. A tinted windshield costs more than a pair of sunglasses, and you can't take it off on a dark night. Other options simply make for more complicated and expensive repair. Except for special items, such as the heavy-duty equipment needed to pull a trailer, you can add options economically after purchase if you still feel that you need them. (Also see pages 197–203, Car Options—The "Doodads.")

- *In choosing a color, remember that white cars can be about 35 degrees cooler than black ones.* The air conditioner in a white car doesn't have to work as hard, and you might be able to do without air conditioning altogether. Lighter colors are also easier to see and therefore are safer. Metallic colors are less visible, and metallic paints tend to deteriorate quickly.

- *Most of the time, it pays to get exactly the car you want,* even if you have to wait a long while for the factory to deliver it. But if there's something close to it on the lot, you may be able to get a good deal because the dealer pays high interest on his unsold cars. In any case, you can expect lots of pressure to buy one of the models on the lot. Use this to your advantage if you're so inclined, but don't fall into the trap of buying a more luxurious or larger car because it's a bargain.

- *Shop hard for a car loan.* Don't go through the dealer. If you belong to a credit union, start there. Credit union rates are usually lowest. Also check with the American Automobile Association (see page 229). They finance car loans so attractively that you'll save even after paying the membership fee. If you rely on banks, shop among several, paying no attention to their ads. The bank that advertises low rates may actually be charging more than the competition. (Also see Financing, pages 212–213.)

CAR OPTIONS—THE "DOODADS"

These are the junk and convenience foods of the auto industry. Although some options, like air-conditioning, increase the trade-in value of the car, few are worth the energy and money it takes to make and operate them.

Why You Don't Need Optional Equipment

- *Consumer Reports* says, "*Few options are necessary for basic transportation. The options to consider first are those that improve a car's safety, comfort, and road-handling.*"
- *Options can increase the cost of your car by a third or a half.*
- *Options can make a substantial difference in your fuel cost* because they add weight and draw power. A lot of this gadgetry will also result in increased maintenance cost.
- *Mark-ups on options are notoriously high.*
- *Don't be talked into a "package" or a "pack."* Car manufacturers have engineered the package to force you to buy several extras to get the one you want. Say you want interval windshield wipers (the kind that pause between strokes and are so useful in light drizzles or mist) for your new VW Rabbit. To get them you'll have to pay $210.00 for their "custom value" package that includes carpeting in the luggage compartment, vanity mirror, rear ash tray, sound insulation, remote mirrors, wheel trim rings, and front vent windows.

  While packages come from the manufacturer, packs are options applied by the dealer and listed on a separate sticker. Examples are undercoating or upholstery preservative. These have the highest mark-ups over the dealer's costs and tend to be the worst deals.
- *Never overlook the fact that what are options on some cars are standard equipment on others.* The cost of options you want should be a determining factor in your choice of car, not an afterthought.
- Know exactly what extras you want and be willing to wait for a model with just those extras to avoid paying more for an option-loaded model on the dealer's lot.

The 25 Most Common Options

1) *Larger engine:*

The extra 5 percent you can pay a car dealer for a larger engine is just the beginning of the extra expense you'll suffer. The difference between a four-cylinder and a V-8 can be eight miles per gallon, broken down as follows: a four-cylinder gets $4\frac{1}{2}$ more miles per gallon than a six-cylinder and a six gets $3\frac{1}{2}$ more m.p.g. than a V-8.

There's also the increased maintenance: Each cylinder you buy needs an extra spark plug, and there's a larger crankcase that needs to be filled with oil.

If you regularly pull a trailer, you can justify buying a larger engine (see below, option 25, Trailer towing packages). Otherwise, even with air conditioning, power steering, and other frills, a standard engine is all that's necessary.

Note: *Learn the relationships among cubic inches, number of cylinders, and horsepower.* A larger cubic inch displacement (the bore and stroke of the cylinders) makes for a more powerful cylinder and lessens the need for a larger number of cylinders. The extra cylinders are the biggest reducers of fuel economy. Cubic inch displacement is the key factor.

2) *Diesels:*

Pros	Cons
Diesel fuel takes less energy to refine than gas and has more B.T.U.'s per gallon but it . . .	causes high levels of polluting emissions until the engine warms up,
	congeals in cold weather so the engine must be prewarmed,
	is not readily available in service stations, and
	requires expensive fuel filter replacement.
Diesels get better mileage but they . . .	must be driven 40,000 miles before the saving in fuel pays for the diesel option,
	need more frequent oil changes,
	must have larger battery and heavy-duty starter (which are far from maintenance-free),
	need tune-ups that you cannot do yourself, and
	will not necessarily last longer.

3) Transmissions:

The more gears, the better, whether the transmission is manual or automatic. Many small cars offer a manual fifth gear option that's worth the money. It's like an overdrive gear that cuts down on highway noise and gives better gas mileage. On larger vehicles you can get as much as 5 percent more mileage from a four-speed automatic than you can from a three-speed.

Generally a manual transmission makes for excellent highway driving while an automatic makes for easy and fuel-efficient city driving. If you plan on trading in your car after a few years, then the automatic transmission has the advantage because it holds its resale value. However, if you keep your car a long time, this resale value decreases over the years until the difference is negligible; in this case you'll have lost nothing in resale value while having saved money by buying and driving a car with a stick shift. A manual is also advantageous in that the car can be slowed more safely by downshifting (especially in snow and ice) with no wear and tear on brakes and tires.

4) Differentials:

A differential is the gear unit used on the rear axle of a car that allows the outside rear wheel to revolve faster than the inside wheel during a turn. Some car manufacturers offer a limited-slip differential as an option. When one wheel is spinning in mud, snow, or sand, a limited slip differential automatically shifts the power to the other wheel. Sounds good, but the increase in traction is minimal and this option tends to be unnecessary. The cost runs around $80.00.

If you as a consumer are given a choice of "rear-end ratio" differentials, the lower ratio (2.5:1, as opposed to a ratio around 4.11:1) gives better gas mileage and strains the motor less at highway speeds, although it can mean lower acceleration.

5) Power steering and brakes:

When these two are not offered as standard equipment, they should be considered unnecessary options. Power steering can make medium- to large-sized cars more easily maneuverable and easier to park while only slightly affecting fuel consumption. But it decreases the driver's sensitivity to the condition of the road, which can result in extra wear and tear on the car. Power brakes let you stop your car with less effort, but some, to quote *Consumer Reports*, can be quite "touchy."

6) Radial tires:

Radials last longer, are safer, and increase your gas mileage about 3 to 5 percent in the city and up to 10 percent on the highway.

Note: *Radials and conventional tires together on a car are a dangerous combination.* Never mix them! The different principles behind radial and regular biased-ply construction make them incompatible to the point where they work against each other, especially during braking, sharp curves, and turns. Some states, such as New York, have gone so far as to pass legislation banning the combination.

7) *"Space-saver" spare tires:*

If a regular-sized conventional spare tire is available, get it. Even though space-saver spares save a few pounds of weight and a little space, they are strictly temporary-use tires, designed only to get you to a gas station in an emergency, and at a reduced speed at that.

8) *Air conditioners:*

Reports are contradictory. Some say that air conditioners are economical because they preserve your car's aerodynamic design; air flowing through open windows acts as a drag, causing you to use more gas than you would with the air conditioner turned on and the windows rolled up. Other sources disagree and say that your fuel consumption can be increased anywhere from 6 percent (in small cars) to 20 percent (in larger cars) by air conditioning; this group is more convincing. In general, buy and use air conditioning when necessary. Some cars have excellent vent systems. Check this when you test drive.

Note: *If you must have an air conditioner, don't get an automatic temperature control unit* (an extra $46 to $175). You can control the temperature better than they can.

Pros	Cons
Improves window defogging and fresh air ventilation.	Costs a bundle to buy.
Prevents or delays driver fatigue.	Consumes fuel, not only while operating, but by the weight it adds to your car; the unit itself, with the heavier-duty springs and the larger engine cooling system it sometimes requires, can mean an extra 100 pounds.
Maintains a high resale value.	
	Increases car service costs.
	Can contribute to your car's overheating.

9) *Tinted glass:*

Yes, it will keep your car cooler and will increase the efficiency of your air conditioner (if you have one) and will reduce glare on sunny days. But something that reduces your visibility at night can't be all good!

10) Sun roofs:

Though they can reduce the need for an air conditioner, let these facts speak against them:

1) As with all windows when open, they increase interior noise and, more importantly, wind resistance (which affects gas mileage).

2) They tend to leak.

3) They can reduce head room.

11) Radios:

Consumer Reports says you might have better luck getting your radio and tape deck from someone other than car manufacturers, whose models (except for AMC's tape deck and GM's FM radio) are rated poorly. By not getting factory-installed sound systems, you can shop around, save, and get exactly what you want. Check "CR" for the best deals.

12) Power-operated seats and windows:

The arguments against them are strong:

- They are initially expensive, mechanically complicated, and expensive to repair.

- They can decrease gas mileage by adding extra weight to the car and by requiring a high-output alternator for the extra energy they need from the engine.

- Power windows can be a safety hazard.

But here's one power seat "pro": Like hospital beds, they can be adjusted in a wide range of positions to accommodate any imaginable human shape, whereas manual seats simply slide forward and backwards.

And while on the subject of seats: if you have a choice between vinyl and cloth, go with cloth. Sitting on vinyl is like wearing polyester doubleknits: they're hot in summer and cold in winter.

13) Automatic speed control:

For $70.00 to $120.00 you can set your speed and forget it. The problem is that a driver can forget too much and be lulled into inattention, lengthening the reaction time in an emergency. But this gismo can reduce fuel consumption on a long trip by maintaining a steady speed.

14) Interval wipers:

They're handy, but are often the only worthwhile part of a manufacturer's expensive package. (See pages 197.)

15) Rear window defogger/defroster:

An expensive ($100.00) but rather useful option that should be standard on all cars driven in ice and snow.

16) *Rear-window wiper/washer:*

Again expensive ($70.00 to $105.00) but advantageous on station wagons and hatchbacks.

Note: An *air deflector* helps keep the rear window clean but is wind resistant and can reduce fuel economy at highway speeds.

17) *Mirrors:*

The mirrors on driver and passenger doors are important safety devices, but the remote-control versions are costly (around $30 per mirror) and awkward to adjust. The ones you adjust by hand are reasonably priced and every bit as efficient.

Some new cars offer a passenger door mirror with a convex surface. This type of mirror expands the field of vision but can be misleading when it comes to judging the distance of vehicles reflected in it.

18) *"Courtesy" lights:*

These go on when you open a door, the trunk, hood, and glove compartment. They can be very high-priced when included in one of those extravagant and unnecessary packages. Buy a flashlight, which you should have with or without courtesy lights. (Courtesy lights won't help as a flashlight will when you have to change a tire by the side of the road on a dark night.)

19) *Luggage racks:*

This $75.00 to $120.00 extra can knock off about one mile per gallon on your gas mileage when it's empty. More, of course, when it's loaded.

20) *Exterior trim strips and bumper protectors:*

For anywhere from $34.00 to $69.00, chrome-and-vinyl strips are placed along the widest portion of your car's sides to prevent parking-lot paint chipping that can lead to rust spots. If you want them, okay, but avoid the more extensive trim packages that only add to wind resistance and a deficit in your savings account.

Bumper facings for $30.00 to $60.00 can prevent the bumpers of other cars from riding over or under yours when you're parallel parked. They are useful for city cars.

21) *Vinyl tops:*

Forget it! A vinyl top performs no useful function and can waste upwards of $165.00. It also precludes the use of car in safari parks (which means unhappy kids)—baboons delight in peeling them off.

22) *Undercoating:*

This $10.00 to $110.00 investment is a sound deadener, *not* a rust preventer. It's a thick, black solvent sprayed onto the underside of the vehicle that does absorb some road noise. Don't confuse the two.

23) Rustproofing:

Forget Polyglycoat and other special wax jobs, but the rustproofing that is sprayed into doors and frames can be useful in areas where salt is heavily applied in winter. If a dealer offers it, ask what kind of a *written* guarantee he can offer. All domestic cars and some imports already have a three-year rust perforation warranty.

Another reason for warranty protection: problems can arise *because* of sloppy and improper applications, and rustproofing is a job that's practically impossible to check up on.

24) Radiator shutters:

These prevent an engine from "overcooling" in winter by partially covering the radiator. Because fuel consumption is greater in winter than in summer, a radiator shutter can help create "summer conditions" under the hood. You see them in use during the winter on semi trucks, and truckers report a winter fuel economy of up to an impressive 70 percent. The same principles and economics apply to automobiles, but radiator shutters are not always available as a factory option for cars. Make your own if you can't buy one.

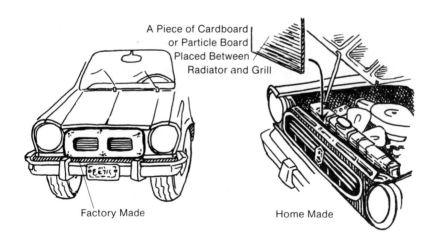

A Piece of Cardboard
or Particle Board
Placed Between
Radiator and Grill

Factory Made   Home Made

Radiator Covers

25) Trailer-towing packages:

Because pulling a trailer can be rough on a car, manufacturers can strengthen both a car's engine and body to accommodate the heavier load and provide a properly attached trailer hitch assembly. These packages are imperative for any vehicle regularly pulling a trailer. Naturally, gas consumption increases because of heavier-duty suspension, electrical, and engine-cooling systems, but you can seriously harm a standard engine by subjecting it to overloading.

CLOSING A DEAL

- *Protect yourself by having the salesman put his offer in writing and getting it approved by his manager.* You may return to a dealer who has given a good price only to have him renege on the deal. If you have the offer in writing, the dealer will stick to it when and if you take him up on it. And you won't lose face by having to renegotiate a price with your other dealers.

- *When your new car arrives, test drive it.* If it's not raining, put it through a car wash to see if it leaks. List the car's problems and have the dealer fix them *before* you pay for the car. Test drive it again after the repairs and before you hand over your check. Be sure you're satisfied. You'll get fast service because the dealer is eager to get your car out of his garage and your money into his pocket, and if the car is a "lemon," you'll find out before you've accepted delivery.

- *Be sure you don't pay the dealer's preparation cost.* This ranges from $50.00 to $200.00 and covers the dealer's expenses for doing the paperwork and preparing the car for you. Manufacturers, except for some in Europe, generally reimburse the dealer for these costs, and you should be careful that you're not being charged for them.

BUYING A USED CAR

It now costs more than $10,000 to purchase a full-size car such as a Ford LTD or a Chevrolet Caprice with the features most buyers prefer. This kind of price tag is making people look at a car as a means of transportation instead of as a status symbol. And if one wants to save money on a car purchase, the easiest way is to recycle: Buy a used car.

Depreciation causes a new car to lose almost one-third of its value in the first year. By the time the car is two years old, more than half its original sticker price is lost to depreciation. But a well-treated car can easily last ten years or more. So you can get 80 percent to 90 percent of a car's useful life for one-third to one-half of its original price.

That may seem to be a conclusive argument for buying a used car, but there are lots of ways to go wrong in buying a secondhand vehicle—many more problems than with a new car.

TWO APPROACHES

1) If you are concerned about your car's looks, then the rule of thumb for optimal savings is to buy an auto that's between one and three years old and keep it for about three years.

2) If you're after a workhorse to haul groceries, peat moss, and kids around the neighborhood, you can probably save lots more by buying a more disreputable car—something in the $200 to $500 range—and using it until the doors fall off. If this is your style, then turn to page 211 for some fast ways of judging the car you've got in mind.

THE FOUR SOURCES TO CONSIDER

The attitude you have towards owning and using your car will help determine where you buy it.

Used Car Dealers

This is the most unpromising source for a used car. First of all, a good many of the cars that wind up on the used car dealer's lot come from taxi fleets; police forces; small, high-mileage commercial fleets; junked cars; and the rejected trade-ins of new car dealers.

Taxis and police cars lead rough lives. It is not unusual for them to rack up 50,000 to 100,000 miles per year. And you may not be able to tell how far the mileage reading has been rolled back on a car like that.

Also consider how many cars are considered "totaled" each year. Once replacements have been found for the original owners, the wrecks are often given a cosmetic overhaul and sent to the used car lot.

Finally, the used car salesman is an expert in short-term ways to hide operating defects in the cars he offers.

All in all, you should steer clear of used car lots.

National Fleet Owners

Corporations like Hertz and Avis sell their cars after about a year or a year and a half of use. The cars have been been used heavily and by many drivers, but they have had regular maintenance. With luck and perserverance, you may find a fleet car with 25,000 miles that is in better shape than a single-owner car with 15,000 miles that hasn't been cared for. Before you buy, you should ask for the car's maintenance record, which will give you a full record of any accidents or problems the car may have experienced.

New Car Dealers

They sell the best of the trade-ins they get from their customers, but they also charge the highest prices. Keep your eye on their lots though, because if a car lingers for a few months, you may be able to get a good deal on it.

Private Owners

Without a middleman you're likely to get the best possible price, so the private owner can be the best source for a used car. But there *are* pitfalls, and you won't have a warranty to fall back on as you would if you bought from a reputable dealer.

Three Things to Ask the Seller Before You Go to See the Car

1) Is the car registered? If it isn't, it may not have been able to pass inspection.
2) Has the car been in an accident? Use your judgment about the response you get. You may be gratified by a direct "yes" and an explanation.
3) Why is the car being sold? You may get a hint of some chronic problem.

Four Ways to Safeguard Yourself When Dealing with a Private Seller

1) Be sure the person you buy from is the person named in the title papers.
2) Be sure the Vehicle Identification Number (VIN) on the title papers matches the one on the car's engine, door, or dash.
3) Be sure that the owner has the title papers and gives them to you. Don't let him tell you he intends to pay off his finance company with the money you pay him and he'll give you the title then. If he doesn't have proof of ownership or at least a note from the finance company saying that the new title is on its way, then either don't buy or confirm matters with the financer before you pay.
4) For a final check before you buy, call the Motor Vehicle Department to check the VIN number and the seller's name.

DO YOUR HOMEWORK

Once you've decided to buy a used car, settle in for the same kind of homework you would do if you were buying a new car.

1) *Project your uses* for the car and decide how fancy it needs to be.
2) When you see the car you want, *check out its resale value* in the National Auto Dealers *Official Used Car Guide* or the *Kelley Blue Book*. You can find them in your library, bank, or loan company. If you are buying from a dealer, ask to see the office copy, and pass that dealer by if the sales people won't show it to you.

3) *Watch out for bargains;* if a car is priced well below the recommended resale price, you can assume that the seller knows something about that car that you don't—and that you won't like to learn about when it's yours.

4) If you're buying from a dealer, *ask for the name and address of the previous owner* and then phone him or her and ask about the car: did the car cause a lot of trouble, was it ever wrecked, what was the reason for the trade, etc. No longer owning the car, this person has nothing to lose by giving you truthful answers.

   Dealers are obliged by law to have a record of who owned the car. They aren't actually bound by law to tell you, but if they refuse or tell you they don't know who owned the car, fold up your checkbook and do business someplace else. (Or, if you're feeling determined, take note of the license plate number—in many states they'll still be on the car—and find the previous owner through the Department of Motor Vehicles. Not every state allows its Motor Vehicles Department to give out this information, however.)

5) Before you buy, *check the car's model* in the *Consumer Reports Guide to Used Cars,* published by Consumers Union, and in sources listed on page 235.

6) The car may have been affected by a recall notice. Most owners ignore recalls, so you should call the federal hot line, (800) 424-9393, and *check for any recalls on the make and model you intend to buy.* Then make sure the recommended repair has been made, if there was one.

INSPECTING A USED CAR

Assuming that you've gotten this far, it is time for an acute inspection.

- *Pick a clear day*—don't try to look at the car at night or on a rainy day. Either you won't be able to see exactly what you're looking for, or you'll be tempted to slight the inspection to get in out of the wet.

- *Bring a friend* with you so you can see how the car looks as it is being driven.

- *Expect to spend about two worthwhile hours.*

A Checklist for the Outside

1) Look down the side of the car and see if there are ripples or different paint colors (indicating body repairs). Blisters or bubbles on the paint may mean rust underneath.

2) Look for rust on the underside of the car near the doors and around the wheels, especially in the back.

3) Check the signal lights by having your companion step on the brake and use the direction indicators and flashers.

4) Check out the tires. Uneven wear (see page 222) is usually a sign of alignment problems. If the tires are worn too far down, consider the expense of replacing them and the implication of poor maintenance. Don't forget to check the spare as well.

5) Check the exhaust system. Look for rust, and make sure the muffler assembly is securely fastened. Check the tailpipe. If it is lined with a sticky black residue, the car burns oil, and that means trouble.

6) Check under the car for oil spots or transmission leaks.

7) Push down on each of the fenders and let go. If the shock absorbers are good, the car should bounce only once.

8) Check under the radiator for leaks.

9) Check around the inside of the wheels for leaks in the brake cylinders, which show up as dark stains.

10) Look for welds and burns on the underside along the frame where the car would be repaired after an accident.

11) Make sure the hood, trunk, and doors open and close properly. Loose door handles usually indicate hard use.

A Checklist for the Inside

1) Look at the general condition of the inside, especially the driver's seat. It may tell you a more accurate story of the car's mileage than the odometer.

2) Check that the seat adjusts easily and that the upholstery doesn't need repairing.

3) Check the pedals. If the odometer shows low mileage but the pedals are worn smooth, then believe the pedals.

4) Make sure that the windows open and close smoothly.

5) Check all the dash gauges, the dash lighting, the horn, and the interior lights.

6) Step on the brake pedal for a count of one hundred. If the pedal sinks to the floor, it could mean there's a leak in the brake system.

7) Look for water marks on the upholstery or on the fire wall between the dash board and the engine. They indicate that the car's been fully or partially submerged.

8) Check the heater and vent controls for smooth operation.

Estimating the Real Mileage

1) If the tires are all of the same make and in the same serial sequences, you can estimate the mileage the car has traveled with them. If the treads are

still good, mileage is less than 15,000 miles. If the tires are well worn, mileage is 25,000 or so.

2) If the battery has been replaced (you can tell by the guarantee date on the sticker), the car has probably seen more than 25,000 miles.

3) If the brake pedal is worn, mileage is about 30,000.

4) If the floor mats and brake pedal have been replaced, don't believe any mileage reports under 40,000.

5) Service stations place stickers on the frame of the driver's door or under the hood to record mileage when a car is serviced. Check these stickers for a record of car mileage and suspect that you're being taken for a ride if they've been removed.

Three Things to Check with the Motor Off

1) Check the oil. If it's low, the car may burn oil or there may be a leak. Check the exhaust again for tarry black residue and under the car for oil spots.

2) Look out for water drops on the dipsticks. They indicate the block is cracked.

3) Check the battery for a bulging top or corroded connections, both of which may indicate that the battery is about ready for replacement.

Three Things to Check with the Motor On

1) Look for cracks on the block, head, and manifolds—you'll see them steam, leak, or sputter.

2) Make sure the idle speed is normal. A fast idle can camouflage a tendency to stall, or can mean that the throttle linkage is worn. An engine that cannot return to a normal idle after it's been revved is a potential driving hazard and fuel waster.

3) Listen for sputters, knocks, hissing, and other sounds. Each indicates a potential weakness in the assembly involved.

TEST DRIVE

If the car is still in the running after your inspection, it is time for the test drive. If the owner balks at letting you test drive it, then move on to your next appointment and let that car pass. *On the test drive:*

1) Check the brakes.
   - The handbrake should hold the car back on an incline.
   - The brakes should work without noise—no squealing or scraping.

- The pedal should be high and should offer resistance to the foot. A low pedal or soft action could indicate that re-lining or adjustment is needed.
- When the brakes are applied, the car should continue in a straight line as it slows. It should not pull to one side or the other.

2) Check the steering.

- The car should not drift and the wheel should be tight, with only an inch or so of play before the car responds.
- Try the steering on a few fast corners, to the right and to the left, and then park.
- To check the wheel alignment, accelerate to about 50 m.p.h. and see if there is any drift. Then drive on a patch of rough road and check for drift again. Drift indicates that front end work is needed.

3) Check for leaks. Take the car to an automatic car wash and run it through. This will show whether the car is watertight or has leaks.

4) Check the frame. Have the car driven through a puddle, or if there's no puddle available, check the tire tracks after the car wash. Tracks of front and rear tires should overlap and there should be only two trails; otherwise the frame has been seriously bent and you should not buy the car.

5) Check the transmission.

- If you are test driving an automatic transmission:
  — The shifting should be smooth through all the gears, including low and reverse.
  — The transmission should be silent. Squeals and other high-pitched sounds indicate problems close at hand.
  — The gear level should move freely. Stiffness may indicate problems with the linkage.
- If you're test driving a standard shift:
  — Check the clutch pedal. If it moves more than an inch or so before it disengages the clutch, the facing needs work.
  — Make sure that the gear shift moves easily into all gears with the clutch pedal down. No gears should clash.
  — Drive for a while shifting into each gear to make sure that there is no grinding sound of chipped gears.
  — Make sure the gears don't slip. That means the transmission is worn out.
  — Be aware of excessive noise. A loud transmission means the bearings are worn.

FINAL TIPS

1) Once you've pretty well decided on the car you want to buy, but before you write a check, take the car to a professional inspector for an appraisal. Make sure the inspector is not a friend of the person from whom you are buying. It will cost you around $30.00 to have the car inspected, but an unsuspected defect may cost much more.

2) Get a signed statement from the car dealer that calls for a refund if the car isn't ready at the time and on the terms agreed upon.

3) Don't deal with salesmen who advertise specials that disappear when you arrive on the lot.

4) Be careful that all the charges are clearly stated and that no extras are added to the purchase price. Outrageous finance-insurance charges and "special" fees are common rip-offs.

5) Be wary of "reconditioned" cars at bargain prices. There are many ways to mask bad problems for a short time, and used-car salesmen don't make bargains because they're altruists.

THE OTHER WAY TO BUY A USED CAR

If you really want to save money during bad times, get a car no one else would. The object is to spend a minimum initial outlay, followed by an absolute minimum in upkeep, with a mind to keeping the car for at least a year without putting any money into it.

Car Tests

Since you've forfeited looks, style, and perfection, scrap the tests on the preceding pages in favor of the following:

1) Start the car a half-dozen times or so. This proves that the ignition, battery, and alternator have some oomph.

2) Drive it. See if it accelerates and stops. If there's noise, smoke, steam, or brakes that go to the floor, don't buy it.

3) If there's no initial problem, drive it at highway speed for about 10 miles or so. Bring it back and check under the hood for leaks, oil, and noises.

4) Start the car again while it is still hot. If it turns over and runs, you can buy it, figuring that it will run for awhile.

While You Own the Car

Spend no money on maintenance and none for repairs, except where driving safety is involved. Replace the windshield wipers, but not the upholstery.

When the car needs a major repair, get rid of it—junk it or offer it for sale to someone who wants an old clunker—and buy another.

The result of this program is very low-cost transportation. *One warning: If you do buy a used car this way, you must exercise extra prudence and care in driving.* Don't make heavy demands on this type of vehicle; you may be taking chances with your safety and the safety of your passengers and fellow motorists.

FINANCING YOUR CAR

The current high interest rates make savvy car financing even more important than usual. There are few true bargains in finance arrangements, so your strategy should be to borrow the least amount of money for the shortest amount of time. You will have to shop hard, but it will be worthwhile to do so.

On a four-year, $8,000.00 auto loan, a difference of one-half of a percentage point in the finance agreement adds up to $329.00. If you've shopped and bargained for the best deal on your new car, don't blow it by accepting the first finance arrangement you're offered.

WHERE AND WHERE NOT TO SHOP

- *Start your credit shopping at a credit union*, if you have access to one.
- *Try your local banks*—all of them, not just the one with the most aggressive advertising campaigns.
- *And don't forget the American Automobile Association* (AAA, see page 229). It finances loans for its members at very advantageous rates. In August 1982 the New York branch of the AAA was charging 17 percent for its loans while area banks were at about 20 percent.
- *The car dealer is very rarely your best source for a loan.* The rates are very likely to be at least 1 percent higher than those you'll find elsewhere.

STEPS TO SUCCESSFUL FINANCING

1) *Make the biggest down payment you can afford.* If you can pay half the purchase price in cash and then pay back your loan quickly in large installments, you can save hundreds of dollars in interest. Certainly try to pay at least a quarter of the cost of the car in cash. You'll be taking a financial beating otherwise.

2) *No matter what you put down on the car, be sure that you fully understand the entire financing agreement.* Ask to see the full and actual cost of financing your loan. You may think that smaller monthly payments are convenient, but can you really afford them in the long run? At 18 percent, the interest on a $1000.00 loan for 12 months is $100.06. For the same amount, at

the same interest, but paid back in small installments over 48 months, the cost is $410.00.

3) *If you have collateral*—a home, stamp collection, fur coat, etc.—*use it to reduce the interest charges on your loan.*

4) *Try to get a loan without prepayment penalties.* You may be able to get a refund of finance charges if you can pay your loan more rapidly than the schedule indicates.

5) *Try to avoid finance agreements that force you to pay all of the outstanding balance immediately if you should miss one payment.*

6) *Don't bother to take life insurance on your credit agreement* unless you have a family that will need your car in case of your death. Let your creditor repossess the car if you should die, rather than pay out for the premium.

7) *Don't make your auto insurance arrangements as a package with your financing.* You'll be paying interest on your insurance, in addition to the cost of your car. You can always get a better deal with your own insurance agent. (See next section for ways to save on your auto insurance.)

INSURANCE

Now that you've got your car, you have to think about insuring it.

THE COVERAGE YOU NEED

- *As long as you are paying back your car loan, keep yourself well covered* for collision, comprehensive (fire, flood, theft, vandalism, and more), and especially liability (what you pay if you hurt someone with your car). Once the car is all yours, most experts agree that you can skimp on collision and comprehensive, but that you should continue to cover yourself generously for liability. (You may want to hold onto some comprehensive insurance until your car is six years old or so to protect against theft.)

- *While you are buying collision and liability, you can save by taking the highest deductible offered.* You can halve your monthly premium by taking a $500.00 deductible instead of a $100.00. This means that if your damage is under $500.00, you are responsible for the bills. You won't report the damage and loss to the insurance company, so it won't raise your rates or cancel your policy because of your accident. In addition, you can deduct any amount over $100 from your income tax. So the larger deductible saves money for you twice.

- *But don't try to skimp on liability insurance.* Juries are awarding higher and higher settlements for personal injury and damage liability. The absolute minimum you should consider is $100,000 per person for injury and $300,000 for total accident liability. The relatively small cost of the additional coverage (usually about 15 percent higher) is well worth it. It is not unreasonable to consider covering yourself for up to a million!

INSURANCE DEDUCTION CATEGORIES YOU SHOULD KNOW ABOUT

1) *Carpool.* Save 22 percent if you drive your car to work two days a week or less.

2) *Commuter.* Save 31 percent if you never drive to work but commute by train or bus.

3) *Senior citizen.* Save if you're 65 or over.

4) *Low use.* Save if you drive less than 7,500 miles per year.

5) *Retirement.* Save 10 to 15 percent now if you used to commute 30 to 100 miles per week; if you commuted more than 100 miles weekly, you may save 20 to 25 percent.

6) *Driver training course.* Graduates under 25 save 5 to 10 percent.

7) *Defensive driving course.* In some states graduates can save up to 25 percent.

8) *Good student.* Students over 16 with a B or higher scholastic average save 25 percent.

9) *Non-smoking, non-drinking.* Sometimes called a "good driver" deduction, this can save 20 percent on some policies.

10) *Farm.* Farm owners can save on policies for vehicles used only on their own property.

11) *Annual payment.* Save by paying your insurance once a year rather than in installments.

12) *Special equipment.* Some companies offer discounts for damage-resistant features on certain cars.

13) *Family grouping.* As long as there are no teenagers, grouping cars under a family policy rather than insuring each singly can save 15 percent per car.

14) *Marriage.* If you're a male under 30, you pay less if you're married.

15) *Theft protection.* Installing a theft protection device in your car can yield a 15 percent credit on the fire and theft portion of your insurance.

OTHER WAYS TO SAVE ON CAR INSURANCE

1) *Skip collision insurance for a car worth less than $1000.00.*

2) *Limit your comprehensive insurance.* If you don't anticipate colliding with a deer or encountering an earthquake in Manhattan, you can save by narrowing your insurance to cover theft, riot, and vandalism only.

ASSIGNED RISKS

Insurance companies are forced to insure people they consider bad risks. Generally these people include those who are young and inexperienced, those who have ticket or accident records, or those who have drug or alcohol abuse records. They must pay high rates and are called *assigned risks.* If you are forced into this category, you should be especially wary of mail-order "bargain" insurers. Ask about the company's reliability by checking with your state insurance regulatory agency. You can also check *Best's Insurance Guide* for a rating of your insurance company. You'll find a copy in the library.

You are eligible to get out of the assigned risk category if your driving record is clean for three years.

A FINAL WORD

If you have a new car stolen, that's when depreciation can really hurt you. An insurance company can settle for several thousand dollars less than what you paid for the car. However, you are entitled to either the cash settlement *or* a comparable replacement of the car you lost. It may take awhile for them to come up with one, but it can save you in the long run.

MAINTENANCE

Detroit has already built planned obsolescence into your automobile; not maintaining your car is playing right into their hands. A poorly maintained car has a shorter lifespan and uses more fuel (plus, it pollutes the environment with its foul exhaust). So in the end it costs *less* to invest in keeping your car tuned up. It seems almost idiotic to do it any other way, but as many as half of the cars on the road are not operating at peak efficiency because of owner negligence. Even a simple tune-up can increase fuel economy 15 to 20 percent. Cars with new emission controls in particular need regular tuning; negligence can slash fuel economy up to 25 percent.

If you don't know how to deal with them properly, car problems can consume a tremendous amount of time and patience. Since you'll be driving the rest of your life, think about taking a course in auto mechanics at a local college or vocational school. This cannot be recommended highly enough. Even if you don't plan to work on your car, a course can be an invaluable aid in assessing the mechanical competence of others. Also, you'll be better able to cope with an emergency situation.

HOW BAD MAINTENANCE CAN COST YOU MONEY

- Misfiring spark plugs can cause a 10 percent loss in fuel. Replace them at least every 7,500 miles.

- Unadjusted brakes that grab unevenly will wear out quickly and put a drag on car wheels, lowering your gas mileage by at least 2 miles per gallon.
- A dirty air filter can cost you a mile per gallon at 50 miles per hour.
- Improperly aligned wheels not only wear down tires but take 0.3 miles per gallon as well.
- Improperly inflated tires cost you around 2 percent gas mileage for every pound they're underinflated. Like poor alignment, incorrect pressure also causes wear.

    Note: A 10° drop in temperature will reduce tire pressure by one pound, so keep tabs on pressure, especially as the weather changes.

TAKING RESPONSIBILITY

13 Important Things to Keep Constant Tabs On

Remember the old days when a service station attendant would actually sweep out your car, clean the windshield, and check under the hood? Now you get gas and little else. It's up to you to be aware of what should always be checked. Making these checks takes only a few minutes and can save you an inconvenient, expensive breakdown.

1) *Oil level.*
    If you can manage to get the hood up, then checking the oil is a snap. Do it every time you go in for gas. The oil is the life blood of a car engine. It's simple to check. With the engine off, pull out the dipstick and wipe it clean, insert it again, pull it back out, and read the level. Add oil *only* if the level is at or below the "add" marking. If the car is hot you may need to wait a few minutes (about the time it takes to fill up with gas) to get a reading.
    Change the oil and filter according to the manufacturer's recommendations—usually every 4,000 to 6,000 miles. It's also a good idea to match oil viscosity to seasonal conditions: thicker in winter (for a warmer engine), thinner in summer (for a cooler engine).

2) *Oil leakage.*
    If your oil is frequently low, and you think you have a leak but haven't actually seen any spots yet, put some newspaper under the front end, then rev the car gently for about five minutes. You'll see oil on the paper if you have a leak.

3) *Radiator coolant level.*
    Always fill the radiator with antifreeze, which prevents boil-over in summer and freeze-up in winter. Check at least monthly. Service stations will gladly do this for you when you fill up.

4) *Other fluid levels—power steering, brakes, and transmission.*

Refer to the owner's manual or have your gas station attendant show you the check points. These fluids are rather vital; if you let them get low, serious damage can result. Usually they should be replaced every 24,000 miles or so. Check the automatic transmission every 3,000 miles, the brake hydraulic-fluid every six months, and the power steering fluid at least every year.

5) *Battery.*

Your battery may give you more trouble in winter, but it needs more care in the summer. That's because summer temperatures hasten evaporation. So check every two weeks to be certain that the water level is high enough. It should come up to the metallic blades inside the battery. Use distilled water if possible, and be careful not to overfill. Also, the terminals should be cleaned periodically with a baking soda solution. After cleaning, smear them with petroleum jelly or grease to prevent further buildups. Batteries generally need replacing after two to four years.

6) *Tire pressure.*

Check your tire pressure at least monthly and before long trips. When you buy a set of tires you should inquire about recommended pressures. Rear tires usually require more than front. Either buy a tire pressure gauge (which also works on bicycle tires) or have the pressure checked at a service station. Underinflated tires wear out faster and decrease gas mileage. Replace your tires when less than 1/16" of tread remains.

7) *Wheel alignment.*

When driving on a flat, straight road, release your grip on the steering wheel. If the car continues on a straight line, your front tires are probably in proper alignment. If the car pulls to the right or left, make sure both front tires are properly inflated. If they are, then the tires are misaligned. An inspection of the tires themselves can also serve as proof of misalignment. Have a mechanic check your wheel alignment at least once a year.

8) *Brakes.*

The same type of driving test can be applied here. When you put on your brakes, if the car pulls to the right or left, the linings could be worn or the brakes could need adjusting. Also, to make sure there's no brake drag, allow the car to coast to a stop. If it does so freely and without any jerky movement, you're OK there. By having linings and pads checked annually, you can prevent costlier major brake repairs.

9) *Hoses and belts.*

Check these periodically—especially if you're planning a long drive. If the hoses are soft or if the belts are flexible, it's time to replace them.

10) *Tune-ups.*

To promote engine longevity, cars with standard ignition should be tuned up every 10,000 to 12,000 miles; cars with electrical ignitions need tuning annually or every 20,000 miles. This involves changing spark plugs and ignition points, adjusting carburetor and ignition timing, and replacing both fuel and air filters. The result is always better gas mileage and longer engine life.

11) *Chassis lubrication.*

To prevent wear and tear on fittings and bearings, you should have the chassis lubricated every 4,000 to 6,000 miles.

12) *Shock absorbers.*

If your car sways like a boat, bounces several times after hitting a bump, or nose dives when you stop suddenly, the shock absorbers might be at fault. Have them checked whenever you have your car serviced.

13) *Body.*

The metal in some cars is the equivalent of three layers of rustable tin can, no match for the heavy concentrations of salt dumped onto icy highways. Washing your car every couple of weeks and waxing it every six months preserves the finish and thwarts body rust and corrosion. Be sure to wash underneath and in areas where salt and other deposits can build up (like around fenders and behind head lights). And after driving on slushy roads, it's a good idea to hose off your car—especially the underside.

"Do It Yourself"

Many motorists who are inclined to do their own auto repairs don't because they don't have the tools and they don't feel their carport is the place to work. Now they have no excuse. There are do-it-yourself auto service centers opening up all over the country. These places charge reasonable hourly rental rates for repair bays and tools, and supervision is sometimes included as well. The larger of these places and a few auto parts manufacturers sponsor do-it-yourself classes, some "for women only." Even if you do only light mechanical work on your car, you can save a substantial amount of money.

Why You Save by Doing It Yourself

1) *You can buy parts cheaper* than a repair service will sell them to you.

2) *You save the high hourly rate of a mechanic.* He gets the same hourly rate whether he's changing a transmission or an air filter.

3) *It's highly possible to save time.* You can often do a job in less time than it would take to arrange and wait for someone else to do it.

Do-It-Yourself Replacements

These replaceable items are listed in order of descending popularity.

- Antifreeze
- Engine oil
- Air filter
- Spark plugs
- Oil filters
- Windshield wiper blades
- Batteries
- Headlights
- Oil additives
- V-belts
- Mufflers

SOME MONEY-SAVING HINTS

- It's the dead of winter and the car won't start. You're headed for the phone to call the garage—but first try your hair dryer. It may save you an expensive service call. Warm air blown over the carburetor will cure the problem in a very high percentage of cases.

- Problem: Your windshield wipers don't *feel* brittle, but they streak your windshield as though they need to be changed. Try rubbing them with some fine sandpaper. It will smooth them and clean up the ragged edges, extending their useful life.

- When you turn your wipers on, run them on low for a bit until they and the windshield are completely wet. This cuts down on friction and damage from dirt and grit, and less friction means longer wear.

- Don't lay out $2.00 for commercial windshield cleaner. Refill the reservoir with a mix of your own by combining a quart of rubbing alcohol, a cup of water, and two tablespoons of liquid detergent. This homemade brew won't freeze until the temperature goes lower than 35 degrees below zero.

- When washing your car, just add about one cup of kerosene to a bucket of water and use this mixture. You don't wet the car down; you don't rinse it off; you don't wax. The oily kerosene will leave a rain-repellent, rust-retardant coat, and you'll save money, water, and your own energy and time.

- Another neat and easy way to wash a car and save water and mess is to use three terry-cloth towels and two buckets—one with soapy

MAINTENANCE AND SERVICING CHART

ITEM	WHEN		
	FALL Major	SPRING Intermediate	OTHER Mileage intervals (owner's manual)
FUEL SYSTEM			
CARB. ADJUSTMENT	●		
AIR CLEANER (dry or oil bath type)	●	●	●
FUEL FILTER	●		●
EMISSION CONTROLS	●		
IGNITION SYSTEM			
SPARK PLUGS	●	●	
IGNITION LEADS	●		●
COIL	●		
DISTRIBUTOR	●	●	
POINTS AND CONDENSERS	●	●	
TIMING	●	●	
COOLING SYSTEM			
RADIATOR	●		
RADIATOR CAP	●	●	
HOSES	●	●	
THERMOSTAT	●		
FLUSH AND REPLACE COOLANT	●		
LUBRICATION			
OIL CHANGE	●	●	●
OIL FILTER	●	●	●
MECHANICAL			
HEAT RISER VALVE	●		
CONTROL LINKAGES	●	●	
COMPRESSION	●		
ENGINE MOUNTINGS	●		
ELECTRICAL			
ALTERNATOR	●		
VOLTAGE REGULATOR	●		
BATTERY	●	●	
STARTER	●		
BLOCKHEATER	●		
EXHAUST SYSTEM Check entire system periodically	●	●	
DRIVE TRAIN AND BRAKES			
TRANSMISSION	●	●	●
TRANSMISSION LINKAGE	●		
DIFFERENTIAL	●		
MASTER CYLINDER	●	●	
PARKING BRAKE	●	●	

Note: The two most overlooked jobs are (1) annually flushing the cooling system, and (2) changing the automatic transmission fluid and filter. If overlooked, either has the potential to cause big trouble.

Tire rotation

	Radials		Non-Radials	
	4 Tires	5 Tires	4 Tires	5 Tires
Routine Rotation				
Putting Snowtires On in Fall				
Removing Snowtires in Spring				

Worn at Shoulders
Underinflated

Worn at Center
Overinflated

Erratic Bald Spots
Wheel Unbalanced

Worn on
One Side

Wheel Out of
Alignment
(Incorrect Camber)

"Shingle" Effect

Wheel Out of
Alignment
(Incorrect Toe)

water and another with clean water. Wash the car a section at a time, starting with the roof. Use one towel and soapy water to wash, another towel and clean water to rinse, and the third towel to dry.

FALL AND SPRING TUNE-UPS

The old adages "A stitch in time saves nine" and "An ounce of prevention is worth a pound of cure" are especially applicable when it comes to car maintenance. We cannot emphasize enough the importance of proper maintenance to save you time, money, and fuel.

The Department of Energy, Mines, and Resources of Canada publishes an informative booklet entitled *The Car Mileage Book: How to Buy, Drive and Maintain Your Car to Save Money and Energy*. It's available free of charge by writing to Car Mileage, P.O. Box 3500, Postal Station "C," Ottawa, Ontario K1Y 4G1 Canada. On page 220 is their maintenance and servicing chart that shows major things you should not neglect.

CAR REPAIR SCHEDULING

Here's a brief rundown of when you can expect certain systems in your car to have problems. This may help you avoid unnecessary costly repairs—and anticipate the ones you really do need.

1) *Tires.*

Under normal driving conditions you can expect around 40,000 miles from a radial tire and somewhere around 30,000 from a biased-ply. To extend the life of your tires, you should rotate them. Front and back tires wear differently because they perform different functions. The following charts show how tires wear and how they should be rotated. A good time to do this is when snow tires are installed or removed.

2) *Air filter.*

Replace your air filter when there are no open spaces visible when the filter is held to the light. This should be after about 12,000 to 24,000 miles for pre-1975 cars and 24,000 to 30,000 for late model cars. If you frequently drive in dust, check sooner.

3) *Alternator.*

Replace the alternator after 50,000 to 100,000 miles. Alternators are often mistakenly replaced, so take you car to a diagnostic mechanic (see page 225) or to an automotive electrical specialist before you have this done.

4) *Automatic transmission.*

This should last at least 50,000 miles and even for the full lifetime of the car. Don't replace the transmission unless you get a second opinion—

but get it fast! Ignoring a bad transmission can do permanent damage to the car.

5) *Brake linings.*

Your front brake pads take more of a beating than the pads on your rear tires. You can expect signs of wear sometime between 20,000 and 40,000 miles. If you can, get only the front pads replaced; the rear pads should last another 15,000 miles. However, your mechanic may not guarantee the work unless both sets are replaced.

6) *Carburetor.*

It should last as long as the car. If you're having problems with it, have it disassembled and cleaned and have the gaskets replaced. That should rejuvenate it.

7) *Fuel pump.*

You can plan on 50,000 to 60,000 miles from the fuel pump. Cheating mechanics have been known to pour some gas over the fuel pump, then claim it's leaking. If the car still runs, however, the fuel pump is probably OK.

8) *PCV (Positive Crankcase-Ventilation) valve.*

Cars with pollution-control systems use engine suction to draw out gases from the crankcase, through the PCV valve, and into the intake manifold for burning. It's important to keep this valve in good condition so that oil doesn't cause carbon buildup in the car. PCV valves should give 24,000 to 30,000 miles of use before needing replacement.

9) *Shocks.*

Under normal driving conditions, shocks should function well for 20,000 to 30,000 miles. If your car bounces more than once when you push down on the front fender or sways when you're going around curves, your shocks probably need replacing. Other signs of wear are drips or oil leaks emanating from them, although a bit of dampness or lubrication is quite normal.

WHERE TO GO WHEN YOUR CAR WON'T

If you are a car owner, there are certain inevitables in life beside death and taxes, and one of them is car trouble. So shop around for a repair service *before* you need it. You need someone you can trust and feel comfortable with. It's rather like selecting a doctor and hospital. Ask around. Positive word of mouth is good recommendation. You can also phone the Better Business Bureau about a place you're considering. Other than inquiring if there have been any negative reports and if the repairmen are licensed, the real test will be how well they treat you. Simply put:

- Do they seem to care?
- Are they interested in whether or not they get your repeat business?
- Will they take the time to explain what they are doing?
- Do they give estimates? in writing?
- Do they guarantee their work? in writing?

One final bit of advice: *Whey you're shopping around, don't necessarily go with the lowest estimate.* Some quotes include more labor and parts than others, in which cases higher can be better.

Four Types of Places That Provide Repair Service

1) *An automobile dealership,* possibly the same one you bought your car from. A rapport with the service manager is important; if he gets to know you and your car, service can be personal and efficient. A dealer also has good stocks of spare parts; having parts available can make a repair job quicker and easier.

   But watch it with some auto dealerships. They'll charge you an hour per problem. For instance, you take your car in to have the wheels balanced and freon put in the air conditioner. The two jobs take a total of 50 minutes, but you get charged for two hours—an hour minimum per job. (This is a true life experience, compliments of Toyota Manhattan in New York City.)

2) *The mechanic at your local gas station,* with whom you should already have a good relationship because you are a regular gas customer. His tune-ups and oil changes can often be less expensive than those at the car dealership. On the other hand, many service stations are not equipped for major repair jobs, and this means that jobs they tackle might not be properly done. When the gas station is one that emphasizes service, however, it can be a good bet, and because you buy gas there it's probably also conveniently located.

3) *The independent mechanic*—his livelihood depends on repairs and servicing only, and upholding a good reputation is a must. He may not be strategically located or do repairs on as short a notice as an auto dealer, but he's still a solid alternative.

4) *Specialty shops* such as Midas, Aamco, and the like can frequently save you money when you need to have your muffler, transmission, brakes, etc., replaced. Specialty shops have the experience, parts, and specially outfitted shops. But here you're losing that valuable personal touch you might have with your mechanic or service manager, and these specialty shops have been known to sell customers repairs they don't need.

   Note: *A nationwide list of repair shops whose employees have passed special auto repair tests is available* from the National Institute for Automotive Service Excellence, Suite 515, 1825 K Street NW, Washington, DC 20006. Send $1.75 and ask for their employers' directory, *Where to Find a Certified Mechanic.*

A Word About Diagnostic Services

One key to keeping repair costs down is to begin the repair process with good diagnostic advice. You will pay for it, but it will probably hold repair costs down in the long run.

The Federal Department of Transportation says that the problem with most auto repairs isn't that mechanics are dishonest, but rather that they don't known how to do their work well enough. That's no wonder, since it's almost impossible to keep up with all the things that can go wrong with each technological change in every make and model.

You can circumvent human error by taking your car to a garage that has an engine analyzer. This is an electronic gadget that does an unbiased job of discovering what your car's trouble is. You may have to shop for a garage that has one, but the time is worth it.

Another way to get technology back on your side is to take your car to a diagnostic center. These facilities are equipped to run elaborate electronic checks on your car. They charge a flat fee and most of them do diagnosis only. They don't even have a repair shop, so their reports are likely to be accurate and disinterested.

Cut down on the time it takes to find these new and relatively rare facilities by calling your local automobile club or association.

Warranties on Your New Car and on Repair Jobs: Some Pointers

- *Always observe the warranty if you've got a new car,* and follow service instructions *to the letter.* You can have your routine maintenance done elsewhere without violating a warranty agreement (but keep receipts showing odometer reading, date, and description of service). However, an authorized dealer must perform repairs under warranty in order for you to make your big saving.

- Once your new car warranty expires, *check if a repair shop offers a warranty on their services and replacement parts* and how long it's effective. Many now guarantee their work for 4,000 miles or 90 days.

- *Always check both mileage and time on warranties* so as not to be misled. A 10,000 mile warranty is of no value if it's good for only 30 days.

- *Member shops of the National Warranty Program give a customer a written guarantee* that covers labor and parts, and any faulty repair will be corrected at another participating shop if the customer is not able to return to the original one. Not bad! For a listing of independent garages and service centers that participate, write to the Automotive Service Councils, Inc., 4001 Warran Boulevard, Hillside, IL 60162.

THE REPAIR JOB

At the Garage

1) Making an appointment for repair work is always sensible. It makes repair jobs easier on both the mechanic and on you. Remember that there are 100 million cars out there and only 800,000 mechanics to go around. Also bear in mind that the busiest days in any repair shop are Monday and Friday. Midweek is less pressured, which gives you a good chance for more efficient service.

2) When telling a mechanic what's wrong, don't muddy the waters. Tell him the symptoms, not what you think the cause is. The symptoms are your department, the cause is his. And be specific about the problem: how frequently it occurs, at what times worse than at others, at what speed, with cold or hot engine, and whether a sudden or gradual appearance.

3) After your thorough description, find out exactly what work is to be done and get a written estimate. Also insist that your approval be obtained if any additional work is necessary.

4) When you pick up your car, bring the itemized estimate and compare it point by point with the bill. Don't accept the car unless everything is complete. (Sometimes they'll tell you they didn't have a chance to do a minor job.) If parts have been replaced, ask for the old ones as proof that the work has been done. Some parts are large or messy; ask to see them and let the mechanic show you what was worn out or broken.

5) The *Manufacturers Flat Rate Manual* indicates according to car make, model, and year how long it ought to take a mechanic to complete any specific job. Garages use it as a guide in determining prices. If you feel you're being overcharged, asking to see the manual should be your first move. Every dealer has one.

6) When you leave, give your car a road test on the way home. If it's not performing properly, turn right around and go back. Don't wait until the next day. You'll have a stronger case returning immediately. (It's preferable to test drive the car before you pay, and if you feel brazen enough to do it, then go right ahead!)

7) If you feel a repair job was really first rate, it's excellent policy to stop by and tell the dealer or service manager. Ask that your compliment be relayed to the mechanic, and tell them that you'd like him to work on your car in the future if possible.

If You're Not Satisfied

- Register a complaint *immediately* with the people who did the work. Be calm, not antagonistic; simply state the problem.

- If a dealership won't give you satisfaction, consult the owner's manual or the warranty for the address of the nearest district company office and telephone or write the customer service representative. If this gets you nowhere, talk to or write the vice president of sales at company headquarters.

- Another alternative is to see if the dealership in question has any arrangement with an arbitration service like the Better Business Bureau (see below) or with AutoCAP (Automotive Consumer Action Panel). If an AutoCAP has been established in your locality, it can be quite effective in resolving your difficulties. True, AutoCAPs are dealer-sponsored organizations composed of local or state automotive trade associations and customer representatives—but they have a good reputation for customer protection. To check if there's one near you, look in the phone book for the Automobile Dealer's Association in your city or county or write to the National Automobile Dealers Association, 1640 Westpark Drive, McLean, VA 22101, for a listing.

- In many states the Motor Vehicles Department will arbitrate between you and the dealer on another type of repair service. Call to see if assistance is available.

- If your car's problems involve safety factors, report this by calling the National Highway Traffic Safety Administration at (800) 424-9393.

- Otherwise, put your complaint in writing. Don't be hysterical—simply state all the pertinent information:

    Your name, address, and phone number

    The name and location of the facility in question

    The make and model of your car

    A description of the problem

    How much it has cost you.

  Send copies to the repair facility; to the city, state, or federal protection bureau; or to the local office of the Better Business Bureau (for the one nearest you write to the U.S. Office of Consumer Affairs, Washington, DC 20201).

- If all else fails you have two alternatives:

    Pay the bill and see a lawyer.

    Take the case to small-claims court; you don't need a lawyer there.

SHENANIGANS ON THE ROAD

You're on the edge of the desert, night is falling and you pull into the Last Gasp Gas Station. You tell the guy to fill it up and check the oil, and then you go in to make your own pit stop. When you get back, the guy is saying, "Tsk, tsk, tsk," and the car sounds like a conga band at a particularly abandoned wedding celebration. It costs you $125.00 to get it fixed. What happened?

What happened is that you got taken. Some unscrupulous garage operators have refined a bag of tricks to make a decent engine sound or look decrepit in a matter of minutes, or to take your money for nothing.

Some of them are:

- Claiming you need an oil change or new filter because the oil is "dirty"
- "Pouring" oil from an empty can
- Claiming your tires are "flawed," or even slashing them when you're not looking
- Draining your battery and replacing the fluid with water so it will test out "dead"
- Putting baking soda in the battery to make it look damaged
- Bending your wiper blades
- Making the engine smoke with a chemical spray
- Cutting the fan belt
- Puncturing the radiator hose
- Switching ignition wires to make the engine run roughly
- Altering the amounts on the credit slip, or using your card to run off additional slips that they can fill out after you're gone.

To thwart these highway bandits:

- Never leave your car alone at the pump. If you have to make a stop for yourself, do so first. Then bring the car to the pump for servicing.
- Get your car thoroughly checked before you start out. The best way to fend off false claims about repairs is to know that your regular mechanic has checked out the car and done all the necessary work before you left.
- Take care of trouble in the early stages, before it stops you. It's better to be able to choose a mechanic than to have to accept the one nearest to where you're stuck. Ask around town; call the local branch of the AAA (American Automobile Association, see below). Or look in the

phone book for a mechanic who is a member of Independent Garage Owners of America; these folks have agreed that any member shop will make good on the work of any other member shop.

- Check your credit slips—all the copies—for the correct amounts. And make sure that your credit card is used for only the one charge form.

A WORD ABOUT THE AAA

Triple A (the American Automobile Association) can be a deal. For a reasonable $29.00 a year you get:

- Free battery jumps
- Towing
- Emergency gas delivery
- Up-to-date maps
- Travel routing
- Insurance discounts
- Lower auto-loan rates
- Even bail for misdemeanor charges.

AAA offices are located in every major city. Membership can pay for itself quickly.

SAVING FUEL

ENERGY-SAVING DRIVING TIPS

- Overuse of the accelerator in starting your car can flood your engine and waste fuel by unnecessarily filling the carburetor. Check your instruction manual. Most of the time one or two pushes sets the choke. Then you can keep your foot off the gas pedal until the engine catches.
- The new, improved viscosity of motor oils makes long warmups unnecessary; 30 seconds is more like it, even on the coldest of days. But you should drive slowly for the first quarter to half mile. And in cold weather, don't turn on the heater until the car's engine is warmed up. It's also a good idea to have the car parked in such a way that you can drive off with a minimum of maneuvering.
- A cold car takes more gas to operate than a warm one, so combine errands to avoid driving with a cold motor.
- Avoid idling the engine in traffic jams or when waiting for a train to pass or a drawbridge to close. *A minute of idling uses more gas than your car takes to restart.* And when restarting, don't press on the gas pedal.

- "Jack rabbit" starts are hard on your car, unnecessary, and immature. They don't get you where you're going noticeably faster, and they wear out tires and use more fuel (as any sharp acceleration does, activating the carburetor's "accelerator pump" that squirts extra gas into the engine).

- Smooth driving is safe and fuel efficient. In stop-and-go traffic your speed should be adjusted to avoid unnecessarily rapid accelerations and decelerations or unnecessary braking. Watch traffic well ahead so constant speed can be maintained. When you see a red traffic light, a stop sign, or a slowdown in traffic ahead, simply take your foot off the gas pedal and coast up to it. Most people prefer to race on, then slam on their brakes at the last instant.

- Driving at 55 miles per hour on the highway conserves fuel; driving slower or faster wastes it. At 70 you're using about 35 percent more, and at 40 you're using 12 percent more. There's also the danger factor—you see less when you drive fast. A driver can see twice as much at 40 miles per hour as at 70; however, at 40 you're inhibiting the flow of traffic.

- On the highway, start building up speed as you approach a hill in order to use less gas. The car will slow on the incline, but it's most important to keep gas flow, not speed, uniform.

- Revving the engine while your car is stopped or before shutting your car off is both unnecessary and uneconomical.

- Brakes and accelerator should be operated with one foot. Resting your foot on the brake pedal is dangerous and bad for your car.

- When you're loading a car, distribute the weight evenly. Doing this also makes for safer driving.

- A trunk that is a repository for heavy items (with the exception of your spare tire, jack, and wrench) costs you gas.

- Listening to radio traffic reports and thereby avoiding jams can save you both time and gas.

- Cut down on your mileage by doing your shopping all on one day and by mapping out the various stops efficiently.

- Share rides and form carpools. When possible shop with a friend (but when you get to the store go your separate ways so as not to make each other spend more). Also share the driving to school and to after-school activities.

YOU AND YOUR GAS TANK

- You get more gas for your money when you buy it in the morning. The heat of the sun hasn't had a chance to expand the gas in the storage tank.

- Try to avoid parking your car in the sun. More gas evaporates from the tank when you can't find some shade.

- When you're down to a quarter of a tank, fill 'er up! In summer, as the level decreases, evaporation increases.

- Don't fill your gas tank to the brim. Some gas always spills out, and the motion of the car causes even more spillage. When you're filling up and the pump clicks off, that's enough. Pay and go.

- Be aware of octane levels that are posted on gas pumps. The price of gas is directly related to them. Using a higher octane than is necessary does not improve engine performance or increase mileage. The indicator that you're using too low an octane is an engine knock or a "ping" when you accelerate. If you hear this, increase the octane until the sound disappears. Then you're at the right octane level.

- In winter, keep your gas tank as full as possible to reduce the condensation of water vapor in the tank and the risk of possible freeze-up in the fuel line.

- With gas occasionally in short demand, a locked gas cap is a good investment. But remember to give the gas cap key to anyone to whom you loan the car.

The Leaded Premium Problem

There are over 15,000,000 cars on the road manufactured during the early '70s (and some foreign models as late as '79) designed to run on leaded premium. All the major distributors except Getty and Union 76 have phased that fuel out. An owner of such a car who simply changes over to unleaded premium or leaded regular can find himself with serious valve problems costing hundreds of dollars. Those engines designed to operate with leaded high test need just that. *Consumer Reports* recommends first trying leaded regular and if there's that telltale signal of ping or knock under the hood (meaning the octane level isn't high enough), add unleaded premium to raise it. Or you can switch over to the following system recommended by Consumers Union: Use half unleaded premium, half leaded regular every tankful; or a first tankful of unleaded premium, a second tankful of unleaded premium, and a third tankful of half unleaded premium, half leaded regular.

Useful After-Market Items That Can Improve Gas Mileage

1) A vacuum gauge can be useful in letting you know if you're applying too much gas-pedal pressure.

2) Gas-line antifreeze. Condensation is almost inevitable in any gas tank. The water becomes trapped in the fuel filter or is vaporized in the engine. However, in extreme weather, condensation has a tendency to freeze and

block the fuel line, incapacitating your car. Gas-line antifreeze prevents this, and it's a good idea to keep some on hand.

3) The shop manual for your car's model and year can be very beneficial. Because of current interest in do-it-yourself repair, many of these manuals are being written with the layman in mind and are included among new car options. Owners of older cars might want to use these to supplement their more technical manuals. (See page 234).

"Gas-Saver" After-Market Aids to Avoid

It's proper maintenance that saves gas, not any of these devices. To illustrate just how far these can go, we list four:

1) "Pass-Saver." This cuts off the air conditioner when you accelerate. It can only pay for itself in a climate where the air conditioner is always used.

2) "Gas Miser," Union Carbide's brainchild. This liquid that you pour into your gas tank costs more than the gas you save.

3) "Goodman Water Injector System" sprays water into the car's carburetor. *Consumer Reports* found it had no significant effect on gas mileage.

4) "Molecular Fuel Energizer" sets up a "force field" that lines up gasoline molecules uniformly to give an alleged 10 to 23 percent fuel savings. Again, actual tests showed no improvement in mileage, and the thing costs anywhere from $140.00 to $395.00, depending on the vehicle's engine size.

SELLING YOUR CAR

Your car should last 15 to 20 years and carry you 100,000 to 150,000 happy miles if you maintain it lovingly.

The longer you keep your car, the lower your average cost-per-mile over the period of your ownership. Depreciation is most extreme during your car's early years, fading away as the car ages to nine to ten. Your financing costs are gone, and your insurance costs have fallen off. The one factor that will rise as your car ages is maintenance. That's when the temptation to sell is likely to come in. You have a valve job in August, the battery has to be replaced in February, and you notice the tires are bald in April, just about the time when the transmission begins to slip. That's about $1,150.00 in maintenance outlays—doesn't that make it time to sell?

Maybe not! If the car is in good condition generally, these outlays can mean an additional four or five useful years. Compare that $1,150.00 maintenance outlay with the additional dollars you would be spending for car payments, insurance, and the cost depreciation on a new car. And if you trade your car in for a used car you very well might be taking on someone else's problems.

In general, our advice is: Don't sell your car until it's value is $400 or less. Then consider the "drive it till it drops" option discussed on page 211–212 in the section on used cars. When some crucial assembly fails, scrap the car or sell it to someone who wants to work on an old clunker.

If you do decide to sell your car, be aware that some unscrupulous used car salesmen are likely to offer an extremely attractive trade-in deal to stop your shopping around. But when the new car is ready, they will begin to find fault with your old car and lower its trade-in value. This is a scam you don't have to fall for. Just get in your old car and drive to someplace where the trade-in offer is a little lower, but for real.

CARS: BREAKING THE HABIT

Now that all your friends have quit smoking, what is there to feel holier than them about? Well, have you considered giving up your car? After all, a car is an antisocial, energy-wasting, air-polluting anachronism that anyone with smarts can learn to do without.

Cars may not be that bad, or that easy to give up—but seriously, consider what you could do with a moped instead of a car, especially instead of an urban car or a second car in the suburbs.

1) A moped is far cheaper: a $400.00 to $600.00 outlay.

2) You can pedal it and improve your own muscles, circulation, and stamina.

3) When you do run the motor, it gets 200 miles to the gallon.

4) With panniers or a small cart attached, there's almost no errand you can't perform.

For the more athletic, the same virtues hold for the bicycle and the adult version of the tricycle.

Of course, most non–car owners resort to public transportation like buses, trains, and subways. They are more energy-efficient, easier on the budget, and easier on the environment than cars. Besides, you can read the paper on the way to the office and arrive rested and well informed.

When you do think about getting free of the car, consider that you'll be winning freedom from the following:

- Parking hassles
- Traffic hassles
- Insurance hassles

- Mechanical hassles
- Gas shortage hassles
- Toll hassles
- Gas price hassles
- Ticket hassles
- Inspection hassles
- Registration hassles
- License plate hassles.

Quite a list! Quite a notion! Think about it!

SOURCES

GENERAL INFORMATION ON CARS

Shell Oil has been publishing pamphlets about energy, car care, and related topics for some time now. There's definitely an oil-company bias in the material, but some good, objective recommendations on how to cut down on waste as well. Request their series of "Answer Booklets" from P.O. Box 61609, Houston, TX 77208. Free.

Basic Car Mechanics

"Car Care: The Inside Story." Booklet on car maintenance for the unmechanical. Write to Atlantic Richfield Co., P.O. Box 30181, Los Angeles, CA 90030. Free.

Time-Life Book of the Family Car. A basic overview of the car and how it works—non-intimidating. Time, Inc. publishes it. 1271 Avenue of the Americas, New York, NY 10019. $15.00

Driving

The Book of Expert Driving by E.D. Fales. Tips to help you become a better driver—safer and more economical. Hawthorn Press, E.P. Dutton & Co., 2 Park Avenue, NY, 10016. $4.95.

NEW CARS

The Car Book. Basic safety information and more about cars. Free from the Consumer Information Service, Pueblo, CO 81009. But write soon; it may be out of print. The Reagan administration considers this useful booklet "antibusiness." However, there are 1.5 million copies already distributed; maybe someone will loan you one.

Car Magazines. These include *Car & Driver, Road and Track, Motor Trend,* and *Automotive News.* They rate new cars for price, performance, safety, etc.

Consumer Reports. Good information on new cars in the December "Buying Guide" issue and the April "Roundup for New Car Buyers" issue each year. Get them at your newsstand, or write for back issues to Consumers Union, 256 Washington St., Mt. Vernon, NY 10550.

New Car Prices and Foreign Car Prices, Edmund Publications. All you need to know to make informed choices based on price. Write to the publisher's Subscription Department, 515 Hempstead Turnpike, West Hempstead, NY 11552. $3.10 per book postpaid.

USED CARS

Cherries and Lemons: The Used Car Buyer's Handbook by Joe Troise. Rates cars back to 1955 and gives you good advice on how to choose yours and maintain it. Warner Books, 75 Rockefeller Plaza, New York, NY 10019. $1.95.

Consumer Reports partially covers the used-car market with their *Guide to Used Cars*, which gives repair records for 1974–1977 vehicles. Cost is $7.50 plus $1.75 postage. They also publish frequency of repair reports in their April issues that can let you know just how trouble-prone a car you're considering is. Check the back April issue for the car that interests you. Consumers Union, 256 Washington St., Mt. Vernon, NY 10550.

Used Car Prices, Edmund Publications. The famous "Blue Book," as it's referred to by the trade, with standard prices for standard models by year and condition. The bible of the business. Write to the publisher's Subscription Department, 515 Hempstead Turnpike, West Hempstead, NY 11552. $2.45 postpaid.

CAR REPAIR AND MAINTENANCE

Basic Auto Repair

Basic Auto Repair Manual. All an inexperienced person needs to know to diagnose, repair, and maintain domestic cars. Peterson Publishing Co., 6725 Sunset Boulevard, Los Angeles, CA 90028. $12.95.

Fixing Cars: A People's Primer by the San Francisco Institute of Automotive Ecology. A basic book with an alternative approach to your car and the car industry. Bookpeople, 2940 Seventh Street, Berkeley, CA 94710. $5.50.

Volkswagen Repair

How to Keep Your Volkswagen Alive: A Manual of Step-by-Step Procedures for the Complete Idiot by John Muir. The title tells it all. A must if you have a Bug— 1.3 million copies sold. John Muir Publications, P.O. Box 613, Santa Fe, NM 87501. $10.00.

Poor Richard's Rabbit Book: How to Keep Your Volkswagen Rabbit Alive by Richard Sealey. If you have a Bunny, not a Bug, you need this book. An instant classic on how to keep your Rabbit hopping. John Muir Publications, P.O. Box 613, Santa Fe, NM 87501. $13.50.

Repair Manuals for Specific Models

Four publishers supply auto repair manuals for specific makes and models of trucks and cars. You can usually purchase them for under $10.00, but prices vary.

Chilton Auto Repair Manuals
Chilton Book Company
Chilton Way
Radnor, PA 19089

Motor Auto Repair and Shop Manuals
Motor
224 West 57th St.
New York, NY 10019

Clymer Shop Manuals
Clymer Publishing Co.
12860 Muscatine St.
P.O. Box 20
Arleta, CA 91331

Haynes Owners Workshop Manuals
Haynes Publications Manuals, Inc.
861 Lawrence Drive
Newbury Park, CA 91320

Keeping an Old Car Running

Drive It Till It Drops: How To Keep Your Car Running Forever by Joe Troise. If you don't care how it looks, you can probably drive your car until it wears out from underneath you. Here's how to do it right. And Books, The Distributors, 702 South Michigan, South Bend, IN 46618. $3.95.

   Why Trade It In? Your Mechanic Can Save You Money by George and Suzanne Fremon. How to get the best value from car repairs and from your car as it ages. Liberty Publishing Company, 50 Scott Adam Road, Cockeysville, MD 21030. $5.95.

Checking Up on Your Mechanic

How to Get Your Car Repaired Without Getting Gypped by Margaret B. Carlson. For anyone who uses a mechanic and worries about the bills. Harper & Row, 10 East 53rd St., New York, NY 10022. $5.95.

AVOIDING AND DEALING WITH LEMONS

DownEaster's Lemon Guide. Which cars and models to avoid. Bureau of Consumer Protection, State House Building, Augusta, ME 04333. $1.00.

   The Lemon Book by Ralph Nader et al. is a 300-page manual for lemon owners. It tells how to fight back effectively when no one wants to listen. Caroline House Publishers, Box 738, Ottawa, IL 61350.

BICYCLES

Anybody's Bike Book by Tom Cuthbertson. Good advice, good price. Get it before you get your bike. Ten Speed Press, Box 7123, Berkeley, CA 94707. $4.95.

The Bicycle: A Commuting Alternative by Frederick L. Wolfe. A general manual, especially good for those who want to get back and forth on their bike, not just use it for recreation. Signpost Books, 8912 192 Street, S.W., Edmonds, WA 98020. $7.95.

DeLong's Guide to Bicycles and Bicycling by Fred DeLong. Well illustrated, general treatment of cycling. Good repair section. Chilton Book Co., Chilton Way, Radnor, PA 19089. $9.95.

INDEX